THE
IMMORTAL
BOBBY

Bobby Jones and the
Golden Age of Golf

RON RAPOPORT

WILEY

John Wiley & Sons, Inc.

Copyright © 2005 by Ron Rapoport. All rights reserved

Published by John Wiley & Sons, Inc., Hoboken, New Jersey
Published simultaneously in Canada

Photo credits: pages 145, 149 bottom, 150 bottom, 151: copyright © U.S. Golf Association; pages 146 top, 147 top: Kenan Research Center at the Atlanta History Center; pages 146 bottom, 147 bottom, 148, 149 top, 152: Special Collections and Archives, Robert W. Woodruff Library, Emory University; page 150 top: AP/Wide World Photos

Design and composition by Navta Associates.

For general information about our other products and services, please contact our Customer Care Department within the United States at (800) 762-2974, outside the United States at (317) 572-3993 or fax (317) 572-4002.

Wiley also publishes its books in a variety of electronic formats. Some content that appears in print may not be available in electronic books. For more information about Wiley products, visit our web site at www.wiley.com.

Library of Congress Cataloging-in-Publication Data:
Rapoport, Ron, date.
    The immortal Bobby : Bobby Jones and the golden age of golf / Ron Rapoport.
        p. cm.
    Includes bibliographical references and index.
    ISBN 0-471-47372-3 (cloth : alk. paper)
    1. Jones, Bobby, 1902–1971. Golfers—United States—Biography.
I. Title.
    GV964.J6R36 2005

2004021909

Printed in the United States of America

10 9 8 7 6 5 4 3 2 1

For Daniel B. Rapoport,
A champion all his life,
And Allanna Beth Chung,
Now at the first tee

Contents

Photo gallery: pages 145–152

Introduction

If Bobby Jones did not exist, the mythmaking sportswriters of the Golden Age of Sports might have had to invent him. And in a sense, perhaps they did.

Just beginning to realize their power to create idols on a scale never before imagined, the writers of the 1920s stood in awe of Jones in a way that left Babe Ruth, Jack Dempsey, Bill Tilden, Red Grange, and the other great athletes of the era behind.

As talented and popular as these others were, they were in it for the money, while Jones, who played as an amateur and never accepted a winner's purse, was not.

They were susceptible to the temptations that fame brought with it in the new age of celebrity, while Jones, who fled to the serenity of his home in Atlanta when not playing golf, was not.

They tended toward showmanship and arrogance, flaunting their talents, taunting and belittling their opponents, while Jones, the embodiment of restraint and southern courtesy, did not.

They courted the public spotlight—or were pushed into it by promoters eager to capitalize on the riches to be found in its glare—while Jones, relying on O. B. Keeler, a hometown sportswriter whose devotion knew no limits, to burnish his reputation, did not.

Occasionally, those who assumed the task of explaining Jones to an increasingly fascinated public would assure their audience that

Jones was not a saint, not perfect. But even the flaws they listed proclaimed a humanity that only added to his mystique.

Jones regularly drank alcoholic beverages, newspaper and magazine readers were told, and had a particular affection for home-distilled corn whiskey. He occasionally swore, on the golf course and off, and was known to enjoy bawdy stories. His temper was notorious in his younger days, and it was not until he learned to control it that he became a champion.

So Jones was seen as that rare combination of noble patrician and regular guy. He was courtly, well-spoken, wise . . . and humble, approachable, one of the boys. By the time the catalog was complete, it seemed almost beside the point that he was also the greatest golfer the world had ever known.

Though Jones was all but an annuity for journalists who were quickly learning that despite its stuffy, country-club origins in America, golf could be an exciting game to write about, he was especially fascinating to the most stylish writers who crossed his path. Among them were those for whom sports was a youthful fancy they would one day leave behind, such as Paul Gallico; a change of pace from weightier concerns to be indulged only occasionally, such as Alistair Cooke; or a blank slate on which something approaching literature could be created, such as Bernard Darwin.

"In all the years of contact with the famous ones of sport," said Gallico in *Farewell to Sport*, the book he wrote before turning to the novels that would secure his reputation and his fortune, "I have found only one that would stand up in every way as a gentleman as well as a celebrity, a fine, decent, human being as well as a newsprint personage, and who never once, since I have known him, has let me down in my estimate of him. That one is Robert Tyre Jones, Jr., the golf-player from Atlanta, Georgia."

"I have done a little digging among friends and old golfing acquaintances who knew him and among old writers who, in other fields, have a sharp nose for the disreputable," wrote Cooke, the long-time American correspondent for the BBC and the *Guardian* who became well known in his adopted land as host of public television's *Masterpiece Theatre*. "But I do believe that a whole team of investigative reporters, working in shifts like coal miners, would find that in all of Jones's life anyone has been able to observe, he nothing common did or mean."

It was left to Darwin, the grandson of the great naturalist and one of the first journalists to devote himself primarily to writing about golf (a friend once called him "the originator of the species") to define the problem they all faced: "A kind friend at St. Andrews said to me the other day that he read everything I wrote except about Bobby Jones; that he never intended to read, since there was nothing to say and superlatives were tiresome things."

These writers were drawn to Jones in part by his education, which was rare among champion athletes, then as well as now. He had a diploma in mechanical engineering from Georgia Tech; a second degree in literature from Harvard; and, after winning two U.S. Amateur and Open titles and one British Open, he returned to study law at Emory University in Atlanta. He passed the state bar in his second year and finally left school for good.

Jones loved opera, pondered Cicero—"If only I thought as much of my golfing ability (I considered) as Cicero thought of his statesmanship, I might do better in these blamed tournaments," he wrote— discussed Einstein and the fourth dimension, and relaxed after a competitive round by soaking in a hot tub and reading Giovanni Papini's *Life of Christ*.

Jones also was at the very least their equal as a writer. His autobiographical works, while not forthcoming about his life away from the golf course, are descriptive, thoughtful, and gracefully written. He is, depending on how you look at it, either the finest writer of any great athlete who ever lived or the greatest athlete of any excellent writer.

In reviewing *Bobby Jones on Golf*, a compilation of instructional articles that set the standard for the burgeoning industry of how-to-play-golf books, Cooke called them "The Missing Aristotle Papers on Golf." He said "Jones' gift for distilling a complex emotion into the barest language would not have shamed John Donne; his meticulous insistence on the right word to impress the right visual image was worthy of fussy old Flaubert; and his unique personal gift was to take apart many of the club clichés with a touch of grim Lippmanesque humor."

Jones, who was amused by the extravagance of Cooke's comparisons, was characteristically modest about his writing talent. "I am not one of those fortunate persons who can sit down before a typewriter and spill out words that make sense," he once wrote Pat Ward-Thomas, a British journalist. "The act of creation on a blank page costs me no end of pain."

But for all his protestations, Jones enjoyed writing and engaged in it professionally and privately all his life. He once estimated his published output at more than half a million words, and more than thirty years after his death, his former law partner Arthur Howell would recall how, as Jones mentored the firm's young lawyers, he would repeatedly emphasize the importance of writing carefully and well.

Occasionally Jones wrote accounts of some of his important matches that would appear in the next day's newspapers alongside the reports of the mere journalists covering the event. To accomplish this, Jones would walk off the course, seek a quiet corner to write his articles in longhand, or borrow Keeler's typewriter. Even after some of his most debilitating matches during his crowning achievement, the Grand Slam, Jones sat down and wrote about them.

As for his correspondence, Jones kept it up until shortly before he died, when even the effort of dictating to his loyal secretary, Jean Marshall, became too much for him. Jones would answer anybody who wrote to him—friend, journalist, or stranger off the street seeking an autograph, the answer to a question, or advice.

Clearly, Jones viewed the carefully written phrase as the mark of a civilized man, and his letters take up the largest part of the thirty-volume personal archive that occupies several shelves at the U.S. Golf Association Library in Far Hills, New Jersey. "He would go out on a fishing boat with his friend Charlie Elliott, the editor of *Outdoor Life*," says Jones's grandson, Robert T. Jones IV, "and for hours they would talk about syntax—sometimes English, sometimes Latin. When his father died, he didn't like any of the sympathy acknowledgment cards he could find—they were all in the passive voice, which he despised—so he wrote his own: 'The family of Robert P. Jones appreciates your kind expression of support and will ever be grateful.'"

Jones also was a masterful public speaker who delivered equal measures of eloquence, humor, and shyness in a languid drawl that cheered the residents of his native South, who did not consider it to be exotic, and charmed northerners and Europeans, who did. And Jones had a facility for making the grand gesture, for saying exactly the right thing at just the right moment. The ovations he received on these occasions may not have been as loud as those he heard on the golf course, but they were just as heartfelt and occasionally accompanied by tears.

Thus was Jones's attraction to some of the most prominent journalists of the generation complete. He was a great athlete, a fascinating person, and a bona fide intellectual who valued their craft as well as his own. What else was there?

As the years went by, Jones was frequently the subject of career retrospectives, often made fresh by the fact that he continued to make news. His very name drew the greatest golfers in the world to the course he had built in Augusta, Georgia, which quickly became host to the game's most famous tournament. Likewise, the constantly deteriorating state of his health, which could be seen in his annual television appearances at the Masters award ceremonies, served to lift the Jones mythology onto a higher plateau.

Consider the published versions of Jones's most-often-quoted response to his friends' distress over his growing paralysis and the terrible pain that accompanied it. Here are some, but surely not all, of them.

To Ward-Thomas: "Well, Pat, I have my heart and lungs and so-called brain. We play it as it lies."

To Charles Price, who helped edit his book *Bobby Jones on Golf,* when Price was reduced to tears on seeing Jones's condition: "Now, Charles, we will have none of that. We just play the ball as it lies."

To Al Laney, a writer he had first met as a teenager: "I've known you longer than anyone in golf. I can tell you there is no help. I can only get worse. But you are not to keep thinking of it. You know that in golf we play the ball as it lies. Now we will not speak of this again. Ever."

There were some, including Cooke, who professed to be skeptical that the exchange ever took place at all.

"The familiar punch line, 'You know, we play the ball where it lies,' was not said in my presence," Cooke wrote, "and, I must say, it sounds false to me to Jones' character, as of a passing thought by a screen-writer that Hollywood would never resist." Alas, Cooke's memory must have failed him, because some years earlier he had succumbed to melodrama himself. In the book that accompanied his highly regarded television show *America*, he repeated the version of the story mentioning Laney.

It is not really important, of course, to know whether Jones said "We play the ball as it lies" (or, in Cooke's debunking, "where" it lies), though it does point up the sort of problems that are encoun-tered in any attempt to separate the life of Bobby Jones from the leg-end. What the "familiar punch line" does illustrate is how the public adulation of Jones, which began when he was fourteen years old, grew with every twist and turn of his career and his life for the next fifty-five years. It also obscures the fact that while Jones did endure his physical affliction with a stoic public dignity for more than two decades, he often complained about it and railed against it pri-vately—in his correspondence if not his conversation.

There are other aspects of Jones's life and personality that stand apart from the legend as well.

He was capable of holding an implacable grudge for years, and of resisting all entreaties by a former friend and fellow golf champion who had offended him to forgive and forget.

He was a man of definite political views that led him to offer sup-port not only to his friend Dwight Eisenhower, on the grounds that he wanted to help establish a two-party system in the South, but also, at a time when his home city and state were choosing up sides on civil rights, to some of Georgia's most powerful segregationist politicians.

And there is compelling evidence that what we have been told about the spinal condition that made his last years so difficult is incomplete and incorrect.

Jones was never more human than when he was on the golf course. He was the most accomplished golfer of his time—of all time, some believe—the most naturally gifted, the most technically proficient, the keenest student, the most determined to win. And yet he was capable of sensational blunders, of unthinking lapses, of letting opponents off the hook time after time.

Part of Jones's appeal to the public lay in his ability to come up with an almost impossibly dramatic shot just when he needed it most. There are many instances throughout his career when he came from behind to beat an opponent, and almost as many when he frittered away a lead to turn an easy win into a defeat or a victory so agonizing he could take no pleasure from it. This was never more true than in 1930, when Jones won the Grand Slam. Though it remains one of the signal achievements in the history of sports, it also was a precarious adventure that was littered with near catastrophes and could have come unraveled at almost any moment.

"Very lately I have come to a sort of Presbyterian attitude toward tournament golf," Jones said in *Down the Fairway*, the youthfully exuberant book he wrote with Keeler that was published when Jones was twenty-five years old. "I can't get away from the idea of predestination."

Another name for it might be luck.

Jones's decision to remain an amateur during his playing days can similarly be viewed through different angles of the prism. Was it a noble example of the ideals of a true sportsman or a simple recognition that professional golf in the 1920s and 1930s was a financially precarious enterprise that required constant travel and self-promotion, neither of which suited him?

Jones never romanticized his choice, but neither did he object to those who did. If it fit some *beau ideal* image to depict him as sacrificing his golf game for a higher calling, putting his clubs away for months at a time while he practiced law, so be it. Even if, as was the case in the winter of 1925, he played golf in Florida with Tommy Armour almost every day for five months.

Sometime before Jones retired from golf, he surely recognized that he could make more money from golf as a former amateur than as a professional. Within months of his announcement that he would no longer play competitively, he was in Hollywood making a series of movie shorts with some of the top stars of the era, and had signed a contract with Spalding to manufacture golf clubs bearing his name. Jones earned an estimated $300,000 in 1931, more than twice the total value of all the money awarded in professional tournament purses in the United States. It would be more than forty years before Jack Nicklaus would earn that much money playing golf in a single year.

In truth, Jones retired because, both financially and emotionally, he could no longer afford not to. He had a growing family to support, and the demand for his services as a public figure could be met only by giving up his amateur standing. As for his health, Jones was finding it so hard to deal with the pressure of competition and the expectations of the public that his friends had begun to worry about him.

"I was writing in the room where he was waiting to know if he had won," Darwin wrote after Jones's final round in the 1930 British Open. "He was utterly exhausted and had to hold his glass in two hands lest the good liquor be spilt. All he could say was that he would never, never do it again. He could doubtless have won more and more Championships, but at too high a price."

And so Jones retired from competition but not from golf, a sport he promoted and earned a living from for the rest of his life. He made movies, designed clubs, and built Augusta National. He wrote books and magazine articles. And he continued to play in Atlanta and elsewhere until the day in 1948 when, toward the end of a round at East Lake Country Club, the course where he had learned to play as a child, he turned to his friend Charlie Yates and said, "I guess I won't be playing with you boys anymore for a while. I've decided to have an operation."

"When the legend becomes fact, print the legend," says a newspaper editor in the John Ford film *The Man Who Shot Liberty Valance*. In the case of Bobby Jones, the legend has the virtue of being the truth. He was a great golfer, an icon admired in his own country and revered in Great Britain, a model of rectitude, an amiable companion, a loving husband, a doting father, a loyal friend.

Can the fact that these were not the only truths surprise us? Does the knowledge that he was subject to the complexities and contradictions that life holds for everyone diminish his stature among the great champions of sport? Surely not because, as the mythmakers suggested with a knowing wink, Bobby Jones was not a saint after all but a human being.

PART I

Little Bob
and
Mr. Jones

1

East Lake Days

Bobby Jones played his first competitive game of golf when he was six years old and lost. They gave him the trophy anyway.

Mary Bell Meador, who owned the boardinghouse where Robert P. Jones had rented rooms for the summer, proposed the match when she saw how much her young son Frank enjoyed playing with Jones's son, a frail but game boy they called Little Bob.

The Meador boardinghouse was across from the tenth fairway of the East Lake Country Club, a golf course that had recently been built by the Atlanta Athletic Club in the rolling countryside six miles outside the city limits of Atlanta. During General George Sherman's march to the sea near the end of the Civil War, one of his generals, John Schofield, had spent a night in a house on the grounds while his troops had slept in the open on what would later become East Lake's fairways.

The recent extension of the municipal streetcar line had helped East Lake become a popular vacation destination for Atlanta residents who wanted to beat the heat and perhaps play some tennis or golf. And East Lake itself offered an inviting beach as well as hotdog and popcorn stands and a penny arcade where visitors could peek at bathing beauties in turn-of-the-century bloomers.

Frank Meador and Little Bob invited two other children spending the summer of 1908 at East Lake, Perry Adair and Alexa Stirling, to play with them in the six-hole match. Stirling, who was ten and the oldest member of the foursome, won.

"We couldn't have a girl beat us," Meador remembered, so the tiny cup his mother gave him went to Little Bob.

"I'll always believe that Alexa won that cup," Jones confessed years later. Of all the trophies and medals he won in his lifetime, it was the only one he ever slept with.

During that first summer at East Lake, Little Bob and his friends fished, killed snakes, picked raspberries, and rode a pony, which Jones named Clara, after his mother, who did not entirely appreciate the compliment. Since the children were too young to be allowed on the golf course by themselves, they marked their own two-hole layout on the road outside the front door. In all, it was a heavenly existence for a six-year-old boy, and just as much a blessing for his parents.

A year before Jones was born, his mother had given birth to a son who had been doomed from the start. None of the doctors in Canton, Georgia, where Clara Jones was living with her new husband, knew why the baby could not gain weight and had no immunity from child-hood diseases. At the age of three months, William Jones, whom Clara had named after her father, died. Clara quickly became pregnant again, and she insisted that Robert P. Jones move his law practice to Atlanta, where there was bound to be better medical care. But when her second son, Robert T. Jones Jr., was born on March 17, 1902, he seemed no healthier than the boy Clara would always refer to as "the baby that died."

Little Bob had an enlarged head and tiny, fragile limbs. He suffered from fits of colic and, more terrifying to his frantic parents, could not seem to eat anything. None of the half dozen doctors his parents took him to had any suggestions other than egg whites along with whatever pablum he could keep down. The child did not eat solid food until he was five years old.

Recalling little William Jones's lack of immunity, Clara kept her son away from other children and, except for an occasional ride on his tricycle in the backyard when the weather was good, indoors. A young black nursemaid named Camilla, whom Jones always remembered with affection—it was her brother who first taught him to swear, he said—provided discipline, affection, and so many readings from Joel Chandler Harris he could recite the adventures of Br'er Rabbit and Br'er Fox almost word for word.

So the prospect of a summer at East Lake appealed to the Joneses because Little Bob could play outside without coming into contact with crowds of people and they could keep an eye on him. And when he thrived at Mary Bell Meador's boardinghouse, the family spent every subsequent summer at East Lake, where they lived in a building near the 13th green called the mulehouse, after the mules that once pulled the mowers for the golf course and had been quartered at the bottom level.

The move was a great one for Little Bob—what better place for a future champion to grow up than on a golf course?—and it was wonderful for his family as well. Jones's father, his legal career thriving as counsel for the newly reorganized Coca-Cola Company, took to the game immediately and played it well enough to compete in tournaments with his son in later years. Even Clara, who was five feet tall, weighed ninety pounds, and had little use for foolishness, enjoyed the game and learned to play it decently.

Robert Purmedus Jones, who was known in Atlanta as Big Bob and the Colonel, could hardly have been more different from his son. The father was loud, gregarious, and creatively foul-mouthed. "He can question a man's ancestry and make it feel like a caress," a friend once said. The son was shy, reserved, and polite. Though he would go on to receive more public attention than all but a handful of other men—ticker-tape parades, huge ovations, and hysterical displays on the golf course that occasionally threatened his safety—he would always maintain a reserve that only a few close friends ever managed to penetrate. And yet the two men could not have loved each other more.

Robert P. Jones had been held in check by his father, Robert Tyre Jones Sr., from the day he was born. He would always regret being denied his father's full name, which would be passed on to the grandson instead.

A self-made man who grew up on a farm in northern Georgia during the Civil War, R. T. Jones put his entire fortune, $500, into a general store in Canton, Georgia. In time, he would all but own the town—the mill where cotton was ginned, the company where it was woven into denim, the town bank and store—and for forty years he taught Sunday school at the Canton Baptist Church as well. By the 1920s, R. T. Jones was earning $1.5 million a year, and when bad times struck he borrowed the funds to keep his employees making denim, which he kept in storehouses he had built for the purpose. As the economy began to recover, he sold the stockpiles to the army at a large profit.

"Stern" is one word for R. T. Jones. "Uncompromising" is another.

"Well, R. T., I guess there's no rest for the wicked," an associate said when he found the boss at work on a Sunday.

"And the righteous don't need it," Jones replied.

Jones saw no need for games and never went to see his son play baseball for Mercer College in Macon. Nor would he allow the boy to play for his mill's sandlot team. A hat was often passed when it played, and he would not countenance the idea of one of his employees losing a chance to make a little extra money so his son could play a mere game. As for the professional contract R. P. Jones was offered by the Brooklyn Superbas (the name was later changed to Dodgers), his father would not consider it for a moment.

"I didn't send you to college to become a professional baseball player," he told his son. And though he was probably doing him a favor—the hardscrabble, ill-paying game of professional baseball was no career for a promising young man at the turn of the century—the missed opportunity stung. His own son, Big Bob vowed, would be allowed to do anything he liked.

Little Bob never had a formal golf lesson, but he had the best teacher possible in Stewart Maiden. Maiden was one of hundreds of young men from the small Scottish village of Carnoustie who left home to work at the growing number of golf clubs in the United States. His brother, Jimmy, who had preceded him at East Lake, left in 1908 to take a job on Long Island. So after an evening of farewell songs at the Carnoustie Golf Club, whose members presented him with a steamer trunk, Stewart Maiden set off to replace him.

"Stewart was just another little Scot, like Jimmy, only Scotcher,"

Jones would recall of the first time he saw him. "He said very little and I couldn't understand a single word of what he said."

But words were the least of what Maiden had to offer a six-year-old boy. Indeed, he hardly seemed to notice as Little Bob followed him around the course for several holes, watching every move he made, then ran back to the mulehouse, where he gathered balls in his cap and tried to imitate what he had seen on the 13th green outside his front door.

Maiden believed in simplicity above all, simplicity in a golfer's swing—feet together, hands low, body upright—and in his approach to the game. He would step up to the ball and, with a minimum of preparation or fuss, swing at it. Throughout his career, Jones would be known for his lack of deliberation over shots and his quick play.

"Hit it hard and it will land somewhere," Maiden liked to say, and his advice was seldom more complicated than that. Once, when Jones was playing competitively and having trouble with his stance, Maiden watched him hit a few balls, then told him to move his right foot and shoulder back a bit and square up his stance.

Jones did as he was told and asked, "Now what do I do?"

"Knock the hell out of it," Maiden said.

Maiden was frustrated by some of the duffers at East Lake— "The best thing for you to do is lay off the game for two weeks, then quit," he told one—but the course also offered him avid young players who would absorb his lessons and make his reputation. Besides Jones, there was Perry Adair, who was two years older and became a highly regarded amateur player. And Maiden was delighted by the natural talent and competitive spirit of Alexa Stirling, who learned the same simple Carnoustie swing the boys had imitated.

The daughter of a physician born in Scotland, Stirling, all long red hair and freckles, was a sort of Renaissance tomboy. Though her mother, a classically trained singer, saw to it that she learned to play the violin, her own interests ran to more physical pursuits—swimming, tennis, golf, and "helping" the family handyman. "I had a natural bent toward hammers, nails and other tools," Stirling wrote, "so I suppose also golf clubs. Boys' pursuits appeared to me the most reasonable and enjoyable, girls' beneath notice." Before long, she was learning to repair automobile engines, and during World War I she served in the Red Cross Motor Corps.

Stirling was serious about her music—"If she would just leave that dashed fiddle alone, she would be a fine player," Maiden once grumbled—and even made herself a violin out of a cigar box. But there was nothing she liked more than playing golf at East Lake with Perry Adair and Bobby Jones, often as much as two rounds a day.

"None of us was very big but our bags were," she wrote. "I thought that anyone who did not have at least three wooden and eight or ten iron clubs was beneath notice. We were all too insignificant for the honor of caddies, and the three of us would trudge round the course nearly hidden by our bags, but happy as could be."

By the time Stirling began to play in tournaments, she had to accommodate herself to the fashions of the day—bulky jackets and long, sweeping skirts—that were as annoying as they were inhibiting. "We could do much better in knickerbockers," she wrote. "The skirt is a big handicap in putting, especially on windy days when it may often hide the ball just as you go to hit it."

There was no hiding Alexa's talent, though. Not for her "the flabbiness and gentleness usually found in feminine play," wrote O. B. Keeler. "She smacks the ball with absolute confidence in beautiful precision; and produces when necessary a powerful backspin that will make even a long iron shot sit down like a poached egg upon the green."

In 1916, Stirling and Jones both made their debuts in the U.S. Amateur national championships. Jones, at age fourteen, won two matches and became the hottest young player in golf. Stirling, four years older, won the first of three straight national titles.

"Hurrah for Sex!" read the telegram Stirling's parents sent her in Massachusetts after she had won, using the family nickname that had innocently changed from Alexandra and Alexa to Sexie and Sex. The message was too risqué for Western Union to deliver, but the members at East Lake made their feelings known when she got home.

Over the years, there would be many dinners held at the club to celebrate the championships won by its favorite son, and today the ornate lobby in the spacious clubhouse and several other rooms serve as a shrine to Jones's trophies and his memory. But in an inconspicuous corner on the second floor there is a photograph from the first gala evening ever to celebrate a national champion from East Lake. It was attended by more than three hundred people, and it was in honor of Alexa Stirling.

2

The Jewel of the South

Atlanta stands for the New South, the New South with all the romance of music, beauty, poetry, idealism, of a fading past; the New South built upon the everlasting granite of imperishable principles—foundations laid by our fathers in sweat, tears and blood. . . . Unique, brilliant Atlanta!

—Dr. Carter Helm Jones, pastor of the Second Baptist Church of Atlanta, 1924

In 1922, the mayor of Atlanta was a member of the Ku Klux Klan. Walter Sims won after a campaign during which he called the incumbent mayor, James Key, a "nigger-lover" as they stood together on a rostrum.

The governor of Georgia and one of the state's U.S. senators also were members of the Klan. So were an Atlanta city councilman, a Fulton County commissioner, several judges, city attorneys, school board members, and municipal employees who recognized Klan membership as essential to their careers.

The Klan newspaper, the *Searchlight*, could be purchased at city newsstands and sometimes contained ads for Studebaker automobiles, Coca-Cola, and Elgin watches. Through its robe-manufacturing company and other enterprises, the Klan was an important economic force in Atlanta and a very public one. With as many as a dozen lodges in the metropolitan area, it sponsored parades, put on minstrel shows, gave money to charity, and donated food to the poor at Christmas and Thanksgiving.

It also beat up union organizers, prevented the rehiring of a Catholic schoolteacher, sponsored a motion in the City Council condemning the Knights of Columbus as un-American, flogged men it suspected of not supporting their families, and carefully monitored the city's housing patterns. Throughout the 1920s, the Klan held rallies and burned crosses, and occasionally bombed homes when black families attempted to move into white Atlanta neighborhoods.

As late as the 1930s, it was a ritual for all new members of the Atlanta police department to stand before a burning cross at Stone Mountain, the birthplace of the modern Klan in 1915, and be initiated into the organization. It was not unusual for police in uniform to escort Klan parades through the black neighborhoods they had been organized to intimidate.

"I can almost say that at one time most of the members of the police department were members of the Ku Klux Klan," Herbert Jenkins, a former Klan member who later became the city's police chief, told an interviewer for *Living Atlanta: An Oral History of the City, 1914–1918*. It was not just the membership of the Klan that was important, Jenkins said, but the number of people who sympathized with its methods and objectives. "That kind of support was the most important thing," he said, "more so than the membership."

Atlanta did not hire its first black policemen until 1947, and though they were greeted with jubilation in their community, they were not allowed to patrol white neighborhoods, arrest white citizens, or enter the downtown police station. There were no black firemen in the city, no black judges or jurors.

Atlanta's neighborhoods and schools were segregated, of course, as were its movie theaters and department stores, its restaurants and train stations, its buses and streetcars, its hospitals and elevators, its drinking fountains, swimming pools, and graveyards. Until the 1920s, black residents were not allowed in any of the city's parks, nor could they vote in the city or state Democratic primaries—the only elections that mattered.

Atlanta's libraries were not desegregated until 1959, when Irene Dobbs Jackson, a professor of French at Spelman College and the mother of a future mayor, received her library card. *The Atlanta Constitution* noted the occasion by printing her name and address, and that night cars circled the family home, their drivers honking horns and shouting epithets. "Doncha know niggers can't read?" one telephone caller informed Professor Jackson.

Yet Atlanta, then as now, was the most progressive city in the South, one that attracted black men and women in great numbers and where they built a thriving and vibrant community.

For long periods, the city was guided by politically astute mayors who navigated the racial currents of the times with something approaching goodwill. Also, many senior members of its business power structure were more concerned with seizing the opportunities a growing city presented than with refighting the Civil War. It was this legacy that helped Atlanta avoid much of the worst violence of the civil rights struggles of the 1960s.

Founded as a railroad center in 1837—it was originally known as Terminus—the town had never been shy about self-promotion. If Atlanta could suck as hard as it could blow, a chamber of commerce official in another southern town once said, it would be a city on the Atlantic. Almost as if to prove the point, Atlanta responded to a land boom in Florida in 1926 that was draining away population and capital by creating a campaign aimed at turning things around.

Ads for "Forward Atlanta" appeared in national newspapers and magazines proclaiming the South as the fastest-growing region in the country and Atlanta as its center. Any large business that failed to place a regional branch in a city with a population approaching three hundred thousand and within a day's travel of seventy million Americans did so at its peril. Atlanta, the nation's businessmen were told, had a congenial climate, a low cost of living, and an "intelligent, adaptable, Anglo-Saxon" workforce.

The campaign lasted three years and was a huge success. Atlanta was soon the home of new factories, warehouses, and sales offices— and more than twenty thousand new employees earning close to $35 million. The promotion of the city as a transportation hub paid even greater dividends in 1928, when City Councilman William B. Hartsfield convinced the federal government to choose Atlanta over Birmingham, Alabama, as a regional airmail center. Hartsfield would later serve three terms as mayor, and the airport that bears his name would become one of the busiest in the world.

Atlanta was can-do in other areas as well. In 1910, civic leaders convinced the New York Metropolitan Opera to visit, and all doubts about the wisdom of the experiment were quickly swept away when Enrico Caruso performed in *Aïda* before more than seven thousand people, the largest crowd ever to hear him sing. Opera lovers came from all over the South and from as far away as Havana, and the company was amazed by the city's hospitality. There were breakfasts, luncheons, dinners, teas, picnics, and dress balls. Members of the company soon began appearing at civic events as well as restaurants around town and at baseball games. The Metropolitan's five Atlanta productions made more money than it had ever earned in a single week in New York, and a return trip was quickly scheduled.

"In the future, anyone who wishes to hear grand opera as given by the Metropolitan Company in America must either go to New York or Atlanta for it," said Otto Kahn, the opera's managing director. With breaks for only two world wars and the Depression, the Metropolitan visited Atlanta annually for decades.

Perhaps this booster mentality, this hunger for advancement and recognition, helps to account for Atlanta's response to its first resident ever to be celebrated on a national and then international scale in the twentieth century.

"He was the first international figure to represent the South since Robert E. Lee," says Dr. Catherine Lewis, the curator of a permanent exhibit devoted to Jones at the Atlanta History Center, of the position Jones would come to occupy in the city where he was born. "Yet, his reputation was not built on defeat, but instead upon character, cordiality, and intelligence. He projected such gentility—he had a distinctive accent and was well spoken. He represented an important symbol for a city striving to grow and thrive in the early twentieth century."

Or perhaps it was just that from the beginning he was such a good story.

Jones first made the Atlanta papers at age nine when he was matched against Howard Thorne, who was sixteen and towered over him, in the final match of the city's junior golf championship. The contest "promises to be a corker," readers were informed, and from a historical perspective it was all of that. Jones won, 5 and 4, over 36 holes.

But it was five years later when the love affair between Jones and Atlanta truly began. That was when George Adair, his friend Perry

Adair's father and one of the founders of East Lake, convinced the Colonel to let him take the boys to the 1916 U.S. Amateur championship at the Merion Cricket Club on Philadelphia's Main Line.

Jones and Perry Adair had played well in several regional tournaments, and not only because they were talented beyond their years. The competition, Jones would note years later, was not very good because many of the top players in the South, and indeed around the country, had not grown up playing golf the way they had. "We were so prominent," he wrote, "because most other competitors had learned to play golf after reaching maturity," and that had held them back.

In the first round he ever played outside the South, Jones shot a record 74 to lead all qualifiers on Merion's new course, and became an instant sensation. Who could resist a small boy who chewed gum and ate ice cream, tugged his cap down over his eyes, hit the ball as far and as straight as his elders, made excellent recovery shots when he got in trouble, and seemed so nerveless on the golf course?

And, indeed, Jones was having the time of his life at Merion. He was just a boy, after all, who was dazzled by his first stay in an elegant big-city hotel and marveled at his first experience on a championship-quality golf course. He was playing the game he loved without a care in the world. What did it matter who his opponents were? It was just golf, wasn't it? What did he have to lose? Knowledgeable observers were impressed at how quickly Jones adjusted to his first experience with Merion's bent-grass greens, which were the most beautiful he had ever seen, and the most deceptive. For the rest of his life, he would remember putting straight past the sixth hole, off the green, and into a brook during a practice round.

Jones shot 89 in the second qualifying round, but when he beat two experienced and much older golfers in his first two matches, and took the defending champion, Robert Gardner, to the back nine of their 36-hole match before finally losing, he was headline news around the country.

"Boy of Fourteen Beats Ex-Champ," read the large type in the *New York Times* after Jones beat Eben Byers, who had won the U.S. Amateur title in 1906.

"Not even Bob Gardner, who is the last word in courage, could outgame the little fellow," the paper concluded after Jones was finally beaten. Gardner was a Yale graduate who had once held the world pole vault record and physically eclipsed the five-foot-four youngster wearing his first pair of long pants.

"Undoubtedly he has the makings of a national champion in the near future," the authoritative magazine *American Golfer* assured its readers. Little Bob Jones, it was unanimously agreed, was someone who bore watching.

But if the nation was impressed, Atlanta went mad.

Accompanying the report of Jones's defeat by Gardner in the *Atlanta Journal* was an editorial cartoon stretched across three columns of the front page. It depicted "Little Bob Jones" standing atop a globe labeled "World of Popular Attention."

"Bobby, you're driving everything else out of our minds," a hat-waving citizen told him, while beneath the globe, figures representing "Politics" and "The Great War" said, "What chance have I?" "I might as well adjourn," said a character wearing a silk hat and a frock coat labeled "Congress," as small men called "Mexico," "Baseball," and "Everything Else" fell out of the picture entirely.

"Gardner Required All He Had to Beat Bob in the Third Round," was the headline atop Grantland Rice's account of the match, but the *Journal* was just getting warmed up. At age fourteen, Little Bob was the subject of poetry.

"The War Cry of the Joneses" was the title of the lead item in Morgan Blake's column.

> In days of old there was a Jones
> If memory serves me right,
> Who shouted from the quarterdeck,
> "I've just begun to fight."
> Today the eyes of Southerners
> Are facing to the North
> And calling on their champion
> Little Bob—to sally forth.
> And as the acid test draws near
> He rises to his might,
> And these—the tones of Bobbie Jones—
> "I'VE JUST BEGUN TO FIGHT."

Though the "wonder child" was now the most famous boy in the United States, *Journal* readers were assured, he was also a fine student who was taking Latin at Tech High School even though it was not required and often set his clubs aside to study. Jones's parents and grandfather also were saluted in the tribute, as was Stewart Maiden.

"Little Bob's father and mother are both fond of golf," the article noted, "so that he comes by the game naturally; or, as Mrs. Jones states the proposition, they come by the game quite naturally from him."

Jones returned home to Atlanta, where during the next few years he went to school, grew from the small child who had wowed the multitudes into a five-foot-eight adult, a bit stocky at 165 pounds, and polished his golf game until it became the standard by which all others would be judged. It would be seven years before Jones became a national champion and began a run of championship tournament performances that has never been equaled. But as far as Atlanta, the city he would live in all his life, was concerned, the era of Bobby Jones had begun.

3

The Keeper of the Flame

In 1926, when O. B. Keeler accompanied Bobby Jones to the British Open, he made a side trip to Ye Olde Cheshire Cheese on London's Fleet Street to have a look at the pub where Samuel Johnson and James Boswell were said to have spent many evenings together 150 years earlier. Keeler was delighted that nobody had thought to fix up the place—in America, he said, some smart operator would have tried to capitalize on its fame by turning it into a café—but he was disappointed he could not sit in Johnson's armchair because it was displayed in a glass case.

The visit to the pub, and the article he wrote about it, were typical of Keeler—learned, puckish, irreverent, clever. So he was Bobby Jones's Boswell, was he? Fine. He would just look in on the original.

In truth, Keeler was far more to Jones than his biographer. Their relationship is without comparison in all of sports. No other writer has ever been as close to his subject for as long. Nor has any journalist ever provided so many services beyond the written word. Keeler saw every one of Jones's championship victories and once estimated that they had traveled 120,000 miles together. When Jones was still in his teens, the Colonel, convinced he was bad luck, stopped going to tournaments with him. Keeler, who was twenty years older than Jones, filled the role of traveling companion and surrogate father as much as journalist.

The two men would ride the trains together, stay in the same hotel rooms, and take their meals in privacy, away from the club cars and dining rooms as much as possible. They would talk into the night, often about subjects other than golf but with a clinical objectivity when that was impossible. "Bobby and his game are two different entities in the mind of each of us, and we can praise or pan it with equal impartiality," Keeler said. "We try to study his game in perfect detachment." For a shy young man away from home with long stretches of time on his hands he might have spent brooding over upcoming tournaments, Keeler was a godsend.

"He had read everything and remembered most of it," Jones wrote. "He could, and frequently did, recite verse for hours. I found the opportunities for a liberal education as we lolled about our hotel room or on a train."

Keeler was an indifferent golfer—it took him years to break 100, and his attempts to get down to 80 never succeeded—but he knew Jones's game inside out. Beyond that, Jones came to rely on him for the kind of support that can only be supplied by the closest of confidants. "I think I have never felt so lonely as on a golf course in the midst of a championship with thousands of people around, especially when things began to go wrong and the crowds started wandering away," Jones wrote. "It was then that I began to look for Keeler, and I always found him."

Once, Jones did not even wait for the match to begin. Afraid he was not going to make the field for the 1927 U.S. Amateur championship at the Minikahda Club in Minneapolis after a mediocre first qualifying round, Jones told Keeler he needed him. "The only way for me to get out of this thing is to go out this afternoon and try to win the medal," he told him, "and I need you to walk with me for a few holes until I get calmed down." What he needed most of all, Jones said, was an understanding soul who would help him get over the "feeling of aloneness which comes when your confidence is gone."

Jones felt more comfortable from the start that afternoon and, after the fifth hole, told Keeler he could leave. He shot a course record 67 to win the medal given to the lowest qualifier, then went on to win the tournament.

Keeler also could tease Jones in the way only a close friend would dare—he referred to his problems keeping his weight down by calling him Rubber Tyre Jones—and he could scold him as well.

"I wonder if I'm *ever* going to win one of these things," Jones said as the two men sat in his berth on the train to the 1921 U.S. Amateur championship at St. Louis.

"Bobby, if you ever get it through your head that whenever you step out on the first tee of any competition you are the best golfer in it, then you'll win this championship and a lot of others," Keeler said.

"Don't be an idiot," said Jones, who may have thought he proved the point after he was eliminated from the tournament to complete the most disappointing year of his career.

So if Jones was one of the best things that ever happened to Keeler—their relationship made Keeler one of the best-known sportswriters in America—the reverse is true as well. Keeler was the rock on which Jones could rely, the one constant during the years when he fought to become a champion and those when he battled to remain one. Keeler also was Jones's link to the outside world, the man other journalists sought out when they needed to fill the ever-growing demand for news of Jones. And though he always held a bit in reserve for his own reports, Keeler was more than generous to his colleagues.

"Keeler made Jones," wrote Ralph Trost of the *Brooklyn Eagle*. "He *was* Jones. He told us what Jones said, what he hoped, his aims. He told us what he had done—and much about what he was going to do and did. Far more than Jones can ever realize, many of us got to know Bobby through O. B."

It never would have occurred to any of these writers to ask Keeler about Jones's private life, of course, just as Keeler would never have imagined trespassing on it himself. Nor did any of his writing, even about Jones's defeats, fail to project the nobility of his subject.

"I am willing to leave the record of my golfing activities to the words this man has written," wrote Jones in a preface to Keeler's authorized biography, *The Bobby Jones Story*. "Why in Heaven's name shouldn't I be? He never once gave me anything but the best of any argument."

"I didn't give myself the worst of it, either," Keeler said.

·   ·   ·

Oscar Bane Keeler was born in Chicago in 1882, and at age four was taken by his family ("without my knowledge or consent") to Tate, Georgia, north of Atlanta. Though he studied Latin and Greek, developed a prodigious memory, and was clearly a young man of talent, he had trouble finding himself in the business world. He knocked around in a variety of office jobs until, at age twenty-six, he showed up at the *Atlanta Georgian* in 1909 and offered to work for free. He would even supply the typewriter. He passed his probation in a short time, was hired at $18 a week, and quickly realized that he had found his calling. After a year, Keeler moved to the *Kansas City Star*, where legend has it he earned that paper's first byline, beating out a colleague named Ernest Hemingway for the honor.

"No matter what the story—murder, sports, opera, or presidential visit—whatever the *Star's* biggest story for that day," the paper's sports editor, C. E. McBride, told Keeler's Atlanta colleague Ed Miles, "it was Keeler who got the call because he was considered the ace and all-around artist of the staff." After several years Keeler went back to the *Georgian*, and in 1920 he switched to the *Atlanta Journal*, where he spent the rest of his working life.

Keeler was a lively writer and a prodigious reporter who covered baseball, boxing, and football as well as golf. For years before he began writing about sports, he covered crime and politics and wrote feature stories on everything from itinerant evangelists to the sinking of the *Titanic*. Keeler's coverage of the lynching in 1915 of Leo Frank, a Jewish factory manager who had been pardoned by the governor of Georgia after being wrongly convicted of the murder of a young girl, was so vivid and sympathetic that a man who was never identified showed up at Keeler's house with Frank's wedding ring and a note asking him to give it to the dead man's widow.

He also befriended Enrico Caruso on one of the New York Metropolitan Opera's trips to Atlanta, and after one late night out, they returned to Caruso's hotel where Keeler, feeling no pain, said that just once he would like to hear the great tenor sing only for him. "What's better than now?" Caruso replied and, standing at the bottom of the hotel staircase at four in the morning, he began to sing. Doors flew open and the hotel guests, wearing slippers and robes, emerged to line the staircase and listen to the impromptu recital.

When Keeler traveled with Jones to the British Grand Slam tournaments in 1930, he wrote columns about the side trip they took with their wives to Paris between events. He was impressed by the Folies Bergère but annoyed that he was unable to order eggs for breakfast in his hotel dining room.

Keeler was a practical joker of epic proportions—once during a rainstorm he called Western Union and had himself delivered to the *Journal* city room in a canvas sack—and a legendary drinker whose house was known as "Distillery Hill." He was extravagantly gallant to women and thought nothing of telling them, upon being introduced, "I love you madly. Shall we flee together?" Whether or not Keeler actually declaimed the lines he said he wrote for a lady who reminded him of a promise to render her charms in poetry, he was not shy about reciting them in public:

> I've indicted a petit jury, On the light in your eyes so fair;
> And I've written a lovely lyric, On the glint in your golden hair;
> And my typewriter's quite ambitious, To ensure your lasting
> fame;
> But the likker we had was vicious, And I can't remember your
> name.

In August 1916, Keeler was sent to cover the first Georgia State Amateur tournament at Brookhaven Country Club in Atlanta. Perry Adair had recently won an invitation tournament in Montgomery, Alabama, and at sixteen was being hailed as the boy wonder of Dixie. The youngster Adair beat in the semifinals in Montgomery, Bobby Jones, also had had some success and might be worth looking at as well.

Keeler would later tell a reporter he had just suffered a paralytic stroke in both arms, was not feeling well, and was hardly looking forward to walking 36 holes on a hot summer day. (This could have been one of his put-ons—it might have been a hangover.) And when an obliging member of the crowd offered to accompany him with an umbrella to ward off the sun, he gladly accepted.

In the years to come, Ralph Reed, the chairman of the tournament committee, would tell of his concern that Adair, who led by three shots after the morning round, would close out the match early and that the large crowd that had come for the afternoon round would not see much golf. Reed said he asked Jones to play out the bye holes.

"Don't worry, there won't be any bye holes," Jones answered.

Keeler later repeated the story—"I recall very vividly how Ralph Reed turned to Bobby Jones and suggested that he stay and play"— even though in *Down the Fairway*, the book he and Jones wrote together, Jones emphatically denied it.

What is not in dispute is that Jones beat Adair on the last hole, and Keeler was hooked. He had seen the toughest boxers of the era, he said—Dempsey, Firpo, Willard, Sharkey—but he had never seen anyone battle like the fourteen-year-old who beat the boy wonder of Dixie.

From that moment on, Keeler told Jones later, he was determined to make a career of writing about golf. And about Bobby Jones's golf in particular.

4

"Emotions Which Could Not Be Endured"

The first great golfer who never won a major tournament was Allan Robertson. Born at St. Andrews in 1815 into a family of caddies and craftsmen who made feather balls by hand, Robertson was often considered to be golf's first professional. The term referred to those who tended golf courses and served the needs of members; there was no thought of their playing in tournaments for prize money.

In 1859, a few months before he died, Robertson became the first player on record to break 80 at the Old Course. The first national championship golf tournament, the British Open, was played a year later. In the years since then, and continuing to the present, fans of the sport have debated who should be considered the best golfer then playing who had not won a major championship. This was golf's way of separating the good players competing regularly at the highest level from the very best.

One of golf's brightest stars of the 1920s and 1930s was Harry Cooper, who won thirty-one professional tournaments in the United States, which is still enough to place him in a tie for fourteenth on the list of all-time winners. But Cooper never won one of golf's highest prizes, and he never got over it. "He was the best player for ten years but he never won a major tournament," said Sam Snead, whose eighty-two tournament victories, the highest total ever recorded, include seven major championships. "I think he destroyed his mind thinking more about the other guy beating him than about beating the other guy."

"I could have won with a break four Opens," Cooper recalled, still rankled at this blot on his record, "but something seemed to happen every time."

In the last half of the second decade of the twentieth century, and into the first years of the Roaring Twenties, the best golfer who had not won a major tournament was Bobby Jones. In a sense, it was terribly unfair that Jones should have carried this burden, because World War I forced the cancellation of the U.S. and British national championships and because he was only a teenager during most of this time. But Jones had brought the problem on himself by doing so well in his first U.S. Amateur championship at age fourteen and becoming the toast of golf. The shotmaking skill Jones exhibited at Merion, and the very idea of a still-growing adolescent playing adults on equal terms drew large crowds, a rush of national press attention, and made him a marked man.

During the next few years, Jones, who was too young to serve in the Great War, participated with his boyhood chums Perry Adair and Alexa Stirling in a series of exhibitions around the country organized to raise money for the Red Cross. These appearances had the dual effect of helping to popularize golf in the United States and spreading the word about this handsome, polite, astonishingly proficient young golfer. They also gave Jones experience against many of the top golfers of the era, including some of the best professionals, in low-pressure charity affairs that took the place of the national championships.

By the time the war to end all wars had ended, Jones was competing regularly in regional and national events and continuing to impress everyone who saw him. The best British golfers, who were spending more and more time in the United States, which had begun to make serious inroads on the game they had invented and always dominated, marveled at his skills.

"Mr. Vardon, did you ever see a worse shot than that?" Jones

asked Harry Vardon, who had won the British Open six times, after
flubbing a shot when they played together during qualifying at the
1920 U.S. Open at the Inverness Club in Toledo, Ohio.

"No," Vardon replied.

But Vardon, who had done much to promote golf both in Britain
and the United States, knew what he was seeing—nothing less than
the future of the sport. "The possibilities of his golf impressed me
enormously," Vardon wrote of that initial encounter with Jones. The
top American competitors also could begin to see that the day might
come when the headlines would read, "Jones against the Field."

But try as he would, and as close as he sometimes came during
what Keeler would later call his seven lean years, Jones failed to win
a major championship in his first ten attempts. He tried to make light
of this failing. All it took to win a major tournament, he wrote, was
"plain brute endurance . . . a strong back and weak mind and a lot of
this stuff they call the will to win—another name for stupid persist-
ence." But this dismissive attitude was expressed only after he had
begun to win important tournaments himself. In reality, the losses
rankled, and he brooded over them.

"If I was really a great golfer—what was the matter?" he wrote.
"Or was I a great golfer? I could hit the shots well; I couldn't help
knowing that. But was I a golfer, or only one of those hapless
mechanical excellencies known as a great shotmaker, who cannot
connect the great shots in sufficient numbers to win anything?" He
said he was getting a championship complex, which he defined as
wanting to become a champion because so many people thought he
ought to be one.

It was in these early tournaments that Jones displayed a flaw in his
game that those who saw him knew he would have to cure before he
could succeed on the level his talent indicated—his inability to control his emotions on the golf course. From an early age, his furious
response to bad shots frightened his family and worried his friends.
Grantland Rice, a longtime acquaintance of Jones's father who often
saw the young man play and would become his lifelong friend, said he
had "the face of an angel and the temper of a timberwolf."

Even as a six-year-old, Jones would dance with rage in the road outside the house at East Lake when a shot got away from him on the makeshift two-hole course he and his friends had improvised. "Let him make one poor shot," Stirling recalled, "and he'd turn livid with rage, throw his club after the ball, or break it over his knee, or kick at the ground and let out a stream of very adult oaths. As I grew into my teens, Bob's temper tantrums began to embarrass me. It was perhaps amusing to see an eight-year-old break his club when he made a bad shot, but not so amusing when the boy was twelve or thirteen."

Even then, Jones's rages had consequences. Stirling tells how she was playing a round with her father, who had once been the British counsel in Atlanta, when they came upon Jones just as he mishit a drive, threw a club, and swore a loud oath. "Unfortunately, one expletive that he used was the most offensive word to the British," Stirling said. "He shouted, 'That bloody shot!' Father drew himself up and thundered, 'Young man, don't you know better than to use language like that in front of a lady?' He took me by the hand and marched me off the course." She was not allowed to play with Jones for two years.

"A lot of good it does me to play with you damn girls," Jones, whose adolescent manners were no better than his temper, told her during this banishment. "If I am ever going to be a golfer I've got to go and play with the men. I'm just glad your old man stopped me."

It was not long before Jones was making his temperamental displays in larger gatherings. At Merion in 1916, Jones engaged in a club-throwing exhibition during his match with Byers, who was thirty-nine years old, had won the U.S. Amateur ten years earlier, and could hardly claim youth as an excuse. At the 12th hole, Byers threw a club out of bounds and would not let his caddy retrieve it. Jones began throwing clubs, too, and the players in the match directly behind them said he and Byers looked like a juggling act. "I think the main reason I beat him," Jones joked years later, "was because he ran out of clubs first."

Two years later, in one of the Red Cross exhibitions during the war, Jones played with Jerome Travers, the winner of four U.S. Amateurs, in a match in Canada. "On the first green," Travers later wrote, "Bobby missed a small putt and became so enraged he hurled his club far over the heads of the crowd into a cluster of trees and stubble bordering the course. The Canadian gallery laughed at this outburst and joined in the search for the putter that had disappeared in the woods."

Stirling was less amused. By 1918 she had won the first of her three consecutive U.S. Women's Amateur championships, and was at least as important to the organizers of the Red Cross exhibitions as Jones. But she was not sure she wanted to play in them for fear of being further humiliated by her friend's outbursts. And sure enough, in an exhibition at Brae Burn Country Club near Boston, Jones hit a poor shot and exploded.

"I saw the blood climb his neck and flood his face," Stirling wrote. "Then he picked up his ball, took a full pitcher's windup, and threw the ball into the woods. A gasp of surprise and shock went through the large crowd watching us. I wished only that the ground beneath me would open and let me sink from sight."

"I don't give a damn what anybody thinks about me," Jones told her when she chastised him after the match. "I only get mad at myself."

Years later, Jones wrote of that moment, "I read the pity in Alexa's soft brown eyes and finally settled down, but not before I had made a complete fool of myself."

Stewart Maiden also was concerned about Jones's inability to control himself, but nothing he said seemed to make any difference. The one constructive suggestion he did make was to tell Luke Ross, who was Jones's caddy for six years beginning with the 1920 U.S. Open, not to run after his clubs when he threw them. Walk slowly, Maiden told Ross, and give him time to cool down.

If Jones's temper didn't create enough problems, a combination of indifferent play, opponents who were often at the top of their form when they played against him, and several weird incidents brought his fragile equanimity to the breaking point when he returned to competitive golf after the war. The memory of his performance at Merion in 1916 and the national attention he received playing in the Red Cross fund-raisers made him one of the players to watch when, after a two-year hiatus, the U.S. Amateur resumed at Oakmont Country Club outside Pittsburgh in 1919.

Jones won four matches, including a satisfyingly easy victory over Robert Gardner, who had beaten him at Merion three years earlier, to make the finals against Davey Herron. A member at Oakmont who had graduated from Princeton the year before, Herron had local knowledge and fan support on his side, but Jones was favored to win his first national championship. After the morning round, the players were all even, which excited the crowd of six thousand that had come to root for Herron and one reporter sniffed at as "generally unlearned." The cheers grew even louder as Herron began to sink long putts. After 11 holes, Jones was three down with seven to play.

On the 601-yard 12th hole, Herron hit into a trap, and Jones had a chance to win the hole and perhaps turn the match around. But just as he was at the top of his backswing for his second shot, an official shouted "Fore!" through a megaphone at a spectator moving somewhere far off in the distance. Jones topped his ball into a bunker, could not get out in two attempts, conceded the hole, and, with his chance to reverse the momentum of the match gone, lost his second U.S. Amateur.

Jones said later that he would have been beaten anyway, but he was clearly rankled that he had been hampered by something that had nothing to do with hitting the ball. What the match suggested to him, he said, was the notion of a golf tournament being decided not by talent but by fate. "There was something about that megaphone blast that seemed to tell me, as clearly as I suppose the Angel Gabriel will call time on us one day, that this was not my turn," he wrote. "That's partly what I mean when I suggest that a golf tournament is all in the book, before a shot is driven . . . nothing ever announced to me as distinctly as that megaphone that I was beaten."

This tournament also supplied the first evidence of the toll golf would take on Jones's nerves during his career. He entered the tournament weighing 155 pounds; when it was over, he was 18 pounds lighter. In future championships, Jones would write, he invariably lost 10 to 15 pounds, and not because of physical exertion. He could play 36 holes every day for two weeks and not lose a pound, he said, but in a championship "the fire seems to be hotter."

The following year, Jones's hopes of winning the U.S. Amateur again fell to simple bad luck, this time in the form of slapstick comedy.

There was no place for Jones to hide in the 1920 Amateur, which was held at the Engineers Country Club on Long Island. He had finished second the year before, after all, and in a creditable tie for eighth at the U.S. Open at Inverness, where he sheepishly admitted he had unwisely finished off lunch between his final two rounds with pie and ice cream. Now all eyes were turned in his direction, and when he easily played his way into the semifinals, his moment appeared to be at hand.

Jones's opponent was Francis Ouimet, the hero of Brookline, where, at age twenty in 1913, he beat Vardon and Ted Ray, two of British golf's greatest veteran players, in an upset that announced the coming popularity of the sport in the United States. Like Jones, Ouimet remained an amateur throughout his career, and the younger man idolized him to the extent that on the night before they were to meet again in the 1924 U.S. Amateur semifinals at Merion, Keeler found Jones in his hotel room near tears.

"I don't want to play Francis," Jones said. "I'm going well, and his game is all shot to pieces, and I'm pretty sure I can beat him, and darn it all—I don't *want* to beat him." Keeler convinced him to act as if he were playing the course, not Ouimet, and after Jones ran away with the match 11 and 10, they walked off the course with their arms around each other's shoulders.

When they met at Engineers, however, Ouimet was playing well and Jones, who had shown some of his temper in the early rounds of the tournament to spectators and a press corps now actively looking for it, exploded. Ouimet won the first two holes and held on all morning when Jones missed a short putt at 18 to fall three back. At which point he picked up his ball and drop-kicked it into the rough.

Jones won a hole back early in the afternoon round and came to the 7th hole still in the match. Both men were on the green in two when Jones had what looked like a makeable putt. Ouimet stood impassively as Jones stood over his ball when suddenly a bee landed on it. Jones shooed it away. The bee immediately flew back to the ball. He waved it away again. The bee landed on the green nearby. An official plopped down a megaphone (*another* megaphone?) on it, but the bee simply flew out of the mouthpiece and headed straight toward Jones. "It seemed to be fond of me," Jones said later.

Finally, with the gallery howling with laughter, and even Ouimet showing the trace of a smile, Jones took off his cap, swung it and his putter at the bee, and chased it off the green. Jones returned, but his concentration was shattered. He three-putted, lost the hole and the next two as well. Ouimet beat him, 6 and 5.

"Sometimes I fancy that bee flew away with a good bit of my juvenile fancy for the game of golf," Jones said. "Anyway, it hasn't seemed the same since the Engineers Club in 1920."

In 1921, when Jones was nineteen years old, he went to Britain for the first time. He was part of an American team that included many of the country's top amateurs, and the British press and public were curious to see the attractive, soft-spoken young golfer whose skills had so impressed Vardon the summer before. But the trip would soon become a full-fledged disaster that contained one laughable encounter, one embarrassing beating and what Jones would term the most ignoble episode of his career.

The Americans won their international match against Britain easily enough, and Jones looked so sharp in his two victories that the British bookmakers installed him as a 5–1 favorite to win the British Amateur championship. But when the tournament began at the Royal Liverpool Golf Club at Hoylake, a seaside community on a peninsula across the Mersey River from Liverpool, he was in trouble almost from the start.

Jones was surprised by what he found at Hoylake. No trees to give shelter from the stiff breezes that blew in off the Irish Sea. Greens that were slow as sand when it was wet and rock hard when they dried out. The fact the greens were not watered amazed him—the hosts applied several buckets of water around the pins of some of the driest holes when the Americans complained—and caused his carefully calibrated pitch shots to bounce off the hard surfaces as if they had landed on cement. Jones made it through the first round without incident, but then played against perhaps the worst golfer he would ever meet in serious competition. He nearly lost.

The British sportswriters were not at all surprised that a florist from the North Wales town of Wrexham bearing the unlikely name of E. A. Hamlet should shoot an 87. But they found it hilarious that he should take the great Bobby Jones to the final hole while doing it. "It really seemed as if he were going to beat Bobby, which, as Euclid might have remarked, would have been absurd," wrote Bernard

Darwin in the *Times* of London. "It was a farcical affair and the crowd were divided between patriotism, fury and laughter." Hamlet's style was ridiculous, wrote George Greenwood in *Golf Illustrated*, and a victory would have been comical. Nevertheless, here he was leading Jones by two holes with four to play.

Nor did Jones's behavior commend itself to the British, who had been so anxious to see him play and now seemed almost insulted by his performance. He had been "petulant and irritable; in short had lost his temper and his nerve as thoroughly as he had lost his putting touch," Greenwood wrote. "He kicked at an inoffensive gorse bush which had the audacity to catch a pulled drive, and generally this glorious boy golfer was a mass of nerves."

Jones was saved from complete embarrassment when Hamlet, intimidated by the partisan crowd and terrified at the thought of how close he was to beating the heralded youngster, lost the last three holes. Jones won the 18th when his ball, partially stymied, hit Hamlet's ball at the edge of the cup and dropped in. Jones had shot an ignominious 86 and been taken to the limit. There was no talk of fate this time. Jones knew it was plain luck that had seen him through.

That luck ran out in the fourth round when he lost to Allan Graham, another golfer the British press couldn't help deriding even as it marveled at his victory. Born in one of the homes that had been built overlooking Hoylake years before, Graham was a tall, sleepy-looking man who appeared bored by the game. As he sauntered around the links, Greenwood wrote, you could almost hear him say, "Oh, confound it, here is another one of those beastly golf balls. I suppose I must hit it." And besides, how seriously was anyone supposed to take a golfer who had borrowed three clubs from his sister to make up a set—one an odd-looking brass putter that Jones still remembered years later—and who, when asked if he had thought of wearing spiked shoes to keep from slipping on the greens, said they were such a nuisance around the house?

But Graham didn't just beat Jones, he routed him, 6 and 5. Jones received high marks for congratulating Graham warmly before his long walk to the clubhouse from the 13th hole, but that was the only positive aspect of his first appearance at Hoylake. He could hardly take any comfort from the fact that the eventual winner of the tournament, Willie Hunter, crushed Graham in the final, 12 and 11, or when the entire U.S. team, which had begun the tournament with such high expectations, was eliminated in the early rounds. But the worst part of Jones's first trip to Britain lay straight ahead.

Jones was not the first golfer to wonder what all the fuss was about when he got his first look at St. Andrews, nor was he the last. "Back home," Sam Snead would say years later, "we plant cow beets on land like that." Jones's description of his first impression of the historic Old Course on Scotland's eastern coast was less colorful but just as direct: "I considered St. Andrews among the very worst courses I had ever seen." St. Andrews, the home of Britain's Royal and Ancient Golf Club, which has been the ruling body of golf for centuries, soon extracted its revenge for this impertinence.

Jones's opening round in the 1921 British Open was mediocre, a 78 that left him six shots behind his playing partner, Jock Hutchison, who led after 18 holes and eventually won the tournament. But a 74 on the second round left Jones in a good position if not to win, at least to make up for his embarrassment at Hoylake. The next day, however, Jones's temper led him to commit an act he would always say he regretted more than any other he ever committed on a golf course.

If only we could be sure exactly what that act was.

It would be helpful if the original accounts of Jones picking up his ball and withdrawing from the tournament were in agreement. It would be helpful if Jones's own descriptions over the years were consistent. It would be helpful if, as time went on, Jones's malfeasance did not take on a life of its own, with almost as many variations as there are those who tell the tale. And it would be helpful if it did not take almost thirty years for an eyewitness report to appear, adding new contradictions.

Did Jones shoot 43 on the front nine that morning or 46? The latter figure is the one most commonly accepted, but the original reports in both the *Times* of London and the *Scotsman* of Edinburgh had the former. In his later writings, Jones told the story both ways.

Did he pick his ball up out of the Hill Bunker on the left side of the fairway on the par-3 11th hole after two—or three or four or even five—futile attempts to escape, or did he finally hack his way out of the bunker and pick up the ball on the green? Again, Jones has it both ways. And what about the report Jones hit the ball out of the bunker *over* the green and into the Eden Estuary? The only thing that is clear is that Jones hit his tee shot into the Hill Bunker, and his inability to get the ball out is responsible for what came next.

"It's the worst bunker on the course, much worse than the Road Bunker," Gordon Moir, St. Andrews links superintendent, says, comparing it to the trap that guards the green on the famous 17th hole. "It's as deep as any bunker on the course, but it's not broad so it doesn't matter where you're standing, something will interfere with your swing."

Eventually Jones did reach the green, but what happened there also is shrouded in myth and mystery. Did Jones tear up his scorecard and scatter the pieces? Most accounts agree that he did, and again Jones cannot seem to remember. In *Down the Fairway* he called the term "figurative," but years later he said his scorecard had indeed "found its way into the river."

Happily, there are two parts of the story as it came down that can be dealt with definitively. Jones did not, once he finally reached the 11th green, walk over to the 12th tee, turn to face the Eden Estuary, and drive a ball into the water. Here it is Darwin who has it both ways, at one point writing Jones "drove his ball into the sea, a very natural proceeding, for which he was unnecessarily apologetic" and, at another, "if he did not, I am very sure he wanted to." And Jones did not, as was still being written more than forty years later, leave the golf course in disgust. Though picking up his ball meant he had removed himself from competition, he continued his round and even came back to play in the afternoon and post an excellent score of 72.

In 1958, a letter appeared in the *St. Andrews Citizen* that represented one last attempt to set the story straight, but only at the cost of adding an additional element. He had seen Jones tear up his card, wrote David Anderson, the owner of a hotel in St. Andrews, not on the 11th hole but the 12th, where there were no more than a dozen spectators at the time. "It happened after Bobby had driven off from the 12th tee," Anderson wrote. "Walking up the 12th fairway, Bobby asked the marker for his card, [and] after a short scrutiny, coolly and deliberately tore it to shreds."

In the years to come, Jones would play some of the most stirring golf the British had ever seen and become one of the most popular

Americans ever to set foot in England and Scotland. He would retain this stature, which would continue to grow after he retired, for the rest of his life. As Jones left for home in 1921, however, the *Dundee Courier* summed up what many in Britain thought after getting their first look at him:

"Master 'Bobbie Jones' is a boy, and a rather ordinary boy, after all."

In writing long after the fact about Jones's attempts to control his temper, O. B. Keeler and Alexa Stirling made much of his performance a month after his British fiasco, in the 1921 U.S. Open at the Columbia Country Club in Chevy Chase, Maryland. Starting his final round well behind the eventual winner, Jim Barnes, Jones shot threes on three of the first four holes, and when he hit a good drive on the 560-yard 5th, he suddenly had visions of a great round that would allow him to challenge for the lead. Then at the 5th, he hooked two straight shots out of bounds.

As his friends looked on in horror, Jones remained perfectly still with only the red color that Stirling recognized so well creeping into his neck and face and the white of his knuckles from holding his club in a death grip, showing how he felt. Finally, Stirling says, he relaxed his hands, smiled in resignation at the crowd, and dropped another ball. He took a nine for the hole and finished with a 77, tied for fifth place. "We didn't let our tempers get the best of us, and returned to the locker room with the same number of clubs we had started out with," said a puckish Gene Sarazen, who played the round with Jones.

To Stirling, Jones's reaction meant Jones had at last mastered his emotions and was now ready to become a champion. Keeler agreed, writing, "I firmly believe that this tournament at Columbia was the ultimate closing of one chapter in the development of this remarkable young golfer. Bobby finally gained control of his temper."

Not quite yet he hadn't.

Jones's loss later that summer to Willie Hunter, in the third round of the 1921 U.S. Amateur at the St. Louis Country Club, might have been his toughest yet. Hunter, who had won the British Amateur at Hoylake, was from thirty to sixty yards shorter off the tee, and the huge crowd of ten thousand was rooting for Jones so rabidly that a

U.S. Golf Association official made several announcements asking for better sportsmanship. Jones led by two holes after the morning round but was not satisfied.

"I don't know why I'm only two up," he told Grantland Rice in the bathroom between rounds, not knowing that Hunter, troubled by diarrhea at this inconvenient time, was in a stall and could hear every word. "I outplayed him more than that."

Jones continued to outdrive Hunter in the afternoon round but still could not gain any ground. Frustrated, Jones tried to drive the 347-yard eighth hole, caught a tree limb, and saw his lead reduced to one hole. Hunter won the next hole, too, and the match was tied. Jones went ahead again on the 13th hole, but Hunter sank a thirty-foot putt at 14. Then Jones missed a two-footer at 15 to fall behind for the first time.

Hunter won the match at 17, where Jones blew up one more time. Disgusted after hitting a poor second shot, he tossed his club toward his bag, which was lying on the ground near the gallery, and once again missed his target. The club bounced off the bag and hit a woman in the gallery in the leg. She was not seriously hurt, but Jones was mortified.

Several weeks later, according to a story that first surfaced more than three decades later, Jones received a letter from U.S. Golf Association president George Walker containing a blunt warning: "You will never play in a U.S.G.A. event again unless you can learn to control your temper." But there is no record of this letter in U.S.G.A. files and no discussion of Jones's behavior at the 1921 Amateur in the organization's minutes. (Nor was Walker the president of the organization then; his term had expired the year before.) Jones himself never seems to have mentioned such a letter, and neither did Keeler. Yet the story persists in various guises, such as the one related by Walker's grandson, former U.S. president George H. W. Bush.

"There is a legend in our family," Bush says, "that Walker—they called him the Old Man—put his arm around Bobby Jones and said, 'Look, you've got all the makings of a great golfer, but you can't do it if you go on like this.' Jones allegedly passed this on to somebody, but maybe this is just a myth in the Bush-Walker family."

. . .

Long after Jones retired, he was still trying to understand where his outbursts of temper came from and decided that it had as much to do with ego as anger. It was, he said, "a childish effort to make known publicly that such a misplay was not to be tolerated by a player of so much ability."

In the end, Jones did learn to control his temper. He was particularly proud of himself for not blowing up when Jess Sweetser crushed him, 8 and 7, in their 36-hole semifinal at the 1922 U.S. Amateur at Brookline. "I just figured that I was playing the best golf I knew, and that Jess was shooting better golf," he wrote, "and for the first time in my life I had absolute control over myself."

And indeed it would not be long before his competitors and other observers would be saying that it was Jones's ability to channel his emotions into his game that accounted for much of his success.

"Those are the ones you have to watch, the fellows who are nervous but have it under control," said Tommy Armour, whose own temper—he once threw all his putters out the window of a Scottish train—was notorious. "They're the toughest to beat."

"These outbursts of temper were safety valves for his nervous system," said 1929 U.S. Amateur champion Harrison (Jimmy) Johnston, who was particularly close to Jones. "As he grew older and saw how undignified it looked to give way to his feelings, Bobby smothered them—and in doing so generated a human volcano beneath the surface."

"The angry golfer gets a zip to his shots and the calm one loses the crispness so definitely needed for the sailing qualities of a well-judged shot," said Chick Evans, the winner of the U.S. Open and Amateur in 1916. "I have no doubt that Bobby felt always strong enough to stand the strain of anger."

But the effort it took Jones to control himself added one more burden to the physical and emotional strain that was beginning to take its toll even as he was moving toward domination of his sport. And no one knew better than he did the difference between controlling his temper and ridding himself of it once and for all.

"To the finish of my golfing days," Jones wrote, "I encountered golfing emotions which could not be endured with the club still in my hands."

5

"By No Means Fit for the Honourable Company"

In the program for the 1923 U.S. Open, Jones was listed as Mr. Robert T. Jones Jr., an indication that he was the sort of gentleman only an amateur golfer could be. Though this designation would soon change—by 1925, amateurs were no longer called Mister in the Open program—the fact that Jones continued to resist the lure of the professional ranks was seen as just one more exemplary quality that set him apart.

Not that the American public found anything wrong with athletes earning money, and tons of it. Babe Ruth made enough to light his cigars with $10 bills. Red Grange earned $100,000 in 1925 playing with the Chicago Bears on a lengthy barnstorming tour that proved the attraction of professional football as a spectator sport for the first time. The second fight between Jack Dempsey and Gene Tunney, at Chicago's Soldier Field in 1927, produced a gate of $2.65 million.

But golf was different. It was the only important sport in which amateurs could compete alongside professionals—no such fraternization was allowed in tennis—and often beat them. The idea that a man such as Jones should play golf only during the spring and summer, that he should then put his clubs away and return home to his family and his studies or his law practice, was simply too charming and inspirational to resist. Even if it was not precisely true.

Jones's explanations that there was not much money to be earned playing golf and that the life of a professional golfer did not appeal to him did not affect the public estimation of him. Neither did the fact that over his lifetime he earned the bulk of his income from the sport, far more than he could have made playing in tournaments. As far as America was concerned, he was Mr. Robert T. Jones Jr., amateur golfer, his entire life.

In part, this had to do with the way Jones was perceived—well educated, mild-mannered, humble, articulate, a sporting breed apart. Refusing to chase the almighty dollar was just another reason he was different from other sports champions. And in part it had to do with golf.

Though it originated in Scotland as a game in which all social and economic groups could mix, it could not escape the sharp divisions the British class system brought to every aspect of life.

"The fine old Scottish 'gentleman golfer' was a great patrician in his own way, and not given to condescending to men of low estate," Garden G. Smith wrote in 1912 in *The Royal & Ancient Game of Golf*. "The butcher, the baker and the candlestick-maker might be very honest fellows, and good golfers and sportsmen, but they were by no means fit for the honourable company of the lawyers, ministers, professors and publishers who hobnobbed with the lairds and nobility in the sacred precincts of the club. The grand seigneurs of the game clubbed and played 'by thame selffes.'"

So while the members of St. Andrews could take lessons from and play with Allan Robertson, golf's first professional, it was unthinkable that they should socialize with him. Robertson's services to the club were so highly regarded that when he died in 1859 the club took up a collection to provide his widow with an annuity, erected a large tombstone in the town cemetery, and hung his portrait in the clubhouse. It is highly unlikely that Robertson ever entered the building while he was alive.

Half a century later, as five-time British Open champion James Braid was beginning his forty-six-year tenure as the head pro at Walton Heath outside London, things had changed only marginally. Braid, who died in 1950, was so revered by the club's members that a braid was added around the base of its emblem as a memorial. But he never entered the clubhouse by the front door or went into the bar without a member's invitation.

Most professionals did not attain the station of Robertson or Braid, of course. They worked as caddies, greenskeepers, and clubmakers and were expected to earn a living selling clubs and teaching the game. If a man was in demand, he could earn a pound a week just giving lessons. By the beginning of the twentieth century, a few pros were paid a small salary, but some clubs rebelled and did away even with that guarantee. Others hit on the idea of auctioning off the right to sell equipment on their premises to the highest bidder, which ensured that even if the local pro won, his profits would be curtailed.

Nor did the immigration of golf to the less class-conscious environment of the United States improve matters much. If anything, it made them worse.

Most of the golf courses in the United States at the turn of the twentieth century were built on private country clubs, and while Donald Ross could earn $30,000 a year for his designs, the professionals who worked at them were very much the social equals of their counterparts in Britain. Indeed, many had learned the game in Scotland and, like Jimmy and Stewart Maiden, had come to the United States to improve themselves. But for most of them, it was as if they had never left. A professional was expected to give lessons, sell clubs, attend to the needs of the members, and use the tradesmen's entrance.

"Golf in the United States is the amusement of the well-to-do classes alone," Garden Smith observed. "The poor man has no place as yet among American golfers and the sport remains as distinctly exclusive as is polo or yachting." The whole point of the game, as far as the gentlemen who played it on both sides of the Atlantic were concerned, was *not* to make money at it—except on the bets they made among themselves. It was to keep it to "thame selffes."

Over the next five decades, golf's image in the United States underwent a huge change as millions of Americans took up the game. But the status of the professionals was hardly affected. Even when something resembling a pro golf tour was arranged, only about a dozen of the best and most determined players could earn a living playing on it. The others remained hired hands at their clubs and played only when they could find the time, usually during the winter, when the tournaments were held in the South and the West.

Byron Nelson, one of the great stars of the 1930s and 1940s, took his first club job in 1933 in Texarkana, Texas, where he earned no salary but was able to clear $60 a month selling clubs and balls, giving lessons, and storing members' clubs for a dollar a month. Living in a room that cost $7 a week, and included two meals a day, helped him get by.

Some club pros were lucky enough to be born into the job, as was the case with Paul Runyan, the winner of twenty-nine tournaments in the 1930s and 1940s. His father worked at the Majestic Hotel across the street from the Hot Springs Golf & Country Club in Arkansas, where celebrities and sports stars such as Babe Ruth, Jack Dempsey, and Gene Tunney vacationed and played on one of three golf courses. A few of his customers in the 1920s were gangsters, Runyan said, including one whose name seemed to change every year and whose front pockets contained something that was interfering with his swing. When Runyan pointed out the problem, the player pulled out a large gun and stuck it in a back pocket of his plus-fours.

Nor did competitive success offer financial stability. When Runyan led all professional golfers in earnings in 1932 with $6,767, his accountant told him he had won $10 more than he had spent. So winning did not mean a pro could neglect his main source of employment. Jimmy Demaret, who won thirty-one tournaments, including three Masters, once won three tournaments in a row and left the tour to return to his club job. Who knew what the members might think if he stayed away too long?

Occasionally, a professional who won an important tournament would get a special dispensation from the members—the Highland Country Club in Pittsburgh gave Gene Sarazen a year's leave to give exhibitions and cash in on his 1922 U.S. Open victory—but the pros learned not to count on it. When Willie Macfarlane won an epic play-off victory over Jones in the 1925 U.S. Open at Worcester Country Club—Macfarlane made up four holes over the final nine and won on the 36th—he was asked if he had any thoughts of joining the professional tour.

"I don't know what I am going to do," Macfarlane said. "This much I do know, however. I am scheduled to do some teaching at the club tomorrow and I've got to get back to Tuckahoe."

Even some of the professionals who had prospered in their club jobs while playing competitively saw no point in continuing on the tour. When Sam Parks graduated from the University of Pittsburgh in

1931, he was happy to get a job giving lessons thirteen hours a day at a resort near Uniontown, Pennsylvania. It certainly paid more than most college graduates could make at that point in the Depression— those who could get a job at all.

But though Parks won the 1935 U.S. Open and parlayed it into some $17,000 worth of exhibition appearances, he saw tournament golf as a losing proposition and gave up competition two years later to devote himself to his club job. In 1942, as U.S. Steel boosted its production for World War II, he left golf altogether to take a salesman's job with the company that he kept for thirty years. Asked if he had any regrets about giving up competitive golf, Parks said, "None. As my wife and I used to say, I'm winning a tournament every month. Plus pension and medical."

Toney Penna, a top player in the 1930s and 1940s who became a favorite instructor of Hollywood actors, was another player who was happy to have a job of any kind. When Penna became the pro at a club in Forest Hills, New York, in 1930, he was shocked at the sight of the unemployed, many of them professional people, selling pencils and apples on the streets. His salary of $150 a month, and the $4 an hour he made giving lessons, made him feel like a lucky man.

The Depression came along just when it appeared prize money might be rising at least to subsistence levels. In 1930, Sarazen was the tour's top money winner with $21,500. Two years later, Runyan led with less than a third as much. Nor did things change quickly once the bad times began to ease. Harry Cooper won the Los Angeles Open in 1927 and earned $3,500, a huge amount at the time. Eleven years later, he won again and made $1,000 less. In 1936, Sam Snead won eight tournaments and a record $20,000. In 1949, he again won eight times, for a total of $32,000.

Money for playing exhibitions also dried up during the Depression, and Sarazen, who had been in such demand after winning the 1922 U.S. Open and PGA that he was able to open a golf correspondence school, make movie shorts, and design golf clubs, decided the best way to get by was to live off the land. He bought a dairy farm, which came with two cows, in Brookfield Center, Connecticut. Before long he was known as the Squire, and he lived there the rest of his life. "When I see the money that goes around today," Sarazen said in 1991 of golf's new generation of millionaires, "I shiver."

So it was the times more than anything else that restrained the growth of professional golf. Jones was not the only top-flight golfer who refused to play for money, but he was among the very few whose decision was not based on the fact that he could not afford it.

"I never gave a thought to playing professionally," says Charles Seaver, a strapping young player who was one of the sensations of the 1930 U.S. Amateur and came within one hole of becoming the last opponent Jones faced in his quest for the Grand Slam. "I was going to get an education, get into business, and continue playing as an amateur." Seaver entered Stanford, went into mining and construction, played on the 1932 Walker Cup team, and won numerous tournaments in California. It was left to his son Tom, who came of age in a different sporting era, to become rich as a professional athlete; he won 311 major league games and was inducted into baseball's Hall of Fame.

It was no different in Britain, where Eric Fiddian, after performing creditably against Jones in the 1930 British Amateur, was told that the Dunlop sporting goods company might offer him a job selling golf balls if he became a professional. But cleaning members' shoes and clubs, mowing greens, and giving lessons did not appeal to him nearly as much as entering his father's business manufacturing and selling spades, forks, shovels, and other tools used by miners and gardeners. Fiddian played as an amateur into his seventies.

Yet the professional game survived, largely through the resourcefulness and dedication of the players. They would stop at hotels near golf courses and talk the management into allowing them to give exhibitions for guests wandering through the lobby in exchange for their rooms. And when they did have to pay, the going rate—$1.50 for a hotel room, $3 for a suite, $1 for breakfast were typical of the times—helped keep expenses down. One of the most popular places for those professionals who did not mind traveling was Pinehurst, North Carolina, where they could get a room and three meals a day for $5 to $7. That was cheaper than living at home during the Depression, said Penna, who would go to Pinehurst early in November and stay all month.

Snead would ask people along the road between tournament stops if he could sleep in their houses or, failing that, would spend the night in his car. Jug McSpadden remembered driving from the

Midwest to California without once traveling on a paved road. When he ran out of gas, he waited until morning for a service station to open. Bill Mehlhorn offered trophies that could be used in tournaments to people he met at clinics and exhibitions if they would sell subscriptions to *Golf Illustrated*. Or he would simply sell the display trophies right out of his traveling case. The players' wives helped, too, and several of them became experts at finding sponsors, setting tournament dates, and making travel and lodging arrangements.

Occasionally there were signs of what, many years into the future, the professional golf tour would become. In 1926, the Los Angeles Junior Chamber of Commerce offered a purse of $10,000 for its first Los Angeles Open. The amount was so large that sportswriters came from around the nation, including Damon Runyon, who was intrigued enough to leave New York's racetracks and ballparks to attend his first golf tournament. After Harry Cooper won the tournament in a quickly played final round, Runyon dubbed him Lighthorse Harry, a nickname he carried the rest of his life.

But while professional golf husbanded its resources and found ways to stay alive during the hard times of the 1930s and beyond, the amateur game withered and died as a competitive force. Few amateurs could afford a part-time approach any longer, and the most talented among them grabbed any jobs they could, whether as club pros or away from the golf course. Others simply gave up tournament golf altogether, and 1933 marked the last year an amateur won an Open championship in the United States or Britain. It was not money that killed topflight amateur golf in the United States, notes golf writer Charles Price, but rather the lack of it.

The irony of the reverence accorded the great amateur golfers in the years after World War I is that it was the professionals who prepared golf for the explosive growth to come. Some of them did not have the education or the inclination to find other jobs, but in one way or another they were committed to the game. So at a time when many amateurs simply stopped playing tournament golf at a high level, it was the professionals who kept competitive golf alive.

When golf first discovered its potential as a spectator sport during World War I, nobody was paying closer attention than Walter Hagen.

Hagen had participated in the Red Cross exhibition tour Jones had enjoyed so much and was fascinated to discover there was a public willing to pay a dollar to watch them. No one had ever thought of charging admission to a golf event before—the U.S. Open did not get around to it until 1922—and Hagen, who had cautiously asked for $75 to appear at exhibitions after winning the 1914 U.S. Open, raised his price to $200 once the war was over. When he got that, he asked for $300. And when he got that, he made a decision that would change his life forever and go a long way toward changing golf as well.

It was not enough, Hagen decided, to be a professional golfer. From then on, he would be a "businessman-golfer," one who would keep his name in front of the public by winning golf tournaments but who would earn the bulk of his income giving exhibitions and endorsing products related to golf. He never worked as a club pro again.

Walter Hagen was everything Bobby Jones was not, and nothing Jones was.

The son of a German immigrant whose first exposure to golf was as a caddy in Rochester, New York, Hagen was boisterous and hail-fellow, while Jones, who never carried a golf bag other than his own, was calm and circumspect.

Hagen was a shameless self-promoter—he may have been the first athlete of the modern age to recognize the benefits of telling the world how wonderful he was—while Jones had to be dragged into the limelight. He liked people all right, Jones said, he just preferred them in small doses.

Hagen was disdainfully arrogant toward his opponents—told late one boisterous night before the final round of a tournament that his opponent had long since gone to bed, he replied, "Ah, but he's not asleep"—while Jones was invariably courteous and respectful to everyone he played against.

Hagen was a womanizer of staggering proportions, while no one ever saw Jones in the company of any woman other than his wife.

As good as Hagen became at making money from golf, he was always better at spending it. A trip to Europe for the British Open and a few other professional tournaments might cost as much as $10,000, once he added in his first-class travel arrangements, hotel suite at the Savoy in London, Daimler car and chauffeur, silk shirts, custom-tailored suits, various parties, and chartered planes for hunting trips on the moors and fishing in the north of Scotland. Nor did the financial reward of winning the Open particularly interest Hagen. After one of his victories, he stunned the tournament organizers by giving his entire check, 75 pounds, to his caddy.

"I never wanted to be a millionaire, I just wanted to live like one" was one of Hagen's most famous sayings. "Be sure to stop and smell the flowers along the way" was another, although the sportswriter John Lardner noted that Hagen picked quite a few flowers, too.

Jones also spent his money, but less ostentatiously and more cautiously. For the first four years of their marriage, for instance, he and his wife, Mary, lived with his mother and father.

Even their golf games fit their different personalities. Hagen, who seemed to lurch into the ball, was wild off the tee, reckless on the fairway and in the rough, a master of gamesmanship, and had a killer instinct that deflated many a hopeful opponent. When someone noted that his penchant for getting into trouble sometimes equaled his ability to extricate himself, Hagen responded with an old golf saying: "Three of those and one of them count four."

Jones, whose swing was close to perfection, drove the ball long and straight, was all but flawless in his approach shots, and preferred to ignore his opponents and concentrate on playing "Old Man Par." His greatest fault was his penchant for turning what should have been easy victories into stomach-churning thrillers that left him trembling and exhausted, or defeats.

The one time Jones and Hagen met head to head when they were at the peak of their powers came in a two-day match-play exhibition in Florida in February 1926. Hagen led almost from the start and crushed Jones, 12 and 11. Hagen said it was his greatest thrill in golf. Jones called it a "glorious licking."

A number of Hagen's fellow pros doubted he would be able to make it on his own, but he quickly proved them wrong. The crowds adored him for his ostentation, his wardrobe, his ebullience, and his go-for-broke approach to the game. And even before he arrived on the golf course, he seldom disappointed.

"We had a regular caravan—three or four Cadillacs or Lincolns, my chauffeur heading the group in one, [his manager, Bob] Harlow in the second, my caddie with my clothes and golf equipment in the third," Hagen wrote. "Guarantees didn't mean much to me. I'd play for the purse and pray that I'd acquired the type of personality and game to draw the crowds. After the matches we'd stuff the money in a suitcase and gun the motors to the next date."

Hagen also had a useful relationship with Jesse Livermore, the fabulously wealthy "Wolf of Wall Street" who allowed him to sit in his office during trading hours. Livermore's suggestion was simple: Buy when he bought, sell when he sold. "Where he gave orders in millions," Hagen wrote, "I bought a few hundred shares." Within a few weeks he had more than enough money to travel to Britain in style.

Through the years, Hagen gave exhibitions all over the world: in Japan, where he was invited to play with the emperor—an earthquake intervened to prevent it—elsewhere in Asia, in Africa, and throughout Europe. Often he was accompanied by Joe Kirkwood, a trick-shot artist who would drive a ball off a watch crystal or a spectator's foot, or pop six stymied balls into the hole in rapid succession. Kirkwood, his fellow pros liked to say, could do anything with a golf ball except hit it straight.

Hagen could be amazingly generous to friends such as Kirkwood, who once guaranteed him $16,000 for a tour of his native Australia that did not pay off because the concept of paying to see exhibitions had not caught on in that country. "Do you know what I think of this scrap of paper, Joe?" Hagen said, pulling out the contract. He tore it up, and they split the take for the rest of the tour, barely making expenses.

Hagen endorsed everything he could lay his hands on—clubs, clothes, sterling-silver "replica" putters—and recorded an album of instructions that sold for $10. Before long he was making so much more money than the small purses the pros were playing for that he would pass up important tournaments to play exhibitions and lucrative private matches against any opponent willing to put up enough cash to make it worth his while.

Charles Seaver remembers hurrying home from Los Angeles High School to the nearby Wilshire Country Club, where he would occasionally be invited to play with his family's neighbor Howard Hughes. The teenager and the famous aviator each had a three handicap and played some spirited low-stakes matches. One day, Hughes

called Seaver and told him to come over to the course for a game with
Hagen and George Von Elm, the reigning U.S. Amateur champion.
Hagen was a notoriously late arrival even during tournaments, so no
one was surprised when the match began as a threesome. It was not
until they reached the seventh hole, along Beverly Boulevard, that
Hagen made his entrance.

"Here comes this big green Packard with a blonde driving and
Hagen sitting alongside her in the front seat and his caddy in the back
holding the clubs," Seaver says. "Hagen kisses the blonde and then
walks over to me and says we'll stand Von Elm for $100 a hole. I must
have turned kind of white. I'd never played for that kind of money
before."

Seeing his young partner's distress, Hagen elbowed him in the ribs
and said, "Don't worry about it, kid. I've got it all."

Hagen then birdied the eighth and ninth holes and proceeded to
win $1,400. "I'm sure Howard Hughes picked up the whole thing,"
says Seaver, who walked off the course with five dollars. "Von Elm
didn't have that kind of money."

When Hagen did play in tournaments, he was a figure of awe and
envy to his fellow golfers. Sarazen, writing about Hagen's arrival at
the 1920 U.S. Open in Toledo, describes his impact:

"Word spread through the locker room that Walter's Rolls-Royce
had just been moored near the first tee. A hush and then a nervous
murmur spread through the locker room. 'Here he comes!' someone
shouted with a tremor in his voice. The door opened and a man in livery staggered in under a load of expensive luggage and Hagen's pon-
derous golf bag. Then Hagen entered, gleaming with that big,
expansive, confident smile. Everybody rose from the benches to
shake his hand.

"'Hi, boy,' Hagen greeted one after another in his high-pitched
voice. 'Hi, boy.' He slapped some of his well-wishers on the back and
followed his footman imperially to his locker. He was dressed just like
the millionaires I had caddied for, and he looked like he had been
born to wealth. As he strode past the bench I was sitting on, he waved
and shot me a casual 'Hi, kid,' as if he had known me all my life."

But the pros of Hagen's era didn't just sit around and admire him,
they also copied him. Occasionally they even found ways to sell themselves that rivaled the master.

In the 1930s, Harry Cooper, Horton Smith, Lawson Little, and Jimmy Thompson went on a tour sponsored by Spalding during which they estimated they averaged two rounds of golf every three days for two and a half years, and routinely spent as many as thirty nights in a row in sleeper cars. Cooper, Paul Runyan, and several other pros also toured Australia and made a profit, despite the fact that it took more than a month to travel back and forth by ship.

"I don't know how you fellows can do it," Jones once told Cooper. "I could no more do what you do than fly to the moon. I couldn't play that much."

Cooper also was lucky enough to be able to supplement his income by playing regularly in $1,000 nassaus in Los Angeles, with Howard Hughes as his partner. (The one thing he would not do with Hughes was fly. Cooper said that the aviator talked so slowly—"You asked him a question and he said, 'Wellll. . . . I do-o-o-n't know, Harry'"—that Cooper didn't trust his reflexes enough to get in a plane with him.)

In 1934, Cooper even hit the vaudeville circuit, traveling to Schenectady, Troy, and Rochester, New York; Minneapolis; St. Paul; and Chicago. As the band played "In the Good Old Summertime," Cooper would hit lightweight fluorescent balls into the darkened theater. Then he would tee up a ball under an egg, swing a club, and catch the egg without breaking it. As a grand finale, Cooper would break the egg to show it wasn't hard-boiled. Hagen received vaudeville offers, too, for as much as $1,500 a week. But as much as the money appealed to him, he declined. He just couldn't think of a suitable act, he said. His talent was more suited to the golf course than the stage.

Nowhere was the second-class status of professionals more clearly defined than in the refusal of the golf clubs where their tournaments were played to allow them into the clubhouse. This was as true in the United States as in Britain.

When Francis Ouimet scored his historic victory over Harry Vardon and Ted Ray at Brookline in 1913, it was considered a great triumph for the unheralded young amateur against two of the most famous professionals of the day. What Hagen remembered about the tournament was that Ouimet, a Brookline member, was allowed in the clubhouse, while Vardon and Ray were not. It must have made the two golfing legends feel right at home, Hagen thought.

There is some debate as to whether Hagen was the first professional to walk into an American clubhouse during a tournament, but none at all that he led the crusade at home and in Britain and that he enjoyed every minute of it.

"Gentlemen, you are in the wrong place," the head locker steward, a little man in a white coat, told Hagen when he entered the clubhouse at Deal, the golf course in Kent where the 1920 British Open was being held.

"This is Deal?" Hagen asked.

"Oh, yes, indeed. But you gentlemen are professionals. You'll be using Mr. Hunter's golf shop for dressing."

"Well, pardon me."

One look at the cramped changing facilities in the golf shop— "one long spike in the wall had several coats hanging on it and in a far corner, many pairs of shoes, the toes turned up like skis," Hagen wrote—and he told his chauffeur to park his car in front of the clubhouse. There, he changed his shoes and ate a picnic lunch in full view of the members every day of the tournament.

Then it was on to La Boulie near Versailles for the French Open, where the accommodations were even worse: a foul-smelling stable full of flies, where the players were expected to eat as well as change. Disgusted, Hagen convinced his fellow pros George Duncan and Abe Mitchell to insist they be allowed in the clubhouse "or else." Mitchell was so surprised when the president of the tournament capitulated that Hagen and Duncan "had to half-push him into the sanctified area of the members and amateurs."

That same year, Ted Ray was made an honorary member of his home club at Oxhey, in honor of his victory in the U.S. Open, but as astonishing as that was to the British golf establishment, nothing really changed. Hagen, who became the first American to win a British Open in 1922, was not allowed in the clubhouse the following year at Troon, where he lost by a stroke to Arthur Havers. After the final round, the tournament secretary invited both men to attend the award ceremonies inside the club.

Hagen walked up a path that was crowded with spectators and British bobbies holding them back. When he reached the door to the clubhouse, he turned to the crowd, announced that since he had not been allowed to enter while the tournament was being played he was not going in now, and invited everybody to join him at a pub where he and his fellow golfers had been made welcome all week. If the committee liked, Hagen said, it could present the trophy to Havers there.

So ingrained was this attitude toward professionalism that even Hagen's friendship with the Prince of Wales could not help. An avid if mediocre golfer, the prince often showed up at championship matches and sometimes awarded the cup to the winner. After Hagen won the 1928 British Open at Sandwich, the prince invited him into the clubhouse for a drink, where they chatted until a nervous club secretary reminded his highness that professionals were not allowed.

Whether or not the prince replied, as legend has it, that he would drink with whom he liked where he liked, it is true that a year later the royal limousine picked Hagen up at his London hotel and took him to the exclusive Swinley Forest Club near Ascot. "From the fence outside the club at Deal, to golf with the Prince of Wales at the Swinley Forest Club was a giant step for me and all golf professionals," Hagen later reflected with satisfaction.

Jones, to his credit, never looked down on the pros or considered himself a more exalted form of golfer. He admired their skills, liked their company, and enjoyed the challenge of playing against them. Even the most skilled amateurs, Jones had to admit, did not always have highly developed competitive instincts. Nobody could say that about golfers trying to earn a living.

"I love to play against the pros, match or medal," Jones wrote. "I found there was the spur of competition, and masters of the game who were all set to drub me—and usually did. . . . When I manage to beat them I am inordinately proud."

Nor did he see any reason why golfers should not play the game for money.

"No question arises in my mind concerning the right of an individual to commercialize his proficiency in sport if his happiness and well-being will be promoted by so doing," Jones wrote. "If enough people will pay to see Walter Hagen play golf to make it profitable for him to play, and if he wants to play, I cannot see why the situation is vastly different from that of Caruso's being paid to sing or of a lawyer's receiving money for drafting a contract." Amateurism, Jones said knowingly, depends on the "financial condition of the individual. . . . In other words, it is fine to be an amateur if one can afford it." Without professionalism, he said shortly before he won the Grand Slam, "men would not have the opportunity to make an honest living at golf and in their stead there would be a great many crooks pretending to be amateurs."

As for his own reasons for not turning professional, idealism was not among them. Amateurism, he said, "is entirely a matter of convenience. It is nice for a man to make a hobby of his favorite sport, to play it or leave it alone as he likes. But to enjoy this luxury he must be able to earn a living from some other occupation or must possess an income sufficient for his needs."

Then there was the muddle surrounding the definition of an amateur, which had long bedeviled the game. Three years after his victory at Brookline had thrilled the nation, Ouimet was stripped of his amateur standing for two years because he was part owner of a store where golf equipment was sold. This created a huge uproar—Ouimet's amateur status was restored in 1918, when he entered the army—and defined the problem.

What *were* the rules governing amateurism? Jones and others wondered. Nobody seemed to have a clear-cut answer.

An amateur could take advantage of his celebrity status to write about golf, and he could accept such gifts as a car from the members of his club after winning a major tournament. But he could not endorse clubs, give lessons, or, as Jones discovered, receive truly expensive gifts. In 1928 a group of friends in Atlanta offered Jones $50,000 to buy a house. He and Mary were grateful to have a place of their own at last, but a few months later he announced he was turning the money down.

While the U.S. Golf Association could point to nothing in the rules that prohibited the gift, the organization was clearly uncomfortable with its size. So Jones gave back the gift and bought a new house himself. The gesture won him fresh accolades for his devotion to amateurism. One tribute said he had displayed "the sportsmanship of a medieval knighthood."

As the years went by, Jones had more problems coming to terms with the meaning of amateurism. He had never made a penny from golf and never would, he said after winning the British Open in 1926, and *Golfers Magazine* soon reported that he had turned down $12,000 to write a series of instructional articles. But a year later, he did exactly that when he signed a contract to write instructional pieces for the Bell Syndicate. That was the turning point. For the rest of his life, Jones made the bulk of his income from golf. He wrote articles and books about the game, made movies, had his own radio show, and put his name on golf clubs and other equipment and more.

This was the ultimate contradiction of his career. Even as he was being hailed as the personification of the spirit of amateurism, as a man who played golf only for the love of it, he was on his way to making more money from the sport than all but a handful of professionals in his lifetime. The public may have viewed him as a lawyer who only played the game for fun, but in truth he was every bit as much a "businessman-golfer" as Walter Hagen.

6

The Long Lane Turns

After four years of being counted among the favorites in every open and amateur championship he entered, and after four years of failure, Jones began to brood. He had the talent to win these tournaments, he heard it said over and over again, or at least that is what he imagined he heard, but maybe talent wasn't enough. Maybe he was just unlucky—a wretched sort of plea, he thought—or maybe he just did not have what it took to *be* a champion. "I pondered that option more than I would care to have people know," Jones wrote.

Certainly there was no reason for optimism when Jones arrived at Inwood Country Club on Long Island in July 1923 for the U.S. Open. He had just completed a year studying English literature at Harvard that had kept him out of serious competition, although his whimsical tenure as assistant manager of the Crimson golf team—he had used up his college eligibility at Georgia Tech—had allowed him plenty of opportunity to practice.

Nor could Jones take much inspiration from his performance the previous year. Trailing Gene Sarazen by one stroke in the final round of the 1922 U.S. Open at the Skokie Country Club north of Chicago, Jones was counting on a birdie on the par-5 18th hole to force a tie, but he did not give himself a chance. His tee shot at 17 kicked off to the left, wound up under a tree, and he could not recover. The resulting second-place finish was his best in an Open so far, but it was Sarazen, the son of an immigrant Italian carpenter who also won the

PGA Championship five weeks later, who suddenly became the most exciting twenty-year-old player in golf. This quest for a championship, Jones thought ruefully, was becoming a bit thick.

Things were no better the following month at the U.S. Amateur at Brookline, where another golfer his age beat him with a single shot. Jess Sweetser, a senior at Yale, played Jones in the semifinals and, on the second hole, hit a ninety-yard approach shot that landed on the green, drew a roar from the gallery, and rolled straight into the cup for an eagle 2. Jones made it exciting, and had the crowd yelling again, with a shot that wound up six inches away, but it wasn't enough. He made a birdie but lost the hole. "Sometimes I think that punch settled it," Jones wrote of Sweetser's sensational shot. "I don't mind in the least saying it jarred me."

He certainly played like it as Sweetser was six up at the turn and closed out the match, 8 and 7, at the 11th hole, the farthest point from the clubhouse. Jones "had to haul my bedraggled self nearly a mile before I could sit down and rest."

The next day, Sweetser beat Chick Evans to win the championship and, when Jones congratulated him, said, "Thank you, Bobby. I beat the best man in the field yesterday." A pretty thing to say, Jones thought, but what it amounted to was one more national championship, his tenth overall, that he had failed to win.

So Jones was nervous and upset when he came to Inwood. His golf game, and his confidence along with it, had hit rock bottom. He had been playing so poorly that he was now entering tournaments *expecting* to be beaten.

Beyond that, Jones was beginning to feel the full weight of not only the public's expectations but those of his friends and family as well. The Colonel, despondent after his loss to Sweetser, had decided he was a jinx and refused to travel with him anymore. There was one unexpected reminder of home, however, a telegram from R. T. Jones, whose feigned indifference to his grandson's fortunes was fading fast. "Keep the ball in the fairway and make all the putts go down," it read. Jones's eyes stung as he read it.

Jones's first practice rounds on Inwood's narrow fairways were a disaster. He could not seem to get a handle on the winds blowing in off the Atlantic, and it was all he could do to get around the course in fewer than 80 strokes. His qualifying rounds, 77 and 79, were another indication of how hard Inwood was playing—Keeler thought it might have been the toughest course ever to host an Open—and he seemed almost desperate as he tried to execute his shots. As the tournament began, Jones was terribly depressed.

And then, without warning, he found the key. The strain he was under suddenly began working *for* him, and as the players began the grueling competition, 36 holes in each of two successive days, he gained control of his game.

Jones shot 71 in the first round, one of only two subpar rounds Inwood would yield during the tournament, then went out in the afternoon and shot 73. He finished the day in second place, two shots behind Jock Hutchison and one ahead of Bobby Cruickshank, who had a total of 145. With only three other golfers under 150, it looked to be a three-man tournament as the final day of competition began.

Hutchison, who had emigrated from Scotland to the United States, taken out U.S. citizenship, and returned in 1921 to become the first "American" to win the British Open, cracked first. He shot 82 in the third round, which made Jones realize he was not the only one feeling the late-round pressure. Maybe that was the answer, he thought—don't try to be perfect, just keep playing. Jones called this approach "the stolid and negative and altogether unromantic attribute of patience." He was about to discover what patience truly meant.

Perhaps nowhere in the history of golf is there a more appealing figure than Bobby Cruickshank. At 5-foot-4 and 125 pounds he was known as "Wee Bobby" to his fellow golfers and the public. But his size didn't keep him from winning seventeen officially sanctioned PGA tournaments in the 1920s and 1930s, enough to place him in the top fifty on the tour's all-time list seven decades later. Nor did it keep him from making a mockery of the concept of a golfer shooting his age. In 1971, when Cruickshank was seventy-seven, he shot a 67 at the Gulfstream Country Club in Florida.

Beyond that, Cruickshank had such a sunny disposition that no less an authority on *joie de vivre* than Walter Hagen said he could literally laugh a ball into the cup. And he was, said Keeler, as courageous a little golfer as ever stepped on a golf course.

Or a battlefield.

Born in the Scottish Highlands in 1894, Cruickshank was preparing to enter Edinburgh University when war was declared. He joined the Seaforth Highlanders and was quickly sent to the front. From the Battle of the Somme to Ypres, from his capture at Arras to his attempt to escape from a prison camp at Lille, Cruickshank left his footprints all over World War I and was lucky to emerge alive.

One day at Ypres ("Wipers, we called it") German artillery let loose such a fearful barrage that Cruickshank swore he could not only smell the cordite but also taste it. When the guns fell silent, 78 soldiers in his company of 110 were dead, among them his brother John, who was buried under the debris. He had almost been close enough to reach out and touch him only a moment earlier, Cruickshank said. He never saw him again. Wounded himself, Cruickshank convalesced in an Irish hospital, then returned home, thinking his war was over. In reality, it had just begun.

"I left on a Friday night," Cruickshank told golf writer Ross Goodner of his departure from the French port of Dieppe after a German assault on Paris in 1918 led to another mobilization, "and by Monday night I had been taken prisoner at Arras." Moved to a camp housing twelve thousand prisoners at Lille, he found Sandy Armour, the older brother of his friend and fellow golfer Tommy Armour, with whom he had served earlier in the war, suffering from acute dysentery.

Cruickshank was sent out on burial duty, an appalling job that was eased only slightly by the ration of schnapps that went along with it, but he soon discovered its saving grace. Any dead horses the prisoners came across were theirs for the taking. He would cut up the meat and take it back to Armour, who was too weak even to walk up and down stairs. They cheered up each other talking of the day when they would face each other in the Edinburgh Club championship.

In October, Cruickshank and three other prisoners escaped, linked up with a woman who lived on a nearby farm, and made it to safety. This time his war truly was over as the armistice was declared the following month. And who could blame him if he shed a tear or two when, in the first Edinburgh Club championship after the armistice, he beat Sandy Armour in the final?

Three years later, Tommy Armour came home from the United States and told him about the golf courses paved with gold for any young pro willing to work long hours at a club job and follow the tournament trail during the winter. Cruickshank packed up his wife and baby, moved to New Jersey, and began a new life.

Jock Hutchison was not the only contender who came to grief in the third round at Inwood. Had Jones shot anything close to the scores he had posted the previous day, he would have turned the final 18 holes into a victory lap. Instead, he blew sky high. Keeler could barely watch as a string of 5s, two of them coming after penalty shots, put him four over par through the first seven holes and led to a ghastly 9-hole score of 41.

But then, just as quickly, the storm abated. From the 8th hole on, Jones played par golf to finish at 76. It could have been worse, and if Cruickshank had not also been feeling the pressure and shot a 78, it would have been. As the afternoon round started, Jones led by three shots. It was his tournament to win. Just let him shoot a 75, he thought. That would force Cruickshank to shoot under par to win—a virtual impossibility under the pressure of the final round of a U.S. Open on such a difficult course.

Teeing off well ahead of Cruickshank in the afternoon, Jones was all over the golf course from the start. In the rough at the first hole for a bogey. On in two at the long 5th hole, where he just missed an eagle. Then, at the 7th, came the first hint of disaster. A long, nerve-wracking par-3—"the most dangerous one-shotter I ever saw," Keeler wrote—the hole traveled a narrow path, with a two-stroke penalty awaiting the poor soul who hit the ball out of bounds either left or right. Trying for the green, Jones hooked his tee shot, which hit the foot of a spectator standing off to the left and bounced under a bridge and out of bounds. Jones went back to the tee and, facing ruin if he was out of bounds again, made the green. If there was any such thing as a good double bogey, he had just made one.

His luck turned at the 9th hole, where his second shot skidded off the top of a bunker onto the green, allowing him to save par. But his outbound score of 39, two over par, showed that he was not at his best, that all his good intentions of playing the golf course, taking care of his game, and letting Cruickshank worry about his, were eluding him.

Long putts at 10 and 11—one for a birdie, the other to save par—put Jones back on track for the moment, but he was in bunkers at both 13 and 15, and only excellent chip shots close to the hole allowed him to save par. He did birdie the long 14th hole, though, and as he stood at the 16th tee he was even par for his round, and the championship was close enough to touch. All the near misses, all the failed expectations, all the self-doubts were gone now. Three more holes—holes on which he had made two birdies and no bogeys during the first three rounds—and it was over. He felt supremely confident.

And then he blew it. Bogey on 16. Bogey on 17. Double bogey on 18. It was the worst failure under closing-hole pressure of his career. The strain of setting the pace, of being in front, had simply gotten to him, and the result was a disaster.

His second shot at 16 was out of bounds into a parking lot, which cost him two more penalty strokes. Only the fact that his recovery shot hit a convenient mound on the side of the green and was deflected toward the hole allowed him to make an eight-foot putt that kept a bogey from being something worse.

At 17, he pulled both his first and second shots and took another 5, and by the time he approached the 18th hole he had lost both his game and his confidence. His tee shot was short, and now he was struck with an uncharacteristic indecisiveness. Which club to use to get over a small lagoon in front of the green? A wood? No, an iron. The shot was dreadful—had he unconsciously tried to compensate for choosing the wrong club? Instead of fading from left to right toward the green, it continued left until it came to rest under a chain near the 12th tee.

For five agonizing minutes, Jones sat down and waited as officials removed the chain and cleared a path to the green. Finally, feeling as if he were collapsing inside and out, he got up and, just as he was hitting the ball, the by-now breathless spectators could see him make a duffer's mistake. The great Bobby Jones lifted his head while swinging his club!

The ball popped into a bunker, and by the time he at last reached the green and two-putted, he had lost four shots in three holes. His 72 had become a 76. He had opened the door to Cruickshank.

Even the people closest to Jones, those who had been with him for years and seen his blackest moods, were shocked by his appearance as he came off the golf course. The deep circles under his eyes and the weary sag of his body gave him the look of a man who had been mortally wounded, Grantland Rice wrote. His age, Keeler thought, seemed to have doubled in half an hour.

Blinking and swallowing hard while trying to think of something to say, Jones finally heard Keeler speak up: "I think you're the champion, Bobby. Cruickshank will never catch you."

"Well, I didn't finish like a champion," Jones said. "I finished like a yellow dog."

Ashamed of himself, Jones went off to his room and sat, staring into space. There was no one to blame but himself for those three closing holes, he thought. Certainly not bad luck. On the contrary, if he had not had some *good* luck, it would have been worse. He felt like a man waiting for the jury to come in.

Back out on the course, Keeler joined the crowd that had rushed over to see Cruickshank bring in the verdict. What he saw made him sick to his stomach.

Wee Bobby was flying. Even the weather seemed to be cooperating as the wind that had been blowing while Jones was finishing his round had died down, and the sky was bright with promise. Keeler watched Cruickshank's short game crackle with precision as his approach shots, which had deserted him in the morning round, suddenly began stopping within a few feet of the hole.

Cruickshank made the turn a stroke under par, and when he birdied the 10th thanks to an extraordinary piece of luck—his chip appeared headed well past the hole, but struck the flag and came to rest a yard away—he led Jones by three shots. By the time Cruickshank stood at the 13th tee, he had the luxury of being able to bogey two of the last six holes and win.

But Cruickshank was feeling the pressure, too, and the bogeys came quickly. A hooked second shot and poor pitch cost him a stroke at 13, and when he three-putted 15, his lead was down to a single shot. His approaches were causing him problems again, and at 16 his second shot landed in the right rough, while his third, a short chip, was also off-line, leaving the ball several yards from the hole.

Cruickshank missed the putt for par and disconsolately walked across the green for a two-footer to remain tied with two holes remaining. He missed! Double bogey. Jones, sitting helplessly in the clubhouse, was back in the lead. Cruickshank would need a birdie on one of the two long closing holes simply to tie.

Feeling dead tired suddenly but much lighter in spirit, Keeler went to the clubhouse, where he found Francis Ouimet and a few others offering their congratulations. Jones was having none of it.

"I don't want to win the title this way," he said. "I know what they're saying. They think I'm a quitter because I had the championship in my pocket and chucked it away, and they're right."

Keeler drew Ouimet aside and asked if he thought Jones's lead was safe.

"No man on earth could play those two holes in seven shots under these circumstances," Ouimet told him. "Bobby has at last earned what he has been deserving a long time."

A U.S. Golf Association official appeared just then and asked Jones to come down in preparation for the awards presentation.

"Not me," Jones told him. "I'll wait until the last putt is down."

Out on the course, Cruickshank had regained enough control to par the 17th hole and, with a grim look on his face, stood at the 18th tee. A birdie on the 425-yard finishing hole that had surrendered precious few over two days of competition to stay alive in the U.S. Open? Call it a 100–1 shot.

Cruickshank's drive was straight enough, but not particularly long. He was hardly the longest hitter around, and the wind had turned, forcing him to drive directly into it. As he stood over his second shot, the narrow fairway loomed up treacherously, and the lagoon guarding the green that had caused Jones such trouble looked even more forbidding.

Cruickshank could feel his heart skipping beats, and he took his time, waiting until he had regained some semblance of calm. Then he hit a 2-iron that sent the ball so straight at the pin more than two hundred yards away that its path appeared to have been drawn on a sheet of paper with a ruler. The ball hit the green thirty feet in front of the cup and came to rest six feet away. To Keeler, who had returned to the course to observe Jones's fate, the reaction of the huge crowd surrounding the green sounded like artillery fire.

He had a chance, Cruickshank thought, as he looked things over, and he took his time to study the line. He struck his putt, then leaped after the ball and grabbed it a moment after it disappeared into the hole.

"You'll no get out a there," Cruickshank said in his thick Scottish brogue as the crowd erupted again, hats flew in the air, and he was joined on the green by a rush of spectators all bent on shaking his hand.

Considering the circumstances, Keeler thought, it was one of the greatest holes ever played, and as gallant a finish as had ever been made in a golf tournament. To Cruickshank, his approach from the fairway at Inwood would always be the greatest shot of his career. The playoff was called for the following afternoon.

Several years later, Jones would write that he was glad Cruickshank had tied him. If his opponent had failed, if he had succumbed to the same nervous collapse that had ruined his own promising round, he would not have discovered whether he had what it took to win a big tournament or whether he was "hopelessly weak under the belt."

The next morning, however, as the hour for the 18-hole playoff approached, Jones looked anything but glad. Ouimet, who was rooming with him during the tournament, told Keeler he had slept well, but the writer was appalled to see how drawn and pinched Jones's face looked, how his eyes seemed located somewhere in the back of his head.

Keeler was feeling the tension himself, and with nothing to do but worry until the starting time arrived, he left Jones in the locker room and convinced Ouimet and two other friends to go for a walk. They sat at the third green and tried to lighten the mood by singing—how silly could you get? Keeler thought—but a line from Kipling kept running through his head: "'I'm dreading what I've got to watch,' the color sergeant said."

By the time the match began, the crowd, which had been arriving all day, had grown until there were at least ten thousand spectators. No longer spread out around the course but intent on getting what little glimpse they could of the two lone contestants, they jammed every fairway, surrounded every tee area and green. As if to emphasize the drama of the proceedings, storm clouds blew in from the west, a promise of the lightning that would light up the sky midway through the round.

At 2:00 P.M., Jones and Cruickshank met at the first tee and proceeded to play one of the strangest and most remarkable rounds of golf in the history of the U.S. Open.

Cruickshank was in trouble immediately when he drove wildly off the first tee and bogeyed the hole. But he quickly recovered with birdies at the second and third. Jones played a little steadier than the day before, but when he missed a two-foot putt at the 6th hole, he trailed by two shots. At the 7th, the hole that had caused him such grief the day before, he faced his first big decision of the day.

Cruickshank, protecting his lead and taking no chances, laid up short of the 7th green with an iron. Should Jones try to pick up a shot by going for the green and take a chance he might drive out of bounds again at a time when he did not dare lose another stroke? Or should he do what Cruickshank had done, play it safe? He decided to go for it.

Jones took his 3-wood from Luke Ross, hit his ball on the green twenty-five feet from the hole, and was down in two for par. Cruickshank's chip landed ten feet from the cup, and when he missed the putt, his lead was down to one. Another missed putt by Cruickshank at the 9th hole, this one from five feet, and they made the turn all square at 37.

Any notion that either golfer would win by conquering the back nine died at the 10th hole. Jones hit his tee shot into a trap and made a bogey. Cruickshank hit his first shot in the rough and his second over the green for a double bogey. A contest of survival was under way.

Jones's lead grew to two shots when he pitched within a foot of the par-3 12th hole, but he three-putted 14 and, *again* taking his eye off the ball as he tried to pitch out of the rough near the 15th green, bogeyed that hole, too. They were even once again.

Cruickshank went from the rough to a trap on 16; Jones led by a stroke. Their nerves shot by now, both men drove off the fairway and hit their second shots into the same trap at 17. Cruickshank made the better recovery to within two feet of the hole, but he nearly blew the easy chance when he hit his putt too hard. As the ball rattled around the lip of the cup, Cruickshank was all but prostrate with apprehension.

Finally, it fell. Jones hit his long uphill putt a bit hard, too, and the ball ran just past.

And there they were. Over 17 holes of the playoff, they had shot the same score only three times, but now, 89 holes and 368 shots apiece after they had begun, they stood deadlocked at the final tee.

Jones would later say the strain of the chance he took at the 7th hole was greater than at the 18th for the simple reason that he was still conscious. For the rest of his life he would maintain he had no memory of what was about to happen.

In a sense, Jones was lucky he had lost the honor at the 17th hole, because it forced Cruickshank to tee off first at 18. He took a nervous moment to rub his hands in the dirt and then, rushing his backswing, half-topped his tee shot, which squirted through the rough on the left and came to rest on a road behind a tree, well short of the lagoon. Cruickshank had no chance of reaching the green in two, so the door was open for Jones. Hit the ball in the fairway, leave himself a make-able approach to the green, and the championship was his.

Jones sliced his tee shot into the right rough 190 yards from the green; not good. It landed on dry, hard ground; not bad.

Cruickshank hit his second shot in front of the lagoon, and now Jones had another decision to make: lay up and match his short game against his opponent's, or go for the green some 200 yards away.

In all the years he caddied for Jones, Ross said, he never saw him make a quicker decision. Jones walked up to the ball, looked at it once, glanced at the pin off in the distance, and asked for his 2-iron. A mistake, Ouimet thought. He was too far away to be sure of making the green. He should lay up.

Ross, seeing the look of determination on Jones's face, felt differently. "Honestly, I think he'd have knocked Jack Dempsey out with a punch if he had been in the way of this championship," he said later.

Jones swung the club without hesitation, and the ball flew through the sky dark with rain clouds straight for the flag. As the noise from the crowd grew in anticipation and then erupted into a roar, it cleared the water, bounced on the green ten feet from the cup, and nearly struck the flag before coming to rest six feet away. It was the shot of a lifetime.

Standing behind Jones, Stewart Maiden pulled off his new straw hat, swung it high over his head in jubilation, and broke it over Ross's head. Ouimet grabbed Jones by the arm to offer what protection he could as the crowd rushed past them to the green.

Cruickshank walked forward to study his shot, then returned and attempted to hit the flag. The ball landed in a bunker at the left of the green. His recovery shot ran twenty feet past the hole, and his putt never had a chance. He walked over to Jones and shook his hand. One last double bogey had finished him off.

One putt and then another and there it was. Jones had shot his third straight 76, four over par, and won by two strokes. Only then did he have the first conscious thought he would be able to remember: "I don't care what happens now. I've won a championship."

The crowd rushed him then and carried him on its shoulders off the green, while in the distance a lone bagpipe played. The jubilation was in celebration of the winner, of course, but it could have been as much a tribute to the tournament itself.

It was a tournament in which both the winner and the runner-up played superb golf and hacker's golf, often from one hole to the next. A tournament in which each forged comfortable leads to come within a few holes of victory and then blew them. A tournament in which each made one of the greatest shots of his career, and in the history of the U.S. Open, on the 18th hole. It was Cruickshank's misfortune that his shot came on the 72nd hole while Jones's was on the 90th.

True to his character, Cruickshank put all disappointment aside and praised Jones to the skies at the awards ceremony. "My, what a golfer that boy is," he said. "He's the greatest champion of them all. To be defeated by him is glory enough."

Over the next fifteen years, Cruickshank would come close to winning three more U.S. Opens and fail each time. "That's the way the Lord makes it," he said five decades after his first and toughest loss. "If you win, you win. And if you don't, you don't."

Jones went home to Atlanta, where hundreds of people at the train station cheered as he embraced the Colonel, who, upon receiving the news of his victory from a leased telegraph wire in the blazing hot city room of the *Journal*, had stood up on a desk and proclaimed, "It has been the ambition of my life to bring a champion to Atlanta and now, thank God, I've done it."

Jones then kissed his mother and, after a moment of modest hesitation, a lovely young woman named Mary Malone.

The Georgia legislature adopted a resolution praising Jones, while an editorial in the *Constitution* called him "nothing less than an idol to the people of the city, the state and the South."

Walter Hagen put it more simply: "He had accomplished as a man what he had failed to do as a boy."

Jones heard further tributes at a dinner at East Lake attended by five hundred people, including the mayor of Atlanta, where Jones gave the first indication that his natural shyness in public did not preclude his ability to move an audience when a speech could not be avoided.

"You gentlemen have said some beautiful things about me and what I've been fortunate enough to do," he said. "But one thing they all have absolutely wrong. They spoke of my honoring the Atlanta Athletic Club. No man can honor a club like this. The honor lies in belonging to it. I am prouder of being a member of this club than I could be of winning all the championships there are."

Jones was on his way now. After losing the first ten national championships he competed in, he would win thirteen of the next twenty-one. Some of these victories would include strokes the equal of his second shot at Inwood's 18th hole, and some would be just as nerve-racking as his triumph over Cruickshank. But coming as it did after the years of disappointment and doubt, he would always remember his first national championship in a special way.

"If the long lane had not turned at Inwood," Jones wrote, "I think sometimes it would have gone straight on to its end in the shadows."

7

"My Lords, Ladies and Gentlemen, Are We Downhearted?"

In 1903, the Oxford and Cambridge Golfing Society made a thirty-nine-day tour of the United States, during which it played ten matches against American opponents and won eight. But John Low, the captain of the British squad, was not fooled.

"Already, I hear the hooting of their steamers in the Mersey," he reported of the American golfers he had seen.

A year later, Walter Travis, an Australian immigrant, became the first American citizen to win a British championship, the Amateur, and though it would take some time for those steamers to become an armada, it was clear what the future held. What no one could have foreseen, however, was that one day Britain's former colony would send back a golfer the mother country would come to regard with a reverence equaling any ever felt for one of its own.

To some British observers, there was no accounting for the passion with which the Americans were embracing golf by the second decade of the twentieth century. Horace Hutchinson, a former British Amateur champion who was the first of his countrymen to write about the sport extensively, spoke of giving exhibitions in the United States in the 1890s.

"It might be a good game for Sunday," Hutchinson was told, a comment he took as an insult both to the game and the Sabbath. But when he returned in 1919, he was astonished by the change. "A quarter of a century ago the businessmen of New York talked dollars," Hutchinson wrote. "Today they talk golf. It is a very sanitary change."

He was particularly amazed to see the Americans taking pains to remove weeds from their greens and even going so far as to water them—sometimes all night long! Any British golfer coming to America, Hutchinson said, should be on guard against three dangers they were not used to at home: "the blaze and glare of the sun, the abounding energy of the native golfers and their abounding hospitality."

Cyril Tolley, one of Britain's top amateurs, also was amazed at what he saw in the United States, both on and off the golf course. The dinners, the parties, the entertainments were all quite remarkable, Tolley wrote of a visit in 1920 to play in the U.S. Amateur. Not to mention the Ziegfeld Follies.

"The spectacle they offer is far finer than anything ever seen in this country," Tolley said. And some of the cabarets he visited featured—he knew his countrymen would find this difficult to believe— a postmidnight breakfast of bacon and eggs.

"As America is a dry country, only soda water is drunk, or, at least, ordered," Tolley wrote. "Every American has special pockets built in his dress clothes, and from these spacious pockets flasks have been known to appear."

As for the speed and the noise of the American trains, not to mention the cars driven on the wrong side of the road by men eating ice cream and talking nonstop to the drivers racing alongside, why, a man could be frightened half to death.

It was not just the enthusiasm with which Americans took to golf that assured the coming revolution, of course. The United States had a larger population; a climate that allowed the game to be played year-round in many regions; and, during the free-spending 1920s, far more resources to devote to its expansion. Hundreds of new golf courses were built around the country—there were forty-five hundred by the end of the decade—and soon they were pushing out from cities and towns into the countryside. Rural America had foisted Prohibition on the cities, said the humorist George Ade, and it had been shackled with golf in retaliation.

Huge sums were spent not only on the courses, but also on

clubhouses—each more elaborate than the last, it seemed—as well as on clubs, balls, clothes, and a large variety of golf paraphernalia that was widely advertised in newspapers and magazines. And whereas in 1908 Theodore Roosevelt had warned William Howard Taft not to be seen playing golf while running for president because it was an elitist game that would hurt him politically, Warren Harding was an avid golfer and did not mind who knew it. With Vice President Calvin Coolidge at his side, Harding attended the 1921 U.S. Open at the Columbia Country Club in Maryland and presented the winner's trophy to Jim Barnes.

Soon, celebrities from Babe Ruth to Charlie Chaplin to John D. Rockefeller were seen playing golf, and the game acquired even greater acceptance and respectability. For every crank such as the Minnesota Prohibition agent who said golf "encourages idleness, shiftlessness, and neglect of business as well as family responsibilities," there was, notes golf historian Herbert Warren Wind, a writer such as Charles Merz, who found the game nothing less than a new American frontier. Plus-fours, Merz said, were a substitute for leather chaps, while loud argyles were "the war paint of a nation."

But even before the American golf explosion of the 1920s, the era of British domination of golf was ending. By 1910 in Britain, the formation of new golf clubs had slowed from the boom years, and social ferment in the country was affecting golf along with many other institutions.

First, there were fears of a railway strike that led the Royal and Ancient Golf Club to stockpile coal at St. Andrews for the winter of 1911. Two years later came letters warning that Britain's militant suffragette movement, which had mounted protests at a number of golf courses and had spelled out "Votes Before Sport" and "No Votes, No Golf" in sulfuric acid on the greens at Woking Golf Club in Surrey in 1913, might attack the Old Course itself.

Politicians who played golf became a popular suffragette target— Lord Asquith, the prime minister, was assaulted by two women on the 17th green at Lossiemouth in northeastern Scotland—and the Royal and Ancient took out insurance against damage to the course and recruited two hundred volunteers to serve as guards during the British Amateur championship.

Then came the war, during which Britain lost almost an entire generation of golfers among its three-quarters of a million dead and was financially devastated. Golf, not surprisingly, was low on the list of the country's priorities.

In the early 1920s, the American rout of British golf began in earnest. When Jock Hutchison became the first U.S. citizen to win the British Open in 1921, the fact that he had emigrated from Scotland only served to emphasize the seismic shift taking place. Before the twenties were over, Hutchison was joined by Jim Barnes and Tommy Armour, who also had left Britain for America. And with Walter Hagen and Jones winning seven Opens between them, the title went back to the United States every year but one from 1921 to 1933.

At first, the British behaved gracelessly when confronted with the evidence that their mastery of the game was slipping away. When Travis won the 1904 Amateur at Sandwich, he was presented the trophy only after having to listen to Lord Northbourne, a British peer, say he hoped such a disaster would never happen again. And when Hutchison won the Open at St. Andrews, the chairman of the greens committee called for three cheers for Roger Wethered, who had lost a 36-hole playoff, and none for the winner.

But gradually the British not only came to terms with the American ascendancy but also accepted and all but embraced it. They even played a role in helping the United States take over the game for good.

"We cannot refuse to meet the Americans as this would show a lack of courtesy," Henry Gullen, the secretary of the Royal and Ancient said when the United States proposed a team match before the British Amateur championship in 1921. The members agreed and abandoned plans to revive a tournament between England and Scotland that had once been a fixture of its competitive season.

Played at Hoylake, the international match was over almost before it began. A large and excited crowd saw Jones, playing in a foursome with Chick Evans as his partner, hit the first shot of the competition and go on to win the hole. He and Evans won the next three as well, and after nine holes they led by five shots. That began a rout of the morning foursomes and resulted in what Hoylake historian Guy B. Farrar called "a shattering blow to our prestige, it practically finished the match."

The Americans won the competition nine matches to three, and a dozen years later, Farrar would remember it as "a triumph from which we have not yet recovered, and it laid the foundation of the present inferiority complex, which grows stronger with each American victory." It was not that the visitors had played so well, he said, as much as the fact that nervous British golfers seemed to regard them as supermen and dug their own graves. "In years to come, golfers of the Western World may well celebrate it as a second Independence Day," Farrar said. This was certainly true from a team standpoint as the Americans won their match with Britain—it was soon christened the Walker Cup and played biennially—the first nine times it was played.

Before long, the British were casting their natural patriotism aside and responding to being beaten at their own game with an amused generosity as the Americans won Open after Open and Walker Cup after Walker Cup.

"We are getting a little jealous, but we always want the best man to win," the Prince of Wales said as he handed Walter Hagen the British Open trophy for the third time, in 1928. "We hope the overseas golfers will continue to come until, as they say in America, we are able to put one over on them."

By then, the final barrier had already fallen when Jess Sweetser became the first native-born American to win the British Amateur, crushing Alfred Simpson, 6 and 5, at Muirfield in 1926. Sweetser, who was so ill with the flu during the tournament that he had considered withdrawing, was given three cheers by the crowd and carried a quarter of a mile to the clubhouse on stout Scottish shoulders.

"Our amateur championship has gone to a citizen of the United States," the club captain said at the awards ceremony. "There is no doubt that the best man won. I hope he will come back and defend his title, and I hope he will be beaten. My lords, ladies and gentlemen, are we downhearted?"

"No! No!" came the cries from the crowd.

"I will come back and I will be beaten," Sweetser said modestly, and there were more shouts of approval.

Afterward, Keeler went to Muirfield's stately old clubhouse, its walls hung with portraits of eighteenth-century golfers in scarlet coats holding odd-looking clubs, where he heard members of the U.S. contingent singing, "The Sidewalks of New York" in Sweetser's honor.

"You amazing Americans," British golf writer George Greenwood told Keeler, "you win our championship, and then you sing songs in the Honourable Company's clubhouse."

"I never thought I would live to see this day," said Frank Carruthers, another British journalist. "There never was a note sung in this edifice before."

"My God, no," said Greenwood. "The members are supposed to wear felt slippers around this place."

The members, as it happened, rather enjoyed the disruption of their decorum. One approached Keeler and asked, "Would you mind asking them to sing 'Drunk Last Night'? It's quite the best thing they do."

Greenwood's written account of the match was more formal but just as sanguine. "We do not begrudge the honor won by America," he said, "but rather do we welcome it, because all good sportsmen of the two great English-speaking races do recognize in it a strengthening of the bonds of friendship between the two countries."

"Defeat may be galling," Bernard Darwin wrote in the *Times*, "but as long as it is accepted in the old public school and university spirit of true sportsmanship it can only make for good."

Even when Walter Hagen said in 1926 that one reason for American superiority was that the British were "too gosh-darned lazy" to work at the game, the reaction was muted. Though the *London Observer* called Hagen's "gratuitous little lecture" ridiculous nonsense, a number of others, including some of Britain's top golfers, could only agree.

"In view of the poor form shown by British golfers in five of the last six Open championships," said Roger Wethered, the 1923 British Amateur champion, "it is surprising to find that some are unable to take a word of advice. Hagen is quite right when he says we are too lazy to win tournaments. Excuses are only another sign of weakness, and excuses stare us in the face."

To a correspondent who found it scandalous that "America has placed her professionals on a similar footing to her amateurs," an editorial in the British magazine *Golf Illustrated* said, "By uplifting the social standing of professional golfers America has set a fashion that must be for the good of the game."

Some of Britain's best golfers explained the Americans' superiority in more practical terms. The beautiful conditions of their golf courses and their more benign weather had much to do with developing their confidence, Cyril Tolley believed, especially when compared with the wind that prevailed at Britain's seaside links and the bad repair of so many courses.

"I know the few times I got on an American fairway, I always had a most magnificent lie, the ball fairly sitting up, asking to be hit," Tolley said. And putting on the slow, perfect American greens gives them a confidence that is "quite impossible to destroy during the short period for which they visit these shores."

Ted Ray noted the Americans' mastery of clubs that gave loft and backspin to short pitch shots as a key to their game. The British, he noted, were still using clubs that sent low shots running up onto the green, while the Americans spent hours practicing high approach shots that landed close to the cup and stayed there.

There were some who looked on the decline of British golf in the face of the American assault as a positive sign, one that marked nothing less than the superiority of the British character.

Under the headline "The Importance of Being Earnest," the *Observer* said, "British golfers regard the game as a means to a lot of fun and healthy recreation, but the impression is gained that in America, at least by the tournament golfers, it is regarded as a very serious business. One would imagine that their very lives depended on the result, so earnest and thorough are their methods."

"They have reduced the game to one of figures," complained James Ockenden in *Golfing* magazine. "The one thing which is uppermost in their minds at each hole is the par score and by hook or by crook they have to get it. By this system, they have driven a great deal of the fun and pleasure out of the game."

After his debacle at St. Andrews in 1921, Jones did not return to Britain for five years. He was no longer a teenager and, since turning professional was out of the question, matters other than golf claimed his time and attention. His studies at Harvard certainly kept him busy enough, as did his start in business, working for George Adair's real-estate firm, where he joined his boyhood friend Perry in the rental department.

And in 1924, Jones married Mary Malone, the daughter of John Malone, a socially prominent Atlanta landowner and tax assessor he had met four years earlier on a streetcar. Luckily for him, Mary was the sister of two college friends, so dropping in for a visit was never much of a problem. In no time at all they were a couple, and they would remain so for half a century.

A beautiful, dark-eyed brunette, Mary was reserved in public—not for her the flamboyance of the 1920s flappers—very much like Jones himself, though without his ability to ingratiate himself when faced with public situations he could not avoid. She was rigidly Victorian in her social views; often stern and distant in her dealings with her children; and, while devoted to Jones, not always pleased with the amount of time his golf kept him away from home or with the public attention it brought.

It is accepted as gospel that Jones never looked at another woman once he was married, and the only speculation of an earlier attachment is, once again, a story that is told several ways. Jones himself seemed to have trouble remembering whether he was attracted to, or even had met, a popular southern debutante named Zelda Sayre, and it was left to her and the man she did marry, F. Scott Fitzgerald, to attach a romantic narrative to the tale.

Many years after the fact, Fitzgerald told his mistress Sheila Graham that shortly after the end of World War I he had stolen Zelda away from Jones. Zelda's version of the story, according to Charles Price, who often wrote about Jones, was that she had tricked Fitzgerald into setting a date by producing a picture from the by-then famous young golfer signed "With love, Bobby," words that she had forged.

In 1962, Jones responded to a letter from Fitzgerald's biographer Andrew Turnbull by saying he had run into Zelda several times at parties in Atlanta but had never had a date with her. But at about the same time, Jones wrote to Price, who had sent him the manuscript of a book he was completing, that he was "surprised you fell for that stupid myth" that he and Zelda had been friends. "I never met her," Jones said, "although I knew of her. . . . Zelda must have been at least five or six years older than I was and would not have looked sideways at me." Perry Adair had spoken of her, and perhaps dated her, Jones said, but "to this day, I have never laid eyes on Zelda."

In truth, Zelda was only two years older than Jones, and Price seems to have taken this into account when, in his 1986 book *A Golf Story*, he quotes him as saying "I only met her once, casually, at a party in Augusta. I assure you that eighteen-year-old girls then, as now, don't pay attention to sixteen-year-old boys, no matter who they were."

Following his breakthrough at Inwood, Jones lost to Max Marston, a top amateur of the day, in the second round of the 1923 U.S. Amateur at Flossmoor County Club, south of Chicago. With only one exception over the next seven years, nothing like that ever happened again as Jones made American amateur golf his own private preserve, winning the U.S. championship a record five times and losing in the finals once.

In 1924 Jones made an emotional return to Merion, the scene of his debut on the national stage eight years earlier, and tore the field apart. He gave a reluctant 11 and 10 thrashing to his idol Francis Ouimet—"Bobby, you could afford to lose that one," Ouimet told him after besting him in one of the only two holes he would win all day—and, in the final, beat George Von Elm, 9 and 8.

In 1925 at Oakmont, Jones avenged his defeat to Davey Herron six years earlier just as authoritatively, winning his matches by an average of eight holes and beating Watts Gunn, 8 and 7, in a final that delighted their friends back in Atlanta. Gunn was Jones's protégé at East Lake, and together they gave the Amateur the only final in its history between two men from the same club.

Jones finished second in the U.S. Open in 1924 and 1925—with only one exception he would be first or second in that tournament the rest of his career—so those two years went a long way toward silencing all doubts, his own among them, that he was now the greatest player in the world.

Nor did Jones's failure to return to Britain for five years affect that country's feelings for him. Yes, he had left ignominiously in 1921 ("a rather ordinary boy, after all"), but feelings changed as time passed. "Nothing but delight was expressed everywhere when the cables flashed the news," George Greenwood wrote of his victory over Cruickshank at Inwood. "Jones is admired not merely because he is a great and wonderful golfer, but because he is an attractive personality. An Englishman loves a man who is frank, boyish, and unspoiled, and Jones is all of these."

How to account for Jones's remarkable popularity in Britain? His attractive looks—he had become almost impossibly handsome by the time he entered his twenties—his well-considered public statements, his modest manner, and the almost aristocratic calm he projected were certainly parts of it, and some observers were left reaching for the sky as they tried to explain what they saw in him.

"Why Bobby Jones appeals to everyone is that he is the essence of simplicity," wrote a columnist in the British magazine *Golf Monthly*, which, on its cover, called Jones "The Napoleon of Golf." "It is the gift of really great men, captains of commerce, and those distinguished in letters and art. Bobby Jones never asserts himself and has nothing of the vain, empty, bumptious manner of the upstart so prevalent in some quarters of golf. He plays his mighty game, leaves his golf to speak for itself, and for the rest, the sweetness and sincerity of his disposition are sufficient."

There also was the fact that by the mid-1920s British golf was on the rise again. After the war there was an almost desperate national desire for a return to the normalcy Americans had been promised by their president, and the resumption of sports was counted as a sign that the worst was finally over. The upper classes went back to their golf courses, and the presence of Jones and other top American golfers at the country's most venerable tournaments was further proof that their way of life had survived.

But there was another factor that helps explain the British infatuation with Jones. They simply loved the way he played golf. His swing was so flawless, his tactics so intelligent, his approach so bold when boldness was required. He seemed to embody everything that drew them to the game.

"I can remember the precise spot at Hoylake where I first saw the swing soon to be familiar in the imagination of the whole sporting world," Darwin wrote years later. "So swift, in that it occupied so little time, with no suspicion of waggle, and yet so leisurely in its almost drowsy grace, so lithe and smooth."

"St. Andrews people, who have golf in their very blood, are shrewd judges of players and in Mr. Jones they see one who is a purist as regards style and method," a correspondent identified as "A Roving Player" wrote in the British magazine *Tatler* after Jones won his second consecutive British Open, in 1927. "Mr. Jones stands to the ball as if he were engaged in ordinary conversation. There is no straddling of legs, no tying of muscles into a knot, no extravagant poses, nothing to suggest that he is thinking of or doing anything in particular."

"It is a symphony in rhythmic movement," Guy Farrar wrote of Jones's putting style. "With his head cocked on one side, he gently pushes the ball towards the hole. 'Heavens,' you think, 'he must be short,' but the ball rolls on and on, until it reaches the lip, gives a last lingering look around, and finally disappears."

"It is comforting," agreed Darwin, "to find a great golfer who does not think much of 'Never up, never in' and holds that it is often made an excuse for banging the ball past the hole, not in any genuine effort to hole the putt but merely to avoid an accusation of cowardice."

Roger Wethered spoke approvingly of how Jones was able to keep his game under control, how he always seemed to have something up his sleeve that would be revealed only when it was needed. "His driving, to take one example, is particularly elastic," Wethered wrote. "He allows the longest hitters the satisfaction of outdriving him when the distance does not matter, only in their turn to find themselves outdriven with ease when length is of utmost importance. Indeed, a fluent variation of stroke runs through every part of his game. . . . I can only describe a match against Bobby in this manner: It is just as though you got your hand caught in a buzz saw."

Eric Fiddian, remembering more than seventy years later the two matches he played with Jones, indicated how distracting competing against such superior form could be. "There was no question of 'hit,'" Fiddian says. "It was as if the ball got in the way of his swing—got *swept* off the tee. If you were playing with Jones, you were sort of watching and saying to yourself, 'By Jove, that's lovely, isn't it?'"

No one contributed more to Jones's mystique in Britain than a man who was among the keenest observers of golf in the world at the time and is still considered by many to be the finest writer the sport has ever produced: Bernard Darwin. Though he was a quarter of a century older than Jones, had observed and written about all the great players of the age, and was by nature cantankerous and hard to impress, his memories of covering Jones left him all but tongue-tied.

"I come now with faltering pen to the greatest of them all," Darwin said in *Golf Between Two Wars*, and the title of the chapter he devoted to Jones gave away his feelings before he wrote a word: "The Immortal Bobby."

Darwin's rise to preeminence among his country's golf journalists was as unlikely as it was fortuitous. Born in Kent in 1876, his mother died in childbirth and his father took him to live with his own mother and father, the world-renowned naturalist Charles Darwin. He called his grandfather Babba.

Writing decades later about the man whose theory of evolution revolutionized science, Darwin would remember insisting on whistling contests in which his grandfather's abilities left him unimpressed and taking occasional walks. A nurse working in the household observed the old man on one of his excursions watching an ant heap for more than an hour. It was a pity, she said, he did not have anything to do.

"The baby was a great delight to both my parents," Darwin's Aunt Henrietta wrote in an introduction to the publication of family correspondence. "Your father is taking a good deal to the Baby," Charles Darwin's wife, Emma, wrote Henrietta. "We think he is a sort of Grand Lama, he's so solemn."

Indeed, Darwin was a solemn boy. With no mother, a father whose work as a botanist took him to Germany for extended periods, and few playmates, he was left to his own devices, which for the most part meant reading. He pored over Dickens, Thackeray, Conan Doyle, and George Eliot, and memorized *Treasure Island*.

Charles Darwin died when Bernard was six, and when his father explained he would not be sick anymore, Darwin was secretly affronted at not being supposed to know what death was. For the rest of his life, he was often reminded of his illustrious lineage.

At the time of the Scopes trial, during which Clarence Darrow and William Jennings Bryan staged their famous battle over evolution, an American promoter asked Darwin to come to the United States and lecture on the subject. Darwin dismissed him, saying "the

State of Tennessee appeared to be making a fool of itself by talking about matters which it did not understand and I did not want to emulate it." He could only laugh when the promoter sold their correspondence to a New York newspaper, which ran it under the headline, "Darwin Kin Finds Scopes Trial Folly." "I have often wondered," he wrote, "whether he got paid for it and, if so, how much."

"Grandfather," Darwin would quickly interrupt whenever anyone asked him, "What relation are you to . . . ?" or, "Was the great . . . ?" And though nobody said so to his face, Darwin was aware that some of his oldest friends called him "Monkey."

Darwin was eight years old when his father introduced him to golf, and he was entranced. He played the game avidly and particularly remembered entering his first pro shop and finding it a "paradise of glue and pitch."

He played golf at Cambridge, where he studied classics and law and was skilled enough to compete in international meets. Though he practiced law until he was thirty, he found it dreadfully boring. In his more depressed moments, he wrote, he felt like Kipps, the draper's apprentice in the H. G. Wells novel of that name, who said, "We're in a blessed drainpipe and we've got to crawl along it till we die."

Then, quite from out of the blue, came an invitation to write a weekly golf column for the *Evening Standard* for thirty shillings each. Within a year he was writing for the *Times* of London and a magazine called *Country Life*. He sold his barrister's wig and gown for five pounds and left for a new life.

Darwin was both the most erudite golf writer ever and the most accomplished at playing the game. Occasionally he would write about the weather; the scenery; the birds on the golf course; and finally, almost grudgingly, about the players and the match. Characters from Dickens and other novelists made frequent appearances in his accounts, never with any identification beyond their names. His readers were expected to know who Mr. Micawber, Mr. Smangle, Mrs. Gamp, and Harold Skimpole were, and to appreciate his transferring them from Dickens's world to his own.

Approving of the way Jones was finally learning to play the troublesome Road Hole at St. Andrews after his early struggles, Darwin wrote, "In short, he had proved the truth of Mrs. Malaprop's saying that 'Tis safest in matrimony to begin with a little aversion.'"

Recalling an epic match played in the rain between Alexa Stirling and the great British woman golfer Cecil Leitch in the 1924 ladies' championship at Turnberry, he wrote, "Think of Madame Defarge leading the women of St. Antoine's against the Bastille, think of anything frightfully grand, and you have a picture of Miss Leitch in that match."

And then he added, "Precisely the number of holes by which she won I do not remember and I do not propose to look it up and so spoil my own imaginary picture by superfluous details."

This was typical of the marvelous disdain Darwin often brought to his writing and to his conversation.

"I say, are those your old school colors," he once asked a golfer wearing a garish sweater, "or your own unfortunate bad taste?"

Of unruly British spectators at a tournament, he approvingly quoted what someone had once said about a large crowd at St. Andrews: "It is disgraceful of the railway people bringing a parcel of uneducated brutes down here when they knew a real match was going on."

Darwin rarely quoted the golfers he wrote about, once telling a colleague at a British Open, "My readers want to know why I think he won, not why that fool thinks he won."

As a golfer, Darwin, who was tall and strong, had all the shots, but his putting was unreliable, and his inability to control his temper did him in more than once. Still, he was skilled enough to play in some of the most important tournaments he covered, and often to do extremely well. In all of competitive sports at the championship level, there is nothing to compare with this: a journalist competing on even terms with the athletes he is writing about.

Darwin would play his matches then come off the course and describe them, as well as the others that had been contested that day. It could be a little exhausting, he said, especially when he had to play two matches in one day, but it was nothing he could not handle.

In 1922, when a British team traveled to the National Golf Links in Southampton, Long Island, for the first official Walker Cup, the captain fell ill and Darwin, on hand to cover the competition, was pressed into service. He beat former U.S. Open champion William Fownes, 3 and 1.

Also that year, Darwin quite offhandedly instituted the Walker Cup's system of matches ending in ties when, after Jess Sweetser and C. V. L. Hooman were all even after 36 holes, they were sent out to break the deadlock. "Heaven knows," Darwin said after Hooman won, "when two men have halved a 36-hole match in the Walker Cup, they have earned an immediate drink with no further demands on them." That judgment has never been challenged, and Walker Cup matches occasionally end in ties to this day.

Twice Darwin reached the semifinals of the British Amateur, most memorably at St. Andrews in 1921, when he lasted longer than any American who had entered, including Jones. Walking down the street after ousting the last U.S. player, Fred Wright, Darwin was approached by a man who said, "Sir, I want to thank you for the way you have saved your country."

By then, Lord Northcliffe, the owner of the *Times*, was sending Darwin urgent messages insisting that he stop writing and concentrate on winning the tournament.

"It was extraordinarily kind of him," Darwin wrote, "but it was easier said than done, and so I played the part of Casabiana and stuck to my post." He never doubted his readers would remember Casabiana as the boy who stood on the burning deck whence all but he had fled.

Darwin lost his match the next day, then came off the course and wrote about it in his unsigned articles for the *Times* and the *New York Herald* as unsparingly as he would have about anyone else who had lost.

"On one occasion when he was reporting a competition in which he was himself playing," wrote Joyce Wethered, Roger's sister and one of England's finest women golfers, "he was so hard on himself that an irate reader wrote to the paper complaining that their golf correspondent had been grossly unfair about Mr. Darwin's golf."

If Darwin ever read that letter, he would not have agreed. "Now then Darwin, come along Darwin, come along, keep it smooth," one opponent heard him say before attempting a short chip to the green. And then, "Oh, Darwin, you bloody fool!"

On other occasions, he was as droll as could be when writing about himself, such as when he met Harrison Johnston, the reigning U.S. Amateur champion, in the first round of the 1930 British Amateur at St. Andrews, the first of Jones's four Grand Slam victories.

"H. Johnston, the Amateur Champion of the United States, was one of the unlucky few who had not drawn byes," Darwin wrote, "and met B. Darwin at the rather grim hour of half-past 8. I was up betimes to see them start and, indeed, saw the whole match, which was an uncommonly good one."

Good enough for Darwin to take Johnston to the 17th hole before finally losing to one of the top amateur golfers in the world. After chastising himself for "missing a nonsensically short putt . . . I had not many hopes of Darwin hanging on," he allowed himself rare public consolation: "The loser need shed no remorseful tears."

Darwin wrote books on many subjects—two on Dickens, one on historic London landmarks, two for children, and an autobiography are just a part of his output—and Joyce Wethered said his literary friends thought his preoccupation with golf kept him from more serious work. In the end, though, they had to agree that his time had not been misspent.

Perhaps he exaggerated the agonies and emotions of playing golf just a bit, she wrote, but "After the drear and tragic years of World War I, British golf was indeed fortunate to have such an interpreter to show us all how once again to enjoy the game."

8

"It Was Perfect and That Is All There Is to Say about It"

The first thing of note Jones did upon his return to Britain in 1926 was thrash the reigning champion, Robert Harris, in the fifth round of the British Amateur. He had seen Jones apply such ruthless pressure to an opponent before, Keeler wrote of Jones's 8 and 7 victory at Muirfield, but never quite as spectacularly as this. It was the worst defeat of Harris's competitive career.

The second thing Jones did was lose to another British golfer who had no business being on the course with him. Just as Allan Graham had so thoroughly embarrassed him in the 1921 Amateur at Hoylake, so did Andrew Jamieson beat him this time, 4 and 3.

Jamieson rode back and forth to the course on a bicycle, enlisted his brother as his caddy, had little tournament experience, and spent the evening before the match practicing his putting on the lawn at his hotel. The next morning he easily beat Jones and then, as if to show just how out of character that was, he shot an 85 that afternoon and was eliminated from the tournament.

Jones's only excuse was that he had played despite a severe crick in his neck he had suffered early that morning, and he had considered defaulting the match. But he chose to continue, and while he did not play poorly, the brilliance he had shown the day before was gone. His round had been limp and spiritless, Darwin thought, and Jones left the golf course feeling not angry so much as disappointed that he had come to such unexpected grief for the second time in a British Amateur. It was all too much for Keeler, who at twilight walked onto the empty course, where he listened to the mournful cry of the seabirds and felt terribly alone.

Jones's passage to Britain had been paid for by the U.S. Walker Cup Committee, but as the *Aquitania* sailed to London, the team learned that Britain's competitive golf schedule was in doubt. A severe housing shortage, unemployment figures that never fell below 10 percent, and a rise in the cost of living had the country's working-class population on edge. The end of a government subsidy to coal miners was the last straw. Labor unions called a general strike, which started on May 3, crippling all public transportation in London and closing many businesses.

William Fownes, the president of the U.S. Golf Association, cabled his concern from the ship and received a stiff-upper-lip reply from the Royal and Ancient: "Shall try to carry out all of the program."

When the American team arrived in London, it found tanks, armored cars, and troops wearing helmets in the streets. But to Keeler the British people seemed stoic and brave as the tension mounted. And then suddenly it was over. The Trade Union Council called off the strike, though the miners stayed out for another six months until, with many of their families all but starving, they went back to work as winter approached.

"Surrender of the Revolutionaries" was the headline in the *Daily Mail*, which informed its readers that the strike had been called in Moscow and been abetted by five hundred Soviet agents in Britain. Of greater concern to the Americans was the fact that their match was on.

Jones played well in the Walker Cup at St. Andrews, and the U.S. team won the competition for the fourth straight time before large crowds that greeted the visitors enthusiastically. Rather than play in the British Open, though, Jones had been determined to sail home. He was homesick for Mary and their one-year-old daughter, Clara, and he wanted to prepare for the U.S. Open, which was coming up in just a few weeks.

But losing the Amateur changed everything. It would look as if he were sulking if he left now, Jones thought. It would be another display of bad behavior to add to his midround withdrawal in 1921. And besides, wasn't it about time he showed the British he could actually play this game? Except for beating Robert Harris, what did he have to show for himself in two trips to Britain? A narrow victory over E. A. Hamlet? Losses to Allan Graham and Andrew Jamieson? One thing was certain, Jones thought as he changed his travel plans and got ready to play in the Open at Royal Lytham and St. Anne's Golf Club in Lancashire. This time he would not pick up his ball or tear up his scorecard.

In his first round of British Open qualifying at the Sunningdale Golf Club in Surrey, Jones shot one of the best rounds of his life—a 66.

"Incredible and indecent," said Darwin. "It was perfect and that is all there is to say about it." Said Charles MacFarlane of the *News*, "The boy's game was as pure and chaste as Grecian statuary."

It was not just Jones's score, which broke the course record by three shots, that caused such amazement. It was the *symmetry* of it—thirty-three putts, thirty-three other shots. Jones made twelve pars, six birdies, no bogeys, and needed only one long putt.

His drives and approaches were so nearly perfect that when he did, just once, miss the green at the short 13th hole and land in a bunker, Darwin thought it must have come as something of a relief to the spectators "who had been feeling that they must scream if perfection endured much longer." Jones chipped out dead to the hole and made the putt.

"It was a staggeringly low score at the time," wrote Henry Longhurst. "I have yet to meet anyone who contests it was the most flawless round of golf ever played."

For once, Jones let the excitement of the moment overcome all modesty. If the British wanted to call it the finest round of golf ever shot in their country, well, they are very polite people, aren't they? And in truth he never expected to shoot a better round of golf than that one, in competition or out. He had showed them a bit of how he could play, hadn't he? He couldn't have been happier.

Jones was so keyed up that when Keeler suggested a walk after dinner, they started at the lake by their hotel and hiked completely around it—ten miles. Jones slept like a baby that night, then shot a 68 at Sunningdale the next day. It was a record two-round qualifying total for the Open, and he led the field by seven shots. The British oddsmakers installed him as a 3–1 favorite to win the tournament, odds that were inconceivably low, Keeler thought.

Then the competition began, and Jones was in trouble again. The 9th hole at Royal Lytham and St. Anne's tormented him in all four rounds, and the 13th as well. As for the six-hundred-yard 11th hole that he always seemed to be playing against the wind, he had never in his life hit three woods as hard as he could and *still* wound up short of the green.

And all those lovely short putts he had had at Sunningdale seemed to be ten- and twenty-footers now. Only four one-putt greens at the end of his first round kept him from disaster and allowed him to finish with a respectable 72. Jones would be the last man in the world to contend that that was any way to play golf.

Still, he was only four shots behind Walter Hagen, whose 68 was such a good score it all but killed the fans' hopes for a British victory. To make the 36-hole cut, a competitor had to be within fifteen shots of the leader, and to that point there were only ten, eight from the United States. The Americans, Darwin wrote, "piled on the agony and rubbed our noses in the dirt."

Jones scraped to another 72 the second day as Hagen faltered with a 77. What did it mean that he could be playing so far from his best and still be tied for the lead? It meant that the 36-hole final on Saturday was going to be a brute.

Jones began the third round tied with Bill Mehlhorn, one of the pioneers of the American professional tour whose ability from tee to green was often undercut by his difficulties putting, one shot ahead of Hagen and two in front of Al Watrous.

Mehlhorn's bid ended quickly as he shot 40 on the front 9 and finished at 79. So the tournament came down to Jones, Hagen, and Watrous, who was Jones's partner for the final 36 holes. Hagen was delighted to be scheduled to tee off an hour and a half after them, since it put him in the position of a gambler looking at his opponents' cards. He would know in advance what he needed to shoot to win.

Watrous was a twenty-six-year-old protégé of Hagen's and had entered the tournament after Hagen had told his club in Grand

Rapids, Michigan, that he might do well there. Raised in Yonkers, New York, Watrous had come up through the ranks, caddying as a boy and then, after serving in the navy, traveling to Detroit, where he had heard there was a job as an assistant club pro.

At age twenty-three, Watrous won the Canadian Open, but he had no illusions about life as a touring pro, particularly after his wife gave birth to the first of their five children. He was content to remain in Michigan all his life, succeeding Hagen as head pro at the Oakland Hills Country Club and winning the Michigan Open and PGA championships a total of fourteen times. On the rare occasions when Watrous did hit the tournament trail—he played in the first two Ryder Cups and the first three Masters—his fellow pros delighted in his company.

"How many children have you got now, Al?" a player who hadn't seen him in a while would ask.

"I don't know," Watrous would reply, "I haven't been home in six weeks." Or, "I haven't been out on the front porch to see how many bottles of milk we get each morning."

So the 1926 British Open was a rare adventure for Watrous, and he began the third round as if he were going to make short work of it. Shooting a 33 on the front nine, he quickly blew past Jones, who bogeyed the 3rd, double-bogeyed the 4th, and did well to make the turn in 37 shots. From a two-stroke deficit, Watrous was ahead by two.

The two men battled shot for shot on the back nine until, after they both hit superb second shots, they came to the 18th green with Watrous leading by a stroke. Jones putted first and missed, to post a score of 73. Watrous sent a twelve-footer straight into the middle of the hole for a birdie that gave him a superb round of 69. As they broke for lunch, his lead was two strokes once again.

With nothing to do but wait—first for Hagen to come in, then for their afternoon starting time—Jones turned to Watrous and said, "Come on, Al, let's get away from here and relax. It's the worst thing we can do, standing around the board waiting for a close rival to come in."

Under the circumstances, two men fighting to win the British Open, it was an extraordinarily generous offer, and Watrous never forgot it.

"Whenever Dad spoke of Jones," says Watrous's son Tom, "it was never just his ability, but what a gentleman he was. I'm convinced that influenced Dad. He was not an educated man, but he had an aura about him—always extremely gentlemanly. I picked up on that when I was a very small boy. I think he owed that to Bobby Jones."

The two men went to the hotel room Jones was sharing with Keeler, where they ordered a lunch of tea, toast, and cold ham, took off their shoes, and lay down—Jones on his bed, Watrous on Keeler's. The writer pulled down the shades, but Jones looked over to Watrous with a warning: "For goodness sake, don't take a nap. That is almost certainly fatal between rounds."

It was a killing thing, Jones thought as he rested, for the leaders to have to play together in the final round of a championship. How was he supposed to concentrate on playing against the golf course, against Old Man Par, when he could see everything his opponent was doing? But that was golf, wasn't it?

Finally it was time to return to the course, and as they left the hotel, he told Watrous, "Remember, Al, the winner and the runner-up are in this pair." It certainly looked that way as they learned that Hagen had come in with a morning round of 74 and was four shots off the lead.

The drama turned briefly into farce when Jones arrived at the course and discovered he had left his player's badge back at the hotel. Failing to recognize the most famous golfer in the world, the gate-keeper would not let him in, so Jones went around to the spectator's entrance and paid the admission fee of five shillings.

The beginning of Jones's final round was maddening. He was hitting the ball better, much farther than Watrous off the tee, and with greater accuracy than in the morning. But his putts still were not dropping. So while Watrous was giving him chances—a bogey at the 3rd, a double bogey at the 5th—he could not capitalize. Three putts at the fifth green cost him a chance at the lead, and when he missed putts at the 9th and 11th holes, Watrous's lead held at two strokes.

"My golf is terrible," Jones told the official accompanying the twosome, although in fact there was little wrong that making a few putts would not cure. All told, he calculated later, he needed thirty-nine putts to get around and three-putted three greens. Just ghastly, he thought. A nightmare.

But then Watrous began to feel the pressure, too. His first putt at

14 overran the hole, and he missed coming back. His lead was down to one. Facing a short putt for par at 15, he seemed to push at the ball with his putter and missed again. With his nerves beginning to crack, he had let Jones catch him.

Watrous steadied himself at the 16th hole, where Darwin wanted to murder a photographer who twice stepped out to take a picture as Jones was chipping onto the green. Jones made his par to maintain the tie, but then hit one of his few poor drives of the day, hooking his tee shot at the 411-yard 17th into a sandy area full of heather, gorse, and thick clumps of grass protruding out of rugged sand dunes. As he watched the flight of the ball, Jones's heart sank.

"It's all over," he told Watrous. "They won't even find it."

Watrous's drive was straight down the middle—he would easily be able to reach the green—and it was clear Jones was in serious trouble. Lose a shot and he would be a stroke back with only one hole to play. And if the ball was lost, that truly would be the end.

Jones walked disconsolately down the left side of the course, until—*no, it wasn't possible*—he saw the ball perched nice and high in the middle of a patch of dry, packed sand. Only six feet square, it looked as if it had been carved out of the thick bushes and wiry grass with a pick and shovel. He had hit his ball into a jungle, and it had landed on a beach. It was a fantastic piece of luck.

Still, there was nothing easy about the task confronting him. The green was around the bend to the left, out of sight from where his ball lay, so he walked far out to the right, almost across the fairway, to judge his prospects. They were not encouraging. He was 175 yards away, and to stay even with Watrous he somehow had to hit a ball off the sand, into the wind, onto a green he could not see, and make sure it stayed there. Let him dig just an eighth of an inch too deeply into the sand and the shot would die in front of his eyes. As for hitting the ball as much as a thought too high, well, better not to think that thought.

Jones took his 4-iron, stood over the ball, took his customary quick glance at the line, and swung. A slight spray of sand rose into the air as the ball flew straight toward the green and, as the gallery held its breath, came to rest inside Watrous's ball.

It was, Darwin wrote, "one of the most melodramatic shots ever played," and Jones would always call it the greatest of his career. Had he dug out just one more teaspoonful of sand, it would have been over. Instead, it was Watrous who was destroyed. Undone by the magnitude of Jones's shot, he three-putted, then hooked his tee shot at 18 and bogeyed that hole as well. With a 74 to Watrous's 78, Jones had beaten him by two shots and was the British Open champion.

Or was he?

Out on the course, with many holes still to play and loving it, Walter Hagen was making his golf ball fly, and the rumors along with it. He had made the turn in 34, came a report back to the clubhouse. No, it was 33. Wait, 32. Finally, an honest count arrived—Hagen had gone out in 36 and would need to match that score on the back 9 to tie Jones. Not an easy thing to do certainly, but he *had* shot 68 to start the tournament, and he *was* Walter Hagen.

Hagen bogeyed the 13th and 15th holes and came to 18 two shots back. It was over, and Jones began accepting congratulatory handshakes. It was over—in everybody's mind but Hagen's. Did he need to make an eagle from the fairway at 18 to tie Jones? Fine; he would just have to try to make an eagle from the fairway.

Walking away from his ball, which lay 150 yards from the hole, Hagen asked the scorer accompanying him to go to the green and take the flagstick out of the hole. Uncomprehending, the official did not move, and Hagen had to ask him again. This time the man walked to the green but stopped short. Hagen walked half the distance to the green himself and then shouted, loud enough for the official to hear, not to mention the thousands of people around the green, "I want you to hold the flag!"

Finally, the official got the message and removed the flagstick from the cup. Up on the balcony of the clubhouse overlooking the green, Jones turned his back. "A guy with that much confidence," he told Hagen later, "would be fool enough to make it."

The shot landed on the edge of the green, rolled quickly toward the cup, and jumped over it—Hagen thought it would have hit the missing flagstick—before ending up in a trap behind the green. He had never really had a chance, of course. He had gone for it just to give the gallery a thrill. But do you know what was just as much fun? he said afterward, thinking he might actually make it.

The episode was pure Hagen—and he would come back to win two more British Opens—but there was no doubt about the meaning of the results of the 1926 championship. And in an emotional gathering in the Royal Lytham and St. Anne's clubhouse, that meaning was made official.

It seemed as if all the great names of British golf from the past half century were there. Harry Vardon, James Braid, Harold Hilton, J. H. Taylor, Ted Ray, George Duncan—British Open winners every one of them. Good lord, there must be forty national championships in this room, Keeler calculated. All congratulating Jones, all shaking his hand, all—British reserve be damned—slapping him on the back and—this was amazing!—hugging him. All saying how proud they were of him.

Though delighting in the moment, Keeler felt a little sad for this great gathering of golfers. Seven of the top ten finishers in the tournament had been from the United States, and another was from Argentina. They gave us their game, he thought, and now we are trampling on them.

Among those who spoke at the cup presentation was J. H. Taylor, who had won the first of his five British Opens in 1894 and who, at age fifty-six, had thrilled the crowd that very morning by shooting 71, a better round than any of Jones's. Bobby Jones, Taylor told the crowd with tears running down his cheeks, was the greatest golfer who ever lived.

Once again, Jones rose to the occasion, gratifying British golfers, officials, and spectators alike by saying that just having his name on the cup with all the great men around him was honor enough. There was more emotion a short time later when he returned to his hotel and met his caddy, Jack MacIntyre, who had followed him around the country from the Walker Cup to the Amateur and the Open.

"Good-bye, Jack, old man," Jones said as they shook hands. "We won it together." MacIntyre tried to say something and failed, then sat down on the floor and sobbed.

Jones received one more British tribute before he left for home. It came in a telegram written in Latin that took Jones and Keeler some time to translate.

"Congratulations from a small nobody who was impudent enough to beat you," it read. It was signed by Andrew Jamieson, who, in his own way, had made Jones's first victory in a British tournament possible.

9

"Like a Hero Back from the War"

T wo weeks after his triumph in Britain, Jones sat in a hotel room in Columbus, Ohio, weeping uncontrollably, his body shaking. His mother, who was packing his bags for the trip back to Atlanta, was so alarmed she said that would be quite enough of competitive golf for her son. At that moment, the phone rang and Jones composed himself long enough to attend a ceremony where he was given the trophy for winning the 1926 U.S. Open.

The stakes seemed to be growing higher with every tournament, and so did the toll the tension was taking on Jones's nerves. For several years now, in the early hours of any day he was to compete, he would find himself on the brink of throwing up, a condition that would last throughout the morning. His neck would swell up so much he could not button his shirt collar and put on his tie for hours. Once, he played a round without a tie and his collar open, a remarkable breach of decorum for a golfer who always observed the game's formalities. He was at the top of his game, and he was acclaimed as the greatest golfer in the world, but the strain of competition was becoming more than he could bear.

Even before Jones went abroad in 1926, the expectations of the public at large and his friends in Atlanta had begun to grow beyond his ability to comprehend them. But his victory in the British Open took him to a higher level of fame and adulation, one that would occasionally seem almost frightening. And as the *Aquitania* made its way into New York, he got his first glimpse of the new world that was waiting for him. The evidence that his life had changed was there in the harbor in front of him.

The port was filled with small boats of every description—ferries, steamers, yachts, all blowing their horns and whistles as the big liner came into view. The city fireboat *John Purroy Mitchell* went them one better, sounding its loud emergency siren and shooting water from its hoses in high arcs through the air.

The official New York City reception ship, the *Macom*, sailed out of the pack and up to the *Aquitania*, bearing a large sign across its deck: "Welcome Bobby Jones." The boat had been chartered by the passengers of the Bobby Jones Special, a line of Pullman cars tied to the rear of the Crescent Limited, which made a regular run between Atlanta and New York. The train had left Atlanta with a delegation of sixty friends and dignitaries, including Atlanta mayor Walter Sims, and stopped in Washington, D.C., to pick up U.S. senator Walter George of Georgia.

Photographers and other well-wishers milled about, while up on the bridge Jones's grandfather, the man who always had been so skeptical of anyone who would waste his time playing games, surveyed the scene. He just happened to be in New York on business, R. T. Jones said. Few believed him. Jones's father, *Atlanta Journal* publisher John S. Cohen, and New York Public Works commissioner Joseph Johnson were supposed to be the only people to board the *Aquitania*, but soon Clara and Mary Jones also were climbing the foot-wide ladder up the towering side of the liner.

"It looks like the whole Jones family is here," Jones said, kissing Mary and his mother.

Jones and the rest of the Walker Cup delegation climbed down to the *Macom*, having been granted special permission by Secretary of the Treasury Andrew W. Mellon to leave the *Aquitania* before it cleared quarantine. Asked by photographers to kiss Mary again, Jones said, "That's silly," and they had to be satisfied with pictures of them standing next to each other, identical bemused smiles on their faces. The *Macom* sped away from the *Aquitania* and into the harbor, saluted by the horns of other boats as they passed.

But if Jones was startled by the shipboard reception, the greeting he received onshore was even more confounding. There were thousands of people, more photographers than he had ever before seen gathered in one place, marching bands, police holding the crowd at bay—it was beyond imagining. He looked, Keeler thought as he saw Jones take in the throngs who had gathered to greet him, like an embarrassed little boy.

Johnson announced the formation of a parade when suddenly it was discovered that the guest of honor was missing; Jones and Mary had sneaked away to the pier shed in search of a taxi. Two city policemen were dispatched to bring them back.

Soon the parade was lined up, complete with bands, a police escort, and the flags of the United States, the state of Georgia, the city of Atlanta, and the city and state of New York. The marchers set off with Jones, solemn and unsmiling, near the front while his father, grandfather, and the other golfers walked immediately behind. The rest of the Atlanta delegation followed, strung out for a block or more, with automobiles carrying the women in the party bringing up the rear.

Showers of colored streamers, long spirals of ticker tape, and clouds formed by small bits of paper came drifting down from the tall office buildings of the financial district. The cheering crowds on the sidewalk occasionally grew so dense that police had to push them back to make room for the marchers to pass. They were not always successful, as a number of onlookers broke through the line to shake hands. "Glory, Glory to Old Georgia," the band played, and "Dixie." The Atlantans responded with rebel yells.

At City Hall, New York mayor Jimmy Walker greeted Jones by saying, "I want to tell you how proud all America and all New York is of what you, as a young American, have done. You have won another triumph for American sportsmanship and American sporting skill." Then Walker added, "I have just learned that you were born on the seventeenth of March. If that fact had been made public before you arrived, the safety of the City Hall would have been imperiled, because the crowd would have flocked to this building and would have carried it away."

When it was time for Jones to respond, he spoke so softly the microphone had to be moved closer. "This is the most wonderful experience I have ever had," he said. "I just can't tell you how much I appreciate it. All I can say is thank you and everybody a thousand times."

In reflecting the following day on the reception Jones had received, the New York press seemed somewhat startled. The city had known ticker-tape parades for sports heroes before, of course. Nor had Jones been the first American golfer to win the British Open; Hagen had won the title two years earlier and also had been welcomed at City Hall. But there had been no parade then, and no celebration that remotely compared to this one.

"Nothing like yesterday's demonstration ever took place in the realm of sport," the *New York Times* noted. "No prince that has ever visited New York received a more royal reception."

"Like a hero back from the war," said the *World*, "Jones was taken off the *Aquitania*, sped to the Battery, marched behind a band through the canyon of Lower Broadway for a reception at City Hall, such as is the meed of royalty."

"I have seen many distinguished guests come up Broadway," said James Eagen, the secretary of Tammany Hall, "but never one who received such an enthusiastic, genuine and affectionate greeting as Bobby Jones."

Some experienced newspaper reporters said the reception for Jones was greater than that for General John J. Pershing at the end of World War I or for Admiral Robert Byrd after his return from his flight over the North Pole. All in all, everyone agreed, the welcome had been quite amazing, and both Keeler, writing in the *Journal*, and *Constitution* sports editor Ed Danforth made sure their readers back home were aware of its magnitude.

That night, a banquet was held at the Vanderbilt Hotel, where the Atlanta delegation continued to celebrate its favorite son and its moment in the national limelight. "From now on, Atlanta will think very highly of New York," Walter George told the crowd. If Jimmy Walker were ever to run for president, Jones's father said, every democrat in Atlanta—and, of course, there were nothing *but* democrats in Atlanta—would vote for him.

The banquet speeches were broadcast on the radio, and Jones, blushing as the band played "For He's a Jolly Good Fellow," could only repeat the sentiments he had expressed at City Hall. "I have had today the greatest thrill of my life," he said. "It is the greatest I have had and the greatest I ever will have. I can say nothing that will express my feelings." The banquet wound down with Hagen asking the band to play something more up to date than "Dixie" and "Swanee River," and bringing down the house as he danced the Charleston.

The end of the dinner did not signal the Atlanta contingent's readiness to retire, however. Instead, its members pursued their newly discovered infatuation with New York at Texas Guinan's 300 Club on West Fifty-fourth Street, where "Bobby Jones Night" was under way and where they received somewhat more of a celebration than they bargained for.

Guinan was New York's most famous speakeasy hostess, and her signature greeting, "Hello, suckers," symbolized much of the spirit of the Jazz Age. Her operating philosophy was simplicity itself: buy bootleg whiskey at $10 a case, sell it for $1 a shot, and make $100 in profit. Nor was accommodating an overflow of customers ever a problem. Guinan would simply set up more tables on the dance floor.

"How could eight couples possibly dance in that space?" one customer asked when Guinan assured him it was possible.

"Piggyback, darling, piggyback," she said.

Paying police protection occasionally cut into Guinan's take a bit, and once in a while her operation was shut down altogether. She would simply wait a decent interval, perhaps leave town for a while, and then open for business at another location. Out-of-towners, high-society swells, theatrical personalities, celebrities from all fields, the Prince of Wales—all had enjoyed Guinan's hospitality at one time or another. And who cared if it was true that during a police raid she had rushed the prince to the kitchen, given him an apron, a carton of eggs, and a frying pan, and told him to pretend he was a chef until the coast was clear? It was such a good story. So much seemed to happen on a nightly basis at the 300 Club, in fact, that several New York newspapers hired tables and kept reporters on the premises so they would not miss anything.

By the time Atlanta stormed New York, Emory R. Buckner, a U.S. attorney who did not see the humor in breaking the laws of

Prohibition, was resorting to extreme measures in an attempt to shut Guinan down. For several nights, two New York policemen were assigned to go to the 300 Club in evening dress and spend as much of the taxpayers' money as necessary to become known as high-rolling regulars.

On July 3, not long after the festivities had ended at the Vanderbilt, the plainclothesmen escorted two policewomen in full flapper regalia to the club, where they spent the evening with the other revelers. At 3:00 A.M., as seventeen-year-old Julia Dunn was performing her "Eve dance," one undercover agent told the doorman he was going out for some air. He returned five minutes later with six policemen who had been waiting on the corner for hours. As they arrived, another officer walked to the dance floor, interrupted the master of ceremonies, and revealed his identity. A third cop went into a small room off the club's kitchen and gathered incriminating evidence: two bottles of gin, one of rye, another of Scotch.

Shocked and far from sober, one of the patrons offered to "lick the cops, one by one," but that was the extent of any protest. As the band played "This Is My Lucky Day," some of the celebrants found themselves ejected onto the street, and possibly relieved to discover that they were free to go.

The police were most interested in Guinan, of course, but also in Julia Dunn, who was taken into an upstairs dressing room by Patrolwoman Margaret Solan and told, "Give me that costume you just wore."

"Not a chance," Dunn replied. "I've got to wear it again."

Justice was swift as Guinan and Dunn appeared before a magistrate at a West Side court the next morning for a hearing that was over almost before it began. A 300 Club official denied liquor had been sold, asserting the club charged a $6 cover and $1.50 for soft drinks, nothing more. Policewoman Solan produced Dunn's costume from a tiny package and told of unsavory comments made by the club's male patrons during her dance.

"Did you ever see a dance like this on the stage?" Magistrate Albert Vitali asked.

"Well, yes," Solan said, "but the people weren't so close."

Vitali dismissed all charges. The 300 Club resumed operations without having been closed down for even a single night.

Guinan was in her glory afterward, and the New York papers were delighted to report another of her escapes from the clutches of the law. Sell liquor? Why bother, she asked reporters, when she could clear $20,000 a month without it?

"Of course, some may bring a hip flask," she said, "but no hostess is going to search her guests, is she?"

And for Julia Dunn, why, she was "a darling child, one of my children, an innocent baby. She was doing a little Eve dance—nothing like the barelegged dances at those Broadway revues—plenty of clothes on, and in come the male and female cops."

Standing nearby, Dunn was asked why she was crying. "They told me that I should," she said. "Aren't all girls supposed to cry when they are arrested?"

Only two more questions remained to be answered. Who was at the 300 Club that night? And who wasn't? Guinan played it for all she was worth.

"There were about four hundred people in my place, having a great time," she said. "We were celebrating Bobby Jones's victory, you know. You'd be surprised if you knew who were here."

The guest list, she said, had included two U.S. senators (Walter George?), the captain of an ocean liner (the *Aquitania*?), a former president of Cuba, a few millionaires, a count, a number of stage stars, "and a lot of the nicest southerners. They were having a marvelous time."

The nicest southerners? She couldn't possibly mean . . . ?

"Aw, Bobby wasn't there," John S. Cohen, the *Journal* publisher, told the *New York Post*, quickly adding he had not been at the 300 Club himself. "How can anybody say that?"

"Who did you say? Texas Guinan?" the *Post* quoted Jones as saying. "I never heard of her, sir. And I was not at any cabaret last night."

As for those from Atlanta who *were* celebrating Bobby Jones Night at the 300 Club, the manager of the Vanderbilt said they had checked out, presumably to head for home, where neither of the city's papers breathed a word of anything having to do with a late night on the town or Texas Guinan.

.   .   .

The following day, Jones left New York for the U.S. Open at Scioto Country Club in Columbus, where more bedlam was waiting for him, on and off the golf course.

More than a hundred reporters were on hand, attracted by Jones's victory in the British Open and the possibility of one man winning the British and U.S. national championships in the same year for the first time. This press contingent was far greater than could be accommodated in the clubhouse, and the writers were sent up to the roof, where they had an excellent view of the 10th tee and the 18th green and where the noise of their typewriters and telegraph machines clacked out over the grounds.

Many of the era's finest golfers also were on hand—Gene Sarazen, Tommy Armour, Bill Mehlhorn, Leo Diegel, Chick Evans, and Hagen, as well as Willie Macfarlane, who had beaten Jones in their epic 36-hole playoff at the Open the year before. "Defeating Jones," Macfarlane said then, "is a greater honor than winning two or three Open championships."

As for the course, the U.S. Golf Association was up to its usual tricks, having allowed the rough to grow so thick that Jock Hutchison laughed about losing a ball and, while looking for it, losing his caddy as well.

"They should mow that bloomin', bloody hay," a British golfer said, although perhaps the last word about the rough came from Hagen.

"What rough?" he said.

Jones was far less jovial. Feeling tired and "overgolfed," and still startled by his reception in New York, he looked exhausted to a number of spectators, who commented on the lines around his eyes. And now he had to contend with the realization that thousands of the fans swarming the course were there not to see the tournament but him. They ran past the marshals trying to get near him, or to see where his next shot would land, and created a tense atmosphere that only added to the stress he was under.

Still, when he shot a creditable 70 the first day, he seemed to have his game under control, and he wound up tied for second place behind Mehlhorn, whose 68 broke the course record. Then Jones fell apart.

Battling the rough in the early going of the second round, Jones needed 39 strokes to make the turn. On the 10th hole, his ball ended up against a stone fence, and he took a penalty stroke. At 15, he called another penalty stroke on himself when his ball, which was lying on a slope of the green, moved about an inch when his putter cut off the breeze that had been holding it in place.

Nobody else had seen the ball move but, as he had done more than once during his career, Jones did not hesitate to add a stroke to his score. There is only one way to play the game, he would say when the subject came up. You might as well praise him for not robbing banks.

At that point, it seemed as if all of Jones's hard-won ability to control himself, to convert the pressure of the moment into his famous steely concentration, had deserted him. Feeling disgusted and sorry for himself, he three-putted 17. "I was tired and stale and sick and mad clear through," he wrote.

What Jones needed to do now was calm down, play the last hole carefully, try for a par—even a birdie wasn't out of the question on the 480-yard par-5 hole—and keep himself in the tournament. There were still two rounds left, after all. A 76 or 77 would not destroy his chances.

He hit his drive at the par-5 18 as hard as he could—far too hard—and the ball flew off to the right and wound up in some of the heaviest rough on the golf course. His chance for a birdie all but gone, there was only one correct shot to play—lay up in front of a bunker 150 yards away with a short iron and leave himself an easy pitch to the green.

But Jones would have none of it. Angry with himself, he took his 2-iron and tried to hit the ball over the bunker, only to have it scuttle no more than twenty yards and remain in the rough. In a fury now, he banged at the ball with the 2-iron again. This time it flew farther—across the fairway into the rough on the other side. Two chip shots later, he was five feet from the pin, but he missed the putt for a dreadful, round-destroying 7. He finished with a 79, as bad a round as he would ever shoot in a U.S. Open, and was six shots off the lead.

Petulance, carelessness, stupidity, Jones berated himself with these words and more, and it all added up to one thing. For all his hard-won mastery of his emotions, he was still capable of acting like the out-of-control adolescent Alexa Stirling's father would not allow in his daughter's company.

The next day, Jones woke up sick as a dog. The weather was hot and sultry, not at all what someone facing 36 holes of golf in a state of nervous exhaustion would wish for. Once again he threw up his breakfast. The strain had simply gotten to him, and he asked Bill Cairns, a friend who had moved to Atlanta from Columbus, if he knew of a doctor in the area. They drove out to Upper Arlington, where, at 7:00 A.M., they woke up the household of Dr. Earl Ryan.

"Doc, I've got Bobby Jones out here and he's sick," Cairns explained. Ryan gave Jones some medicine to settle his stomach, and Jones offered him two tickets to the tournament in return.

"Just give me a ball you use today and we'll call it square," Ryan said. The two men sat and chatted for forty-five minutes before Jones returned to the course.

The cure had an effect as Jones shot 71 in the morning round and moved into third place, three shots behind Joe Turnesa, and one in back of Mehlhorn, who had slipped to a 76. Turnesa, one of seven brothers from Westchester, New York, who all played golf at a high level, teed off two groups ahead of Jones, who fell four shots back when he bogeyed the short 9th hole that had given him trouble the entire tournament. The shots he had wasted the day before—how could he have been so foolish?—were coming back to haunt him.

But at the 12th hole, it was Turnesa who began to crack. He drove into the rough and took a bogey 6. A few minutes later, Jones hit a huge drive and a good second shot, which allowed him to chip on and, as his gallery roared its approval, sink a birdie putt. Turnesa's lead was down to two. Turnesa took another bogey at 13, out of a bunker this time, and when Jones saved par there by putting out of a trap, he trailed by a single shot.

Turnesa's irons deserted him at 16 and 17—he was over the green at the former, short of it at the latter—and suddenly Jones was ahead. But not for long. Turnesa rallied and birdied the last hole, leaving it up to Jones. Here he was again at the last hole, where he had self-destructed so completely the day before. If he could make a par this time, he could drag himself through a playoff the next day. A birdie and he would win.

Jones hit his tee shot through a difficult crosswind with everything he had. It was not, Keeler judged, the farthest he had ever hit a ball in competition, but at 300 yards it was surely the farthest under this kind of pressure. And unlike his shot of the day before, it was under control. The ball came to rest near the left edge of the fairway, 180 yards from the hole. He was facing a tricky shot: if the ball landed on the humpbacked green too hard, it might bounce off, but if it was played right, a birdie was possible.

As Jones stood over the ball, his knees were shaking and he wished only that they would stop long enough for him to hit the ball. What would it be like to fail now? he wondered. And why was he *thinking* about failure?

He swung his 4-iron, the same club he had beaten Watrous with at St. Andrews two weeks earlier, with a firm half stroke. The ball flew in a low trajectory toward the green and, as Jones had planned, hit in front of the green, then bounced and rolled until it came to rest twenty feet past the flag. Keeler could swear he saw Jones's knees buckle as he began to walk down the fairway. It was an accident, Jones thought, when he saw his excellent position. Don't tell him there is no such thing as fate. And don't think for an instant he could have made the shot again.

Jones pushed his way through the cheering crowd, judged his putt, and hit the ball. It nearly went in for an eagle. A tap-in and the Open was his. As he had promised, he gave Dr. Ryan the ball—it would become a treasured family heirloom—and, while the throng continued to celebrate, dragged himself back to his hotel. He did not know if any-one still out on the course had a chance to catch him and, to tell the truth, he was beyond caring. Jones poured himself a drink, sat down, and burst into tears. No more golf, Clara Jones said sternly. For the first time in his life, Jones began to wonder if that was not such a bad idea.

In the years to come, Jones would remember 1926 not for the unwanted changes it had made in his life—the intense public scrutiny when he was off the golf course, the impossible expectations when he was on it—or for the crying jag in Columbus at a moment when he should have been at his happiest. He had won the British and U.S. Opens in the same year, after all. He had achieved the kind of success he could only have dreamed about.

"I'll always feel kindly toward 1926," said Jones in *Down the Fairway*, the book he wrote with Keeler a year later. "It was the biggest golfing year I'll ever have."

He could hardly have been more mistaken.

10

"He Belongs to Us All"

By 1927, Jones had every reason to cut back on his competitive schedule. He had entered law school at Emory University in Atlanta; Mary had given birth to their second child, Robert Tyre Jones III; and his reputation as the best golfer in the world was secure. He knew it was time to get on with a career away from the golf course more substantial than the two years he had spent promoting Florida real estate for George Adair's firm. He had not enjoyed the glad-handing and salesmanship that job required. He likened the work to selling used cars, Jones's law partner, Eugene Branch, told Stephen R. Lowe, the author of *Sir Walter and Mr. Jones*. It was definitely not for Jones.

And at first, Jones was determined to play in fewer tournaments. His studies cut into his practice time, though not enough to keep him from winning the 1927 Southern Open in March by a huge margin over an excellent field. And while, of course, he would play in the U.S. Open and Amateur championships, he would not return to Britain to defend his Open title there. There was only one problem with this plan: Jones's fierce competitiveness would not allow it.

"Here's a telegram you may be interested in," U.S. Golf Association secretary Tommy McMahon told Keeler when he dropped in at the organization's headquarters in June. It was from Jones, asking if entries for the British Open were closed and, if not, would McMahon cable his entry to the Royal and Ancient?

"It's cabled," McMahon said. Jones would defend his title after all.

Jones had played simply dreadful golf in the U.S. Open that had just been completed at Oakmont, and had tied for 11th place, his worst finish ever in the national championship. Making his showing all the more galling was the fact that he had managed to creep within a shot of the lead on the back nine of his third round, when he took a pair of 6s and wound up with a 79, tying the personal Open high he had set the year before.

He could have shrugged it off as an aberration or offered two perfectly acceptable excuses: his legal studies and Oakmont's tough bunker-strewn course, which had been at its diabolical worst. Tommy Armour and Harry Cooper had tied after four rounds at 301, the highest Open score in eight years, before Armour won in a playoff. But the stakes were higher now, and Jones felt the losses more keenly. He went home to Atlanta, sat in his office, and brooded until one day he found himself idly looking at a calendar of upcoming tournaments. The British Open, he realized, was still two weeks away. Impulsively, he telegraphed McMahon.

Keeler, who had been married in New York two days earlier, counted himself lucky that he had arranged to begin his honeymoon aboard the *Aquitania* as it sailed to Europe. They would be taking a little side trip, he informed his bride, Eleanor—to St. Andrews. A few days later, Jones, his father, and Stewart Maiden sailed to Glasgow on the *Transylvania*.

The news that Jones was returning to defend his title reached Britain before he did and created a sensation. Thousands of fervent golf fans, holiday trekkers, and the just plain curious descended on St. Andrews, where they were greeted by the buzz of anticipation and warm weather that was as delightful as it was uncharacteristic of Scotland's windswept east coast. So many reporters came to cover the tournament that some had to write their articles in a hotel near the course. Among those not admitted to the cramped press tent was George Bernard Shaw. More than the usual number of journalists from America made the trip as well, and they were startled by the pro-Jones sentiment among the crowd. No British golfer would ever be received so enthusiastically in America, they noted, and one told a

British colleague that the fans' attachment to Jones was quite the finest thing he had ever seen.

A few of the area's legal bookmakers created some excitement during the practice rounds when they cheekily stationed themselves beside the starter's box and shouted out odds: "Ten to one Jones! Thirty to one Barnes!" They were quickly shooed away. The Royal and Ancient, whose headquarters are in the clubhouse beyond the 18th green, did what it could to control the crowds, but it was licked from the start.

At Royal Lytham and St. Anne's the year before, admission had been charged for the first time at an Open, not to make money but as a means of "limiting the number of undesirable spectators." But St. Andrews was a public course subject to acts of Parliament that banned selling tickets. The best the club could do was to paint white lines around the greens, indicating that the crowds should stay off. That worked reasonably well, but there was no solving the problem of how to handle the thousands of spectators who had come to see one man only.

The fans "constantly scurrying across the line of play" and "conducting themselves in total disregard to the players coming up or preceding the star attraction" made the competition unfair, the British magazine *Golf Monthly* said.

Henry Cotton, for instance, was still in contention at the start of the third round, "but he never had a fair field." And when Archie Compston drove out of bounds as a spectator walked directly behind him, he was so upset he put a second tee shot in the same place. The distraction, Compston said, was like a blow to the head with a hammer. At one point during the tournament, The *St. Andrews Citizen* noted the poignant scene of Harry Vardon, one of the great names in the history of golf and a six-time winner of the Open, standing unnoticed over his ball trying to protect it from the crush of people rushing past him in their quest to keep up with Jones.

In his first practice round, Jones played quite poorly, fluffing a number of shots and missing putts. But Bernard Darwin, who seemed determined to witness every shot the defending champion made, was not fooled. "A man who can make so very many mistakes and yet have a 76," he wrote in the *Times*, "is a very terrible person."

And indeed Jones had made his peace with St. Andrews since his

1921 debacle and was eager to redeem himself. In large part, his conversion was due to Tommy Armour, with whom he spent so much time playing in Sarasota, Florida, while promoting real estate the year before.

Armour, who was one of golf's most flamboyant personalities, said he first learned of a boy wonder named Bobby Jones while he was in the trenches in France. Like his brother Sandy and Bobby Cruickshank, he had fought in World War I, leaving the University of Edinburgh to become a machine gunner in the newly formed British Tank Corps. Legend had it Armour once captured a German tank single-handedly and, when its officer refused to surrender, strangled him with his bare hands. Armour lost the sight in one eye at Ypres and, in another battle, an explosion shattered his left arm and caused head injuries, both of which required the insertion of metal plates.

After the war Armour came to the United States, where he won fourteen PGA tournaments, including the PGA championship and the U.S. and British Opens. A master bridge player and storyteller, Armour became one of golf's most renowned teachers—his book *How to Play Your Best Golf All the Time* became a best seller—and larger-than-life characters. "Nothing was small about Tommy Armour's reputation," said golf writer Ross Goodner. "At one time or another, he was known as the greatest iron player, the greatest raconteur, the greatest drinker and the most expensive teacher in golf."

As they played together in Sarasota, Armour was entranced by Jones's swing, calling it "as near perfection as you could get it; he was like a ballet dancer," as well as his timing, balance, and concentration. For his part, Jones admired Armour's iron play and competitiveness, and though their daily rounds during the winter of 1925 and 1926 were nothing more than two men out playing golf, they were fiercely fought.

"Our friendly matches almost invariably were gentle, pleasant little affairs," Armour wrote. "Just like the Dempsey-Firpo affair. By the fourth hole we were not talking to each other."

"They played for keeps," said Armour's wife, Estelle. "The first time I followed them, I expected them to socialize with me a little bit. I didn't expect them to talk to me while they were playing, but I did think they'd at least speak to me on the first tee. But, no. They started up the middle of the first fairway together and then all conversation ceased between them."

On the rare occasions when they did talk during their rounds, Armour would needle Jones, "just to see for myself if anything ever could puncture the battleplate of Bob's concentration." Jones would get angry, snap back, and then they would grow silent again. But both men understood the real value of these matches—the honing of their games to a razor sharpness. "It's not easy to find someone who can give you that competition every day," Jones said.

In the years to come, it would often be noted how remarkable it was that Jones could play in relatively few tournaments, put his clubs away all winter, and yet still be the greatest golfer on earth. The first part of this equation is true enough—Jones played in about sixty regularly scheduled tournaments during his career, as many as a busy professional might play in three years today—but the second is not.

The rounds of golf Jones played when the game was out of season were seldom as competitive as his matches with Armour, but he generally found plenty of time to practice. And it may not be a coincidence that his winter in Sarasota, playing head to head against a golfer who was close to being his equal, preceded the most productive five years of his career. The matches did not hurt Armour, either; he won a dozen tournaments himself during that period.

It was during these matches that Armour got Jones to understand that he was wrong about St. Andrews. So convinced was Armour that "Divine Providence had had a part in the construction of the course, that I went there determined to like it," Jones wrote. "I really did not have to try very hard. Before I had played two rounds I loved it and I love it still."

What Jones finally learned to appreciate was that it was the infinite variety of the Old Course that made it so fascinating. At first glance it did not appear to be particularly difficult to play—there are no trees, no real hills, no water but for the Swilken Burn, a narrow stream at the bottom of a six-foot-wide ditch that bisects the first and 18th fairways. "The maddening part of the whole thing," Jones wrote, "was that, while I was certain the course was easy, I simply could not make a good score."

What Jones had to learn was that the ultimate challenge of St. Andrews lay in what *cannot* be seen: the blind bunkers, the small but thick gorse bushes, the wind that might require a different shot in a different direction with a different club from the one a golfer had used from the same position the day before. Add St. Andrews' huge two-hole greens into the mix—only four holes on the course do not share a green—and the golfer finds himself confronted with a layout that requires the maximum amount of planning, course knowledge, and shot control all at the same time.

In his first round of the 1927 Open, Jones took St. Andrews apart. There had never been, everyone agreed, anything quite like it in championship competition. Driving brilliantly, recovering with ease every time he found himself in trouble, and putting like a dream, Jones shot a 68, tying the course record.

Jones faced long putt after long putt during the round, one of them for a 120-foot eagle on the 5th green, which shares its vast acreage with the 13th. "This is the longest putt I ever saw," Jones thought as he walked toward his ball. Then, with the huge gallery laughing and cheering at the same time, he sank it.

On and on it went through the round. Three thirty-footers, one twenty-footer, only a single miss on a putt of fewer than twelve feet. The absurd thing about Jones's round, Darwin noted, was that his short game was far below his usual standards, but his putting saved him every time.

"The cumulative luck of a dozen years was upon him about the greens," Keeler wrote, "and the putts that had denied him in a score of championships went down that day."

By the time Jones got to 18, the crowd in the vast area between the green and the clubhouse took up every available bit of room. As Jones pitched up short of the hole and faced a ten-foot putt for a 67, Andra Kirkaldy, a grand old man of Scottish golf who had lost a play-off for the Open title in 1879, stood in his customary position holding the flag. For the first time all day, Jones missed a putt of medium length.

"Man, ye're no' a gowfer, ye're juist a machine," Kirkaldy told Jones when he tapped in and then made his way through the cheering crowd, which included throngs of schoolgirls begging for his autograph.

Jones had benefited from the excellent weather, which had cleared up after some rain earlier in the day that had softened the greens and allowed his shots to stick where they landed rather than bounce away.

A stiff wind and harder terrain would have made the round more interesting, Darwin wrote, adding that "the battlefield was hardly worthy of the victorious hero." Still, it had been a stunning round, and rumors began to circulate that that Royal and Ancient would meet after the tournament to discuss ways to toughen the course for future championship competition.

During the round, careful observers noted how drawn Jones's face looked, how the shadows beneath his eyes seemed so dark, and more than one of Keeler's acquaintances asked if he were physically well. It was just the concentration, Keeler believed, and Jones confirmed it.

"It was the hardest decent score I ever shot," he said as he sat in a corner of his room in the Grand Hotel, near the 18th hole, with his father, Stewart Maiden, and Jack MacIntyre. "I have played harder rounds, scoring worse, but I have never scored so well in so hard a round."

The rest of the tournament was a victory lap for Jones, who shot 72-73-72 for a final score of 285, the lowest ever shot in any British or U.S. Open. This left him six shots clear of the field, a margin Darwin called "wholly indecent and profane."

But Jones would not have been Jones if he did not create a few anxious moments, and his easiest victory in any major tournament was no exception. Leading by four shots at the start of the final round, he was three over par after just five holes as the huge gallery grew silent, and Keeler became sick with fear that the strain might lead to disaster.

But after another bogey at the 8th hole, Jones entered the loop that leads out to the Eden Estuary and doubles back and, in the next twenty minutes, settled the tournament. He made four straight threes from the 9th to the 12th holes, which allowed him to play 6 through 12 in just twenty-four shots. Though there were none of the long-putt heroics of his opening round, it was a championship-clinching stretch of golf that Darwin called "consistently better than perfect."

As Jones approached the 18th tee, the crowd had grown all but completely out of control. Children who had been let out of school early to witness the historic event added one final measure of excitement, and one of them, thirteen-year-old Gordon Christie, would speak more than seven decades later of squeezing through the crowd and being boosted over a fence by a friendly gentleman just in time to

see Jones tee off. Later Christie would become St. Andrews' town historian, collecting artifacts and devoting himself to learning all there
was to know about the Old Town's place in the history of golf.

From the Swilken Burn to the terrace behind the green, the spectators jostled for position, spilling over onto the course, and delaying
play until some sort of order could be restored. When Jones's tee shot
landed just beyond the road that cuts through the course, the gallery
was so thick he could not see the green. Sweating stewards labori-
ously moved people back as Jones sat down in a small clearing the
crowd had left him near his ball and waited for a path to be opened.

At last he was able to swing, and he sent his ball into a little hollow in front of the green known as the Valley of Sin. The crowd
surged forward in a mass wave toward the green, obliterating any
sight of Jones from the gallery area in front of the clubhouse. After
much pushing and shouting, a lane was cleared, and Jones putted up
out of the hollow to come within a few inches of ending the tournament with a birdie. He knocked the ball in, shook Andra Kirkaldy's
hand, and all hell broke loose.

"I thought that Bobby was going to be killed in the very hour of
victory," Darwin wrote. "Even Captain Lindbergh in Paris cannot
have been in more imminent fear of asphyxiation than was the champion for one or two anxious moments. . . . He popped his ball in, and
in the next instant there was to be seen no green and no Bobby—
nothing but a black and seething mass from which there ultimately
emerged the victor bourne on enthusiastic shoulders and holding his
famous putter, Calamity Jane, over his head in a frantic effort to preserve it."

Finally, Jones was rescued by six burly Scottish policemen, who
helped him navigate the short distance to his hotel, where his father
was waiting. Four years earlier, the Colonel had refused to attend his
son's tournaments for fear he was a jinx. Now he had traveled across
the ocean to see him defend his British Open championship.

"I'm mighty glad that's over," Jones told his father as they
embraced.

Keeler took off his glasses to wipe them, only to discover that the
mist was not on the lenses.

Jones was called back to the course for the trophy presentation
where Colonel Bethune, a past captain of the club, said that while the

champion was obviously no respecter of golf courses—it was unseemly for anyone to shoot a 68 at St. Andrews—his golf game and sporting spirit had shown him to be a model player.

"If the cup is to go overseas," Bethune said, "I am glad that it should go to one who is a most distinguished member of the Royal and Ancient Club."

Jones, who had been made a member of the R&A after winning the year before, responded with a graceful speech.

"I have achieved the ambition of my life," he said. "Whatever I have done in the past, or whatever I do in the future does not matter two straws. This wonderful experience will live in my memory until my dying day. If I never win anything again, I am satisfied."

And then Jones said one thing more, which turned the affection the Scottish crowds already had for him into something approaching reverence.

"You have done so many things for me," he told the crowd, "that I am embarrassed to ask one more, but I will. I want this wonderful old club to accept custody of the cup for the coming year."

Once more, the cheers were deafening as the thousands of people out on the lawn stretching down from the clubhouse realized that Jones meant to leave the championship trophy behind. Hats flew, fathers lifted children to their shoulders, and, said one reporter, "stolid old Scots who have not danced a step for decades threw themselves into the Highland Fling with the utmost abandon."

"Such things touch deep the chords of sentiment," *Golf Monthly* wrote of Jones's gesture. "Such things do convince that golf is a great brotherhood and that, after all, Robert Tyre Jones does not belong to America alone, but that he belongs to us all."

For his part, Darwin suggested that for all they may have wished to see one of their countrymen at last win another Open, the fans believed that "Bobby was so superior that it would have been a shame and an outrage if anyone else had dared to win. For a visitor to be able to force that conviction upon the whole of any intensely patriotic Scottish crowd is an astonishing thing, altogether outside the power of any other golfer in the world."

11

"You Can Never Know How I Envied You"

Several weeks after returning home from Britain, Jones traveled to the Minikahda Club in Minneapolis where, with brutal efficiency, he won his third U.S. Amateur championship and unwittingly set in motion the one truly bitter feud of his life.

After shooting a 75 in the first qualifying round and fearing he might miss the tournament altogether, Jones won several competitive matches before breezing to the title by routing three of the top American amateurs of the day: Harrison Johnston, who would win the Amateur two years later, 10 and 9; Francis Ouimet, the hero of Brookline, 11 and 10; and, in the final, Chick Evans, 8 and 7.

Along with Jones and Ouimet, Evans is one of the three great names in the history of American amateur golf. His victory in the 1916 U.S. Amateur at Merion, the tournament in which Little Bob Jones made his debut, came shortly after he won the U.S. Open at Minikahda with 286 shots, a record that would stand for twenty years, while using seven hickory-shafted clubs. It was the first time a player had won both national championships in the same year, and it made him the newest hero of American golf.

Evans was inundated with offers to turn professional after his double triumph: Spalding golf clubs, the Orpheum Theater vaudeville circuit, books, exhibitions, all of the endorsement opportunities that inevitably flowed to a player of his stature. He refused them all.

"My mother and I talked it over," Evans said, "and we decided that I would remain an amateur—forever."

This decision helped create the sort of adulation among the press and public that would be bestowed on Jones in the following decade. "He is an idol for those who love the game for what there is in it," said the *New York Times*, "not for what they can get out of it."

Evans's devotion to amateur golf extended even beyond that of Jones, who renounced his amateur standing when he retired, and Ouimet, who was suspended from the amateur ranks for two years for his part ownership of a sporting-goods store. Evans competed in an astonishing fifty U.S. Amateur championships in a row—he won his second title in 1920—and for many years presided over the Western Open, a popular stop on the PGA tour and in which he made his final appearance at age seventy-seven.

Evans also won praise for refusing to play in the Western Amateur, a tournament he had already won four times (he would later win four more), when the Western Golf Association ignored a U.S. Golf Association decision to suspend competition during World War I. He would only play in Red Cross benefits, Evans said, and he helped raise more than $300,000 in fund-raising exhibitions, including some in which Jones, Perry Adair, and Alexa Stirling appeared. Among the golfers who did play in the much-criticized Western Amateur in 1917 were Ouimet, who was still serving his suspension and won the tournament, and fifteen-year-old Bobby Jones.

At a time when golfers tended to be grimly serious—Walter Hagen being a notable exception—Evans was a gallery favorite. The combination of his smooth, simple swing, engaging personality, and ability to remember names and faces added up to project the image of a man enjoying what he was doing. Sometimes Evans actually *talked* to the people following him during tournaments. Some of his contemporaries, says golf historian Herbert Warren Wind, maintained he would even go so far as to lose a hole or two when he was winning a match to extend his time in front of the crowds. Nor did Evans's playing partners always appreciate the fact that he liked to joke with them when they were supposed to be trying to beat each other.

In 1923, Evans accepted an offer of $5,000 plus royalties to make instructional recordings, but only after his mother, a librarian, came up with an idea after his own heart: he would use the proceeds to create college scholarships for caddies.

Growing up in Chicago, Evans had been the most popular caddy at the Edgewater Golf Club, where he made 35 cents a round, plus tip, and where he endeared himself to members with his special method of recovering lost balls: he stretched out full length in the rough and rolled around until he turned over on top of them. But to protect his amateur status, Evans gave up caddying the day before his sixteenth birthday—U.S. Golf Association rules were uncompromising on the point—and he later dropped out of Northwestern University after a year for lack of money.

He experienced no small satisfaction, therefore, when the first two caddies to receive Evans Scholarships entered Northwestern in 1930. He expressly noted that minority youngsters were to be included, and his mother's suggestion has since grown to become the largest privately funded college scholarship program in the United States, one that has made tuition payments of some $80 million to some eight thousand former caddies. When he died at age eighty-nine in 1979, Evans was remembered as one of golf's great patriarchs and benefactors.

But despite his good works and sunny disposition, there was a dark side to Chick Evans, and in the years ahead it would lead him to engage in an angry dispute with Jones that would embarrass Evans in public, tear him apart in private, and have him begging Jones for forgiveness.

For all his successes on the golf course, Evans was most consumed by the championships he did not win. His dream of becoming the first amateur to win the U.S. Open was snatched away by Ouimet in 1913, and his early losses in the U.S. Amateur were almost as comical as they were frequent. Five times between 1909 and 1913 he made it to the semifinals and five times he lost, on several occasions blowing leads late in the round when his putting, always the weakest part of his game, failed him.

"Heaven knows what his scores would have been had he been a good putter like many of the others," said Ducky Corkran, one of Evans's victims in the 1916 U.S. Amateur.

"If Evans could putt like J. Walter Travis," said four-time Amateur champion Jerry Travers, "it would be foolish to stage an amateur tourney in this country."

Evans seemed most rankled by his belief that he was a better golfer than those who were beating him. His problems with his peers stemmed from the fact that he did not mind letting them know it.

Evans particularly resented Ouimet's success, and his status as the first golfer whose fame extended beyond the game and into the American consciousness. Evans often compared their overall records in national events, particularly in the qualifying rounds of the Amateur where he had the edge, and occasionally he would note the views of those who considered him the country's best amateur player. The fact that Harry Vardon was among them gave him particular satisfaction.

Even at the time of Evans's greatest triumph, his two 1916 championships, some of this bitterness was evident. A few eastern observers noted that his victory in the U.S. Amateur that year was clouded by the absence of Ouimet and Travers, who had won the tournament the year before. Evans replied that he would have beaten them both.

"There is a certain provincialism about the East," he said. "In the West it is generally understood that when a leading player fails to enter an event, he knows he has little chance to win it."

Jones was nine years old the first time Evans saw him. Evans had come to play at East Lake in 1911 and was standing in front of Alexa Stirling's house hitting some balls when a solemn and silent Jones, carrying a club almost as tall as he was, watched him for a few minutes and then wandered away.

The first hint of a rivalry may have revealed itself even at that early date when Evans, self-conscious about his slender build and lack of strength, was discovered by Jones's father squeezing a pair of spring-loaded hand grippers in an attempt to build up his wrists. The sight of a golfer engaging in such exercises struck the Colonel as comical and, to Evans's embarrassment, he teased him about it in front of his Atlanta cronies.

Five years after their first meeting, as Jones was creating a sensation at Merion, Evans was fascinated along with everybody else. The small nine-year-old had grown into a youngster of great promise. But it was not just his rapidly developing skills and physical presence that Evans admired. The fact that he was carefully watched as he played by George Adair and a few other adults who had made the journey from Georgia was of great importance, he thought.

Throughout Jones's career, Evans would shrewdly note, a few close friends, Keeler chief among them, always seemed to accompany him "to protect him from the troubles of the links and the larger troubles away from the links . . . I wonder if Bobby realizes what they mean to him."

As for Little Bob's highly publicized temper tantrums, which included his club-throwing contest with Eben Byers at Merion, Evans had a tolerant view. "I had suffered from a few such exhibitions, and unlike most grown-ups I had not forgotten them," he said. "I remember a favorite club that went to the bottom of Long Island Sound, and another favorite club that went out a taxicab window in Paris, thereby endangering someone. Here, I thought, was a golfer of tender years whose heart was really broken by a poor shot. After all it was an artist's feeling."

Jones appreciated these remarks, and he admired Evans's skill and competitiveness. What he remembered most about the 1919 U.S. Amateur at Oakmont, he later wrote, was not losing to Davey Herron in the final, but an epic second-round match between Evans and Ouimet. Both players were ill—Evans with rheumatism, Ouimet with a severe cold—yet they played under par on the difficult course before collapsing on the final nine and struggling to finish in a contest of survival. "Human machinery couldn't stand it," Jones wrote.

Evans tied Ouimet at the 35th hole, only to lose when he missed a ten-foot putt and Ouimet made a nine-footer. He was "pop-eyed with interest and excitement," Jones wrote. "It was a battle of giants, to me."

Keeler had a soft spot for Evans, too, ever since he first saw him play as part of a World War I Red Cross exhibition in Kansas City. He had never watched a championship golfer practice, Keeler wrote, and as Evans fired shot after shot downrange to a caddy who caught his balls on the first bounce, he was mesmerized.

"How did he do it?" he wondered, and as he watched, he began to understand. Evans's talent was due in large part to the fact that he hit the ball the same way every time. He had never known what to look for in a golfer before, Keeler thought, but he was learning.

In 1920, Jones and Evans met for the first time in a tournament, in the semifinal of the Western Amateur in Memphis. Playing well in the early rounds and buoyed by the presence of a large Atlanta contingent, Jones, though only eighteen, felt he had a chance to beat one of golf's greatest players. And when he made up a three-hole deficit on the final nine of the two-round match, Jones believed he would win.

Evans gave Jones added confidence by hitting his second shot at the 17th hole into the rough while Jones made it onto the green. But Evans played a good recovery shot and then overcame both his self-doubts and his reputation by sinking a ten-foot putt. Jones three-putted and lost the hole and the match. Despite the defeat, Jones was exuberant afterward from the sheer excitement of the contest.

"We had one of the greatest matches I ever took part in," he wrote, "and I want to say that the way he beat me proved, to my mind, that Chick is one of the gamest and best competitive golfers the world ever saw."

Keeler was equally complimentary of Evans's fighting spirit, but back home in Atlanta, Jones's father had another view of the man he had once derided for using artificial means to build up his wrists.

"He'll never beat him again," the Colonel said.

Evans was thirty-seven years old and his best days on the golf course were well behind him when he returned to Minikahda, the scene of his triumph in the U.S. Open eleven years earlier, for the 1927 U.S. Amateur. Though he made it to the final, he stood no chance against Jones and won only four holes.

Jones led by five holes after the morning round and added a triumphant note with a second shot of more than two hundred yards to the elevated 9th green that rolled within two feet of the hole. It was the only eagle that had ever been made there. Jones closed out the match at the 11th when Evans, facing a four-foot putt for a half that would only prolong the inevitable, accidentally touched his ball with his club. He was penalized a stroke and conceded the match.

"Smiling, he picked it up and held out his hand to Bobby," Keeler wrote. "He had called the stroke on himself, and for a moment the gallery did not realize what had happened. Then they sent up a resounding cheer for Bobby's superb golf, and a tribute to the man who had fought so bravely when there was no chance to win."

"It was worth a good drubbing to see such a marvelous exhibition of golf," Evans said.

For many years, that is how the matter stood. Jones's greatest victories lay directly ahead, while Evans, though still competitive in regional tournaments, and later in senior events, faded into the background. His time had come and gone, and so had any claim he might have had to being the greatest amateur golfer the United States had ever produced.

A small hint that things had not been as they appeared on the 11th green at Minikahda came in an article Evans wrote for *American Golfer* before the 1930 U.S. Amateur, Jones's last Grand Slam tournament. At first he praised Jones effusively, told several charming stories about their early encounters, and closed with a touching scene in which he described members of the U.S. Walker Cup team sitting in a room discussing the vagaries of the stock market.

"I close my eyes and think of the Stock Exchange Way, and the wrecks that lie along it," wrote Evans, who was a stockbroker for a time, "when I am startled by a remark from Bobby Jones. 'What is the use of all that money?' he said. 'Just enough to be even and kind to every one.'"

But then, as he discussed what had happened at Minikahda, there were intimations of conflict, although carefully couched in a way to give credit to Jones's competitiveness and will to win.

"I, broken with worry and trouble, he, young, confident and unworried, protected by his friends. He said only two or three words all day long. He did not dislike me; he was merely out to win. Now and then I would see him in the center of [the large gallery], but his very expression said, 'Do not speak to me! I have a job to do.'"

And then Evans gave his version of how the match had ended:

"I have just lost three holes in succession. I am seven down and eight to play. Soon I have a very tiny putt to make it seven and seven. I fuss with it, wondering why he does not give it to me. He cannot lose, and it seems such a waste of time not to say, 'Take it!'"

Ouimet would have let him have it, says Evans, in whose memory the length of the putt has been reduced from four feet to "very tiny." So would Jess Sweetser and Harrison Johnston, and perhaps even Walter Travis. But not a word from Jones.

"Do not misunderstand me, I was not expecting a gift—just a little concession to expedite the game," Evans wrote. "In my surprise I fuss a little with the shot and accidentally my club touched it. Did it turn over? Bobby nodded, saying nothing. I congratulate him. What is the difference? Eight or seven, or one up? The better golfer won."

Though he had all but accused Jones of being responsible for his error, Evans insisted he was not telling this story out of anger or resentment. Rather, it was to show Jones's powers of concentration. "No outside interest shall interfere? A white ball on a tee, and a white ball in a cup; nothing anywhere between. It is not a social matter, but a hard, stern business. The game over, and there is a different Bobby, courteous and friendly."

The fact that the two men were feeling anything but friendly toward each other as they shook hands on the 11th green at Minikahda remained hidden for more than three decades. It might never have come to light had Evans not given an astonishing interview to Charles Chamberlain of the Associated Press in Chicago on July 18, 1963.

Evans's most explosive charge was that Jones had turned professional before completing the Grand Slam in 1930. "I know for a fact that Bobby pocketed a $25,000 check from Jack Warner after he won the National Open at Interlachen," he said. "It was for his appearance in a golf movie." Thus Jones had become "an out-and-out professional when he won the National Amateur."

But Evans was just getting started, and Chamberlain, in the best wire-service tradition, strung the quotes together, paragraph after paragraph, in his story. The result was both a damning indictment of Jones and a revealing look at the depth of Evans's bitterness toward him.

"In 1916–18, I took Jones around with me for more than 10,000 miles playing Red Cross benefits," Evans said. "I think he will admit he learned a lot of golf from me. But when he became a champion,

I guess he got too big for me. He turned down my requests to make appearances.

"Jones developed his game with his clubs rather than his skill. When I beat him 1-up for the Western Amateur in Memphis, he had 22 clubs in his bag. I had seven. . . . The fewer clubs you have the more skilled you are."

And while in the past Evans had always gone out of his way to praise Jones's skill on the golf course, now he tore it down.

"Perhaps the best part of his game was the ability to sink long putts," Evans said. "He had to, because from 50 yards out he was pitiful. Jones the greatest golfer? Not by a long shot, in my book. I know it's tough to argue against the record. But I don't think he could hold a candle to Walter Hagen, when Hagen really wanted to play. There was the greatest."

As for what had happened at Minikahda in 1927, Evans could barely contain himself.

"It wasn't the beating so much as the way it was done," he said. "On the first tee, Jones told me I had teed my ball in front of the markers. Later he called me for putting my finger into the grass—a habit I had formed to test its depth and thickness before hitting my ball on the fairway."

As he waited in vain for Jones to concede the putt at the 11th hole, Evans said, "I looked at him and he just stood there, about a yard from me, and stared at me. I went up to my ball, and when I put my putter head down, it touched the ball.

"I looked at Jones. 'The ball didn't move,' I said. 'It sure did,' he replied. I just shook his hand and said, 'Congratulations for your great victory,' and walked away."

In one conversation with a reporter, Evans had accused Jones of being a cheat, an overrated golfer, and a poor sport. In short, a fraud. Had these charges been made by anyone else, they would have been shocking. Coming from one of the most revered players in golf, someone who had known Jones for more than fifty years, they were all but impossible to comprehend.

In Atlanta, where he was contacted by Ed Miles, a friend since high school who worked for the *Atlanta Journal*, so quickly that his reaction ran alongside the story containing Evans's indictment in some papers, Jones spoke in measured tones. "It's difficult for me to believe that Evans said these things," he said. "He knows things that I don't know. I find it mildly amusing. I didn't even meet Warner until the following year. It's too bad he takes this position. If he really meant to say these things then I'm truly sorry he said them."

Jones did not have this quite right. He had signed his Warner Bros. contract in November 1930, not the following year, and was first approached about the film series during the U.S. Amateur, when he "declined even to discuss the subject." But he was correct on the essential point: Evans's charge that he had taken money to make movies while still competing as an amateur was false.

The Associated Press also contacted Jack Warner in Hollywood. While he could not remember the details of his studio's contract with Jones, Warner said, "he is a very honorable man and what he would say I would back to the limit."

As for refusing to make appearances with Evans, Jones said, "I played a lot of golf with Chick, both in exhibition matches and in amateur championships, and I learned a lot of golf from him, but I don't remember turning down any matches."

The more Jones considered Evans's remarks over the next few days, the more he was inclined to laugh at them. "Based on the part of it you read to me last evening over the telephone," he wrote Miles, "I said that I thought it was mildly amusing. I now consider it to be hilarious. I have been sitting here for some time enjoying the picture of myself as described by Chick, glaring at him from a yard away as he prepared to hole a putt of two inches which would still leave him seven holes down with seven to play. Somehow, the picture does not come through, but the idea is funny as hell."

In the coming days and weeks, as Jones's friends began to write and call with messages of outrage and support, he decided that Evans's charges were not so amusing after all. And while he was content in public to deny them with his usual casual grace, privately he responded with the cold, hard fury of a very angry man.

"I am only sorry that the correspondence had to be inspired by one of our friends who is suffering either from retarded mental development or premature senility," Jones wrote Henry C. Mackall, a governor of the Minikahda Club who had been on the 11th green in 1927 and sent Jones a copy of a letter he had written to Evans chastising him and backing Jones's version of events there.

"I think you may have seen the enclosed which represents some fairly typical tripe from the estimable Mr. Evans," Jones wrote Joe Dey, the executive director of the U.S. Golf Association, which had presented Evans with its annual Bob Jones Award for distinguished sportsmanship in golf three years earlier. "I am sure you have already recognized it as such."

And now it was Jones's turn to break through the veil of false cordiality that had existed at Minikahda. He was explaining it to him, Jones told Dey, because his knowledge of competitive golf in the United States would not be complete if he did not know more about what had really taken place.

After he took an early lead in the morning round, Jones said, Evans had begun clowning around behind his back, at one point tipping his hat when he failed to concede a three-foot putt on a slick sidehill green. During the lunch break, he said, U.S.G.A. president William Fownes, who was the referee for the match, told him, "Bob, if you want me to, I will call this bird on some of the things he had been doing out there." Jones asked him not to interfere.

On the 11th hole, Jones said, Evans was facing a putt of 10 or 12 feet and "plainly shoved it at least half an inch with his putter blade."

"I guess it moved, didn't it?" Evans said.

"Yes, Chick, I guess it did," Jones replied.

He could not say what had caused Evans's ball to move, Jones said. Perhaps it was just nerves. On the other hand, he rather suspected Evans "preferred being the apparent victim of a misfortune to playing the long 12th hole up the hill away from the clubhouse."

Three months later, in an exchange of letters with golf writer Lester Rice, Jones added another complaint about Evans's conduct at Minikahda.

"Chick was always a malicious fellow who made a great play to the gallery with that big, toothy grin of his," he wrote. "As we were being photographed before the start of the match, he draped his arm around my shoulder, flashed that big grin, and rattled on in a loud voice about how much fun it was going to be to have a game with me, that neither of us cared who won. We would just go out and have a real good time, and all that sort of bosh. Naturally, I preferred a guy who frankly hated my guts."

Though the length of Evans's final putt had changed once

again—four feet by contemporary accounts, "very tiny" in Evans's memory, ten or twelve feet according to Jones—there was no question about whose account would be accepted.

"I have long been aware of Chick's weakness for maliciousness—toward many people—but he has now exceeded himself," Dey wrote Jones. "The most charitable reaction I can muster is that maybe he *isn't* himself. But even that does not mitigate the disgust felt by everyone who has mentioned the matter to me."

Everyone else in the golfing community who expressed an opinion on the matter felt the same way, and Evans was helpless against this onslaught. It was all such a surprise to him, he wrote to Mackall. He was dazed, it was all propaganda, he had no idea what it was all about. While never actually denying what he had been quoted as saying, he said he had spent only a few minutes talking to Chamberlain and had no idea he was being quoted. The "so-called interview," he told a friend, was almost entirely a fabrication.

Mackall and others relayed Evans's distress to Jones, who responded coldly.

"I find it difficult to understand why Chick should feel imposed upon," he told Mackall, "since he has never taken the trouble to deny the lies he circulated about me."

And when representatives of the Western Golf Association, which sponsored the Evans Scholarships, expressed their regret in several letters and in a meeting with Jones, Clifford Roberts, the chairman of the Masters, kept the pot boiling.

"It would seem you get everything except a *public* apology," Roberts wrote in a memo to Jones.

In fact, Jones was not at all happy with the Western Golf Association's private apology, particularly a line in a letter from its president, W. F. Souder, saying should it happen again Jones would now know it did not represent the opinion of the organization.

"You say, 'Should it happen again . . .'" Jones responded. "I do not think that I can afford to accept the sort of tolerant approach you suggested should this slander be repeated."

By now, Jones was conducting a behind-the-scenes campaign against Evans. Jones wrote to Augusta National member William D. Kerr, who was an acquaintance of Souder, to say he "was showing very little concern about the possible repeat of Mr. Evans' tantrum.

... You might feel like suggesting to him that he provide that word of caution for Chick concerning any future outbursts."

The Western Golf Association had cautioned Evans in no uncertain terms, Kerr assured Jones, adding that "their principal concern for the future comes from the fact that Evans has reached the stage in his mental processes where they are not completely dependable."

Evans never did issue a public apology, or, as far as can be determined, did he attempt to speak with Jones in the immediate aftermath of the uproar he had caused. Perhaps he was too embarrassed or perhaps the warnings he was getting from Western Golf Association officials indicated how Jones would respond. The one public peace offering he did extend was a contribution to a page of tributes from prominent golfers in the *Augusta Chronicle* prior to the 1966 Masters in celebration of the fiftieth anniversary of Jones's debut at Merion.

"I pick Bob Jones as the greatest champion of them all," Evans wrote, and he told a self-deprecating story of that long-ago tournament. A man asked his female companion if she were going out on the course to watch Bob Gardner, the defending U.S. Amateur champion, or Evans, who had recently won the U.S. Open. "No, I don't want to see them," the lady replied. "I want to see the Georgia kid putt those long putts."

"Golf has gained great ground because of Bob Jones," Evans wrote. "New names are springing up and becoming household words, but none greater than he. He is entitled to be the greatest champion of them all."

Though Jones would surely have read Evans's praise, any doubts that it might prompt a measure of forgiveness were answered a year later when Charles Price submitted a list of people he planned to interview for a television documentary on Jones's life.

"All are acceptable except Chick Evans," Jones wrote. "I do not want Chick to be connected with the program in any way."

In 1968, five years after his outburst, Evans finally wrote to Jones directly, plaintively pleading for absolution.

"I should like you to know that if I ever offended or hurt you in any way, I truly regret it," Evans, who was nearing his seventy-eighth birthday, wrote. "I feel guilty and ashamed of having ever made any remarks concerning you that were considered derogatory. Truly, I hope that at this late time in our lives you will overlook and forgive and remember only the years long gone when we could and did play so happily together."

And then, in a cry from his heart, Evans all but crawled before Jones in supplication.

"I have not been at the Masters for a number of years," he wrote, "but come next May, if you invite me and if I am able physically and financially, I should like to be one of the gallery at Augusta National. Certainly, I have missed not seeing you. I do see a few of our friends occasionally, but many have left us for the land of the shadows. I know it is asking a good deal to expect you to read this letter, but I hope it will rest you and give me the kindness of so remembering you."

By this time, Jones was wasting away with the spinal condition that had turned his life into one of indescribable pain. All but completely paralyzed, he had deteriorated to such an extent that the 1968 Masters, which had taken place the month before Evans wrote to him, marked his last trip to Augusta National.

Yet not even Evans's evocation of lost friends and their own approaching mortality could soften his heart. The Chick Evans whose brave struggle to the finish with Francis Ouimet in the 1919 U.S. Amateur had left him limp with excitement was dead to Jones. Gone, too, was the man he had once considered to be among the gamest and best golfers the world had ever known. All that remained was the Chick Evans whose betrayal could never be forgiven.

"Of course, I shall accept your expression at face value," Jones wrote. "I am no more interested than you are in keeping alive any embers of resentment that may have been left over from long extinguished flames. On the other hand, however, I cannot resist reminding you that our differences did not arise from any misunderstandings. You wrote certain things and were quoted as having said others, none of which you chose to correct. . . . The remarks affecting me that were quoted in the press were never denied by you. Nevertheless, as I have said, by all means let us forget whatever in the past may have been unpleasant."

As for Evans's request to attend the Masters the following year, Jones coldly replied that he would receive the honorary invitation that went to all former U.S. Open and Amateur champions. "I hope you will come to the tournament," Jones said. Masters records show that Evans was invited to the tournament but did not go.

A few weeks after hearing from Jones, Evans wrote him one last letter in which he cut to the heart of all that had come between them.

"You can never know how I envied you," he said.

Jones did not reply.

12

"Don't Kill the Star in the Prologue"

When it came to golf partners, eighteen-year-old Charles Seaver was a hard young man to impress. The son of a prominent U.S. Golf Association official, Seaver was already used to a friendly vice principal letting him out of school early to keep his regular golf dates with Howard Hughes at the Wilshire Country Club. And throughout the summer of 1929, Seaver had driven up from his family's beach home in Santa Monica to the Riviera Country Club, which was on Sunset Boulevard in the open country between downtown Los Angeles and the Pacific Ocean, for rounds with Douglas Fairbanks, Harold Lloyd, Richard Arlen, Randolph Scott, and other members of Hollywood's growing community of devoted golfers.

Still, it was something else to join a group at Riviera that included Bobby Jones, and Seaver brought along a movie camera he had recently begun fiddling around with to memorialize the occasion.

Jones was visiting Los Angeles in advance of the 1929 U.S. Amateur at Pebble Beach Golf Links, up the coast on the Monterey Peninsula. It was the first time a national championship had been held in California, and he was greeted with an enthusiasm that startled the local golf establishment, which was every bit as insular and restrictive as its counterparts back east, and which would remain so for many years.

When Victor Mature, a popular movie star in the 1940s and 1950s, was turned down for membership in the exclusive Los Angeles Country Club because of his profession, his response—"Hell, I'm no actor and I've got twenty-eight movies and a scrapbook of reviews to prove it"—went down in golf lore. To this day, that club, which is considered one of the finest in the country by the few nonmembers who have seen it, has resisted every effort by the U.S. Golf Association to stage a U.S. Open there.

But when Jones arrived in Los Angeles, this upper-crust sport was suddenly on the front pages. The public was fascinated, and movie stars were vying to play, or at least be seen, with the handsome patrician young Georgian who was unanimously hailed as the greatest golfer of the age.

"Will Rogers' ranch was right below Riviera," Seaver remembers. "He came down and watched us with a piece of straw in his mouth. He laughed and said we were playing cow-pasture pool."

By now, Jones was twenty-seven years old and his life had become more complicated. Recently admitted to the Georgia bar, he had joined his father's law firm, where he discovered he was no more suited to the courtroom than to selling real estate.

"I am not the sort of fellow who can do much standing on his feet, spouting a lot of words," he said, and the rest of his legal career would be confined almost exclusively to office work, which he was not particularly keen on, either. "I like to have something to do, all right," Jones told Paul Gallico, "but I don't like to have to do it."

Years later, Jones expanded on this theme in a letter to Charles Price. "I love to play," he wrote. "I love fishing and hunting and trapshooting and Ping-Pong and chess and pool and billiards and driving a motor car, and at times I love golf, when I can get the shots going somewhere near right. It seems I love almost any pursuit except work."

What Jones was beginning to discover was there was not as much difference between himself and the best professional golfers as he once thought. "I don't believe that a sporting champion, as a rule, is much good at anything outside his game," he said almost wistfully, "but I've got a family to support."

In the previous few years, Jones had been torn about how to

proceed. For one thing, he had accomplished so much—three U.S. Open championships, two British Open titles, four U.S. Amateur titles. What more did he have to prove? And for all the excitement and revenue his appearances in national championships created ("What makes the Open a moneymaker?" an envious PGA vice president asked; "Bobby Jones!" the organization's treasurer replied), he still could not profit from playing golf as an amateur. Nor had dealing with the public aspect of his fame gotten any easier.

There was another problem as well. After Jones's two great triumphs in 1927, his competitive golf game had turned into an amazingly mixed bag. At times he was still the greatest player anybody had ever seen. At others, he was capable of throwing away tournaments with the best of them.

There was no disgrace in Jones's losing the 1928 U.S. Open to Johnny Farrell in a 36-hole playoff. The dapper Farrell—he was called "the beautiful Irishman" and was consistently voted the best-dressed golfer on the tour—won twenty-two professional tournaments during his career and six in a row in 1927, a record that stood until Byron Nelson won eleven straight in 1945. The embarrassment was in *how* Jones lost.

The Open was held at Olympia Fields Country Club south of Al Capone's Chicago, and spectators thought they could smell bootleg gin overflowing from stills upstream into a brook running through the course. Olympia Fields legend would later have a member of the Capone gang, Machine Gun Jack McGurn, being arrested while playing in a tournament under an alias.

Jones and Farrell saw a lot of each other in the Open. They were paired in the first two rounds, which forced Farrell to contend with the gallery intent on following Jones from hole to hole, with no regard for the man playing with him. Shorter off the tee than Jones, Farrell was bothered early on by spectators running to the next hole once Jones had finished putting, even if he was still on the green.

"It was a little disconcerting," Farrell said, "so I asked Bobby if he would mind marking his ball until I finished putting." It was a measure of Jones's sportsmanship, Farrell said, that he agreed to slow down the pace of play.

Jones had problems of his own as he struggled with his tee shots and seemed to grow increasingly more frustrated as the tournament wore on. Still, his putting was good enough to give him the lead after two rounds, and when he shot a 73 the morning of the final day, he was two shots clear of the field and five ahead of Farrell. Five holes into the final round, Jones had picked up two more birdies and was threatening to run away with the tournament. The toughest part of the course was behind him, he told himself. All he had to do was coast home. That bit of overconfidence cost him dearly.

At the par-3 6th hole, Jones hit his tee shot into the fragrant creek and wound up with a 5. Another double bogey followed and then three straight bogeys. Needing to score nothing better than three or four over par to win his third U.S. Open, he had wasted seven shots in five holes and allowed the field to catch up to him.

For a time it appeared that Roland Hancock, a professional from North Carolina nobody seemed to have heard of, was on his way to victory. Working on a 69, Hancock came to the 17th green needing only a pair of 5s to win.

"Make way for the new champion!" somebody in the gallery yelled. Unnerved and forced to wait an agonizing thirty minutes while officials moved spectators back from the fairway, Hancock finished with two 6s and wound up third.

Farrell came in with a 72 just as Jones, who had regained control of his game on the back nine, arrived at the tee for the par-5 18th hole not yet knowing he needed a birdie to win and par to tie. Two shots later, it looked as if he would lose.

Jones's tee shot landed in the rough, and his second shot flew across the fairway and onto the bank of a ditch on the other side. Just then, word of Farrell's score reached the gallery. The two bad shots presented Jones with his just reward, a terrible lie buried in the muck about ninety yards short of the green. No golfer could possibly reach the green from such a lie.

Jones placed his left foot high on the bank, his right foot in the sloppy grass, and, swinging his 7-iron as hard as he could, he reached the green, his ball rolling to rest twenty-five yards from the hole.

"You never heard a greater shout than the shout that went soaring along with the ball," Don Maxwell wrote in the *Chicago Tribune*. After missing a twenty-five-foot birdie putt that would have won the tournament, Jones tapped in for a par that gave him a score of 77 and forced a 36-hole playoff.

In a gloomy rain the following day that did not keep eight thousand spectators away from the course, Jones played some excellent golf. But Farrell played better, with birdies on the last four holes of the morning round to take a three-shot lead. Though Jones caught him and even went ahead by a shot in the afternoon, he fell behind again at 16, when his approach shot bounced off the green and rolled into the rough. What followed still ranks among the greatest two-man finishes in U.S. Open history.

Farrell's approach shots had always been the strongest part of his game, and now they rose to a higher level. His second shot at 17 landed five feet from the hole, and Jones had to sink a thirty-foot putt to remain tied. After Farrell's first two shots at the par-5 18th left him in the rough sixty yards short of the green, he hit a brilliant pitch that wound up ten feet from the flag.

Jones chipped dead to the hole for his easy birdie, while Farrell sank the putt for his difficult one. Both men had birdied the final two holes of a U.S. Open playoff, and Farrell, shooting 70-73 to Jones's 73-71, had won the only national championship of his career. One shot in a match that lasted 108 holes decided it all.

But if the pros were giving Jones all the competition he could have asked for in the Open—and he was certainly holding up his end of the bargain by finishing first or second in six of the last seven national championships—the U.S. Amateur remained his private domain. In September he won his fourth Amateur title, at Brae Burn Country Club in West Newton, Massachusetts, where his final three matches were over shortly after they began: 14 and 13 over John Beck, 13 and 12 over Phillips Finlay, 10 and 9 over Philip Perkins.

Jones had now tied Jerry Travers for most U.S. Amateur victories, and this much was abundantly clear: the only man who could beat Bobby Jones in an amateur championship was himself.

During much of the competition at the 1929 U.S. Open at Winged Foot Golf Club in New York's Westchester County, it appeared as if the tournament would be a rerun of the events at Olympia Fields the year before. Jones played some superb golf over the extremely difficult course and appeared unbeatable. Jones played some dreadful golf and appeared beaten. And once again, it came down to a 36-hole playoff.

Jones began the tournament by shooting 69, the first time he had ever broken 70 in a U.S. Open. He ended it by shooting almost 80. It took the most excruciating putt imaginable on the 18th hole to give him a 79 that placed him in a 72-hole tie with Al Espinosa, a pro from Monterey, California, instead.

"This tournament was a contest to see who could throw away the championship the greatest number of times," one reporter wrote, and Jones could only agree. With a three-shot lead going into the fourth round, and with his closest competitors self-destructing—Espinosa, playing well ahead of him, needed eight shots on two different holes—there was no excuse for what happened to Jones. Or how.

The trouble began at the 8th hole, when he went from one green-side bunker to another and then back to the first and took a 7. So *that's* the way it's going to be, he told himself, and he grew so fearful of landing in any more bunkers that he began trying to steer his second shots rather than hit them. The remainder of the round was "an agony of anxiety."

Still, Jones led by five shots with six holes remaining. Espinosa had only come that close, in fact, by thinking the eight strokes he took at the 12th hole had ended any chance he had to win. With the pressure off, he finished with four 4s and two 3s for a round of 75, which was not so bad after all. Jones responded by throwing away every shot of his big lead.

A bogey at 13, a *triple* bogey at 15—the second 7 on his card—a bogey at 16. Now he needed a pair of 4s just to tie. He got the first one easily enough, but when his second shot at the 18th hole rolled into the long grass at the edge of a bunker, he faced a tricky pitch that he hit too thinly. The ball came to rest twelve feet from the hole, which was downhill and would require a putt that took into account both the slickness of the green and a slight left-to-right slope.

Keeler couldn't watch. A cameraman's ladder was nearby, and Keeler could have stepped up to peer over the crowd, but the putt would not go in if he looked, he told himself, and he turned away. All he could think was what a disaster it would be if Jones shot 80 for the first time in a U.S. Open and lost by a stroke. To be beaten was one thing, but to be beaten like this would be an eternal disgrace, a permanent blot on Jones's record.

The late afternoon shadows spread across the green where Jones's playing partner, Al Watrous, a man who knew all there was to know about what Jones was capable of at a time like this, crouched so he would not obstruct the view of the gallery. Herbert Ramsay, a vice president of the U.S. Golf Association, took the flag out of the cup and did the same. All Keeler could hear was the crowd breathing and, somewhere far in the distance, the slow ringing of a bell. Then the click of a golf club hitting a ball.

A sigh rose up from the crowd, grew in volume—how *long* this was taking? Keeler thought—and then turned into a moan. *No! He had missed!* And then, like a bolt of thunder striking at his feet, came a roar. Once again, Jones had sent his putt just to the lip of the hole, watched it hesitate for a fraction of a second, and then fall in. If the hole had been a circle on the green, Watrous told Keeler after a few stiff drinks in the clubhouse, the ball would have stopped dead in the center.

Espinosa never had a chance in the playoff the next day—he shot 84-80 to 72-69 for Jones, who had now won his third U.S. Open title. But as Jones went home to Atlanta for some rest before packing up his wife and parents for a leisurely train ride to the Grand Canyon and then on to California, Keeler kept coming back to that one agonizing putt. Taking everything into account, he thought, it was one of the great shots of Jones's life. But it was something more than that. He would always believe that if the putt had not fallen, none of the great events of the following year would have been possible.

Keeler could not be sure about this, but nobody knew Jones's temperament better than he did. Nobody knew how much harder the strain of championship competition was becoming. Nobody knew how much more difficult Jones was finding it to accept losing through his own careless play.

"He would have been a beaten man, broken in spirit," Keeler said two decades later. "It's a guess but he couldn't have taken it in the future had he failed to win that 1929 championship."

•   •   •

In 1954, on the twenty-fifth anniversary of Jones's victory at Winged Foot, a hole was cut in the 18th green approximately where the cup had been that day in 1929, and four U.S. Open champions—Gene Sarazen, Tommy Armour, Johnny Farrell, and Craig Wood—tried several times to duplicate Jones's putt. None of them could.

The Monterey Peninsula was in a frenzy over Jones's arrival. Cars jammed the roads, special trains rolled in, yachts sailed into Monterey Bay, all carrying people eager to get a glimpse of Bobby Jones. There seemed to be no limit to the curiosity he aroused, even among those whose knowledge of golf was limited.

"Shoot for the camera," a director from a movie company who had been sent to film Jones's swing told him.

"You mean aim right for him?" Jones said, looking at the cameraman perched up in a tree.

That was exactly what he meant, the director said. Jones's shot knocked both camera and cameraman from the tree.

Despite the expense of traveling such a long distance, most of the country's top amateur players came to Pebble Beach because the results would go a long way toward determining the selection of the Walker Cup team that would go to Britain the following year. A number of the top sportswriters of the day made the journey as well, and along with many players and high-rolling fans they congregated in a nearby lodge where Prohibition took a week off and where many bets were placed. San Francisco millionaire Henry Lapham was said to have wagered more than $50,000, including $23,000 to purchase Jones in a Calcutta pool the night before the tournament began.

For his part, Jones was fascinated by the California golf courses on which he was invited to play, which were like none he had ever seen before. The Los Angeles Country Club, Riviera, Pebble Beach, they were all so beautiful—the turf, the trees, the flowers, and particularly the surroundings. Was there anything like the bay at Carmel? Keeler said it was the dream of an artist who had been drinking gin and sobering up on absinthe.

Jones was particularly taken with Cypress Point, a stunning layout near Pebble Beach, where thick stands of trees are home to deer that occasionally wander onto fairways that later emerge onto windswept cliffs overlooking the Pacific. The designer of the course, Jones learned, was Alister Mackenzie, a name he would remember when he decided to build a golf course of his own.

Jones played excellent golf while practicing at Pebble Beach—a course record 67 was one of the best rounds of his life, Keeler thought—and tied for the qualifying medal with Eugene Homans, a young player from New Jersey he would encounter again. Among those who failed to qualify for the tournament were Charlie Seaver, who spent the rest of the tournament shooting movies of the matches he followed, Chick Evans, and Howard Hughes.

So there was not a reason in the world to think Jones would not become the first man to win five U.S. Amateur titles—and the first to win three in a row—as well as the only golfer other than Evans to win the U.S. Open and Amateur the same year. Certainly that is what the fans were expecting, and thousands of them crowded around the first tee when Jones began his rounds. There were so many officials, marshals, and photographers in the area, one reporter said, that the scene resembled the introductions at a championship boxing match.

Jones's opponent in the 18-hole first round was a pushover, twenty-year-old Johnny Goodman of Omaha, Nebraska, who had finished twenty-four shots behind him and Espinosa in the U.S. Open. The most remarkable thing about Goodman's performance at Winged Foot and Pebble Beach was that he made it to the tournaments at all.

Goodman was one of nine children whose father deserted the family when he was a child and whose mother died when he was eleven. Several of his younger brothers and sisters were placed in an orphanage, and Goodman went to a foster home. He learned golf as a caddy, and though he had little time to practice, he quickly became the best young player in town.

Goodman's big moment came in 1928 when, on the night of his high school graduation, he and a few friends drove a Model T to Colorado Springs, where he entered the Trans-Mississippi championship at the exclusive Broadmoor Hotel. The Trans-Miss was an important amateur tournament and drew an excellent field that year, including George Von Elm and Harrison Johnston. Goodman won and came home a celebrity.

He qualified for the Open at Winged Foot the following year, but had no way of making the trip until a wealthy admirer who owned a share in Omaha's stockyards arranged for him to ride to New York as a drover in a cattle car. Undaunted by his poor showing, he decided to make the trip to California, and another drover's pass was arranged. When he was paired with Jones in the first round of the tournament, it appeared that his stay would be a short one.

Jones lost the first three holes. The huge crowd was stunned to see the great man, who was unaccountably nervous, botch shot after shot and actually concede the first two holes. Still, Jones won two of the next three holes, and even when he three-putted 7 to fall two holes behind, he appeared to be back on his game. At the turn, he trailed by one.

Goodman hung on to his lead with a thirty-foot putt at 11, but was wild off the tee at the par-3 13th, and Jones tied the match. When Goodman hit a poor drive at the 14th and knocked his second shot into the rough under a tree, Jones, who was in the fairway some fifty yards from the green, went for the kill.

"I wanted desperately to get my nose out in front," he wrote, "because I figured once there, I could stand off any challenge Goodman might make."

Rather than go for a safe shot well onto the green, Jones tried to place his ball just over a bunker at the front. It came up short, landed in the sand, and Goodman, who made a nice recovery shot, won the hole to go back into the lead.

At 17, Jones faced a ten-foot putt to tie the match that rimmed the cup and hung on the lip. "I'll never forget how his shoulders sagged," Seaver remembered. "He looked like a tire someone had let the air out of."

Goodman played the par-5 18th hole, which stretches along Monterey Bay, perfectly and, when Jones missed a thirty-five-foot birdie putt, Goodman scored the biggest first-round upset in the history of the U.S. Amateur. The deflated tire was suddenly the tournament itself.

"The ancient Scottish pastime in this age is a one-man sport," Ring Lardner wrote of Jones's debacle, "and the one man is public property, like Lindbergh or Charlie Chaplin or Babe Ruth. If you're giving a show, don't kill the star in the prologue."

"The whole place was like a Greyhound Bus station," Seaver said of the mass exodus that began immediately after Jones was eliminated. "People were lined up in their automobiles to get out. There just wasn't anybody left to watch the rest of the tournament compared to the crowds that had been there."

Keeler was disconsolate after the loss, writing that "while Omaha doubtless regards Johnny Goodman as a prime hero, California considers him a painful accident that came over two thousand miles to happen . . . the general feeling was that it was a type of misfortune, like breaking a leg or running into a lamp post."

Goodman's moment of triumph was short—he was ousted from the tournament that very afternoon by Lawson Little—but he would gain more significant prizes in 1933, when he became the last amateur to win a U.S. Open, and 1937, when he won the U.S. Amateur. But he would always be best remembered for shocking Jones, and the world, at Pebble Beach.

Not that he was under any illusions about what his victory meant. As thrilled as he was to beat Jones, Goodman said, "I will never make the mistake of thinking I can beat him again."

The person who seemed least concerned about the loss was Jones himself. "The clubs weren't working," he told reporters. "We had a great match, though, and Goodman is a fine golfer and a game boy."

Rather than join the mass evacuation from Pebble Beach, Jones remained for the rest of the tournament and even served as referee for the third-round match between Harrison Johnston, who would eventually win the tournament, and George Voight. The contest was a thriller, lasting 39 holes, and Jones enjoyed it despite his embarrassment at receiving as much applause as the golfers themselves every time he stepped onto the green to judge who was away.

Jones was having such a good time, in fact, that he and Mary went to San Francisco after the tournament where, first-round loss be damned, he was given a parade and motorcycle escort.

But beyond his display of good sportsmanship, Jones took away an important lesson from his loss to Goodman. As much as he disliked the 18-hole matches that were played in the first round of the U.S. and British Amateurs because he thought they left too little margin for error, he had to deal with the fact that they were a part of the game.

"Whether or not Johnny Goodman should be thanked for the result," Jones wrote, "it is true that never afterwards did I face an 18-hole match with fear and trembling. I was to feel nervous again, and there would be times when I found the short route distasteful, but from that day on, I was able to play all the matches the same way."

Actually, Jones had lost only one other 18-hole match in the previous five years, to Andrew Jamieson in the 1926 British Amateur. And that earlier defeat, in the one important tournament he had yet to win, also had given him something to think about.

Suppose he had beaten Jamieson at Muirfield that year, which he very well might have but for that painful crick in his neck. That would have given him three of the four major championships in a single year. And he had lost the 1926 U.S. Amateur by a narrow margin to Von Elm in the final.

What, he wondered, was to keep him from trying to accomplish something nobody else had ever thought of doing? What was to keep him from trying to win all four major championships in the same year?

Jones kept his thoughts to himself, not even telling Keeler, though perhaps confiding in Mary, but the more he thought about it, the more the idea appealed to him. He even had a year picked out: 1930, when the U.S. Walker Cup team returned to Great Britain.

Bobby Jones at age six. His simple, upright golfing stance was in evidence even then.

Bobby Jones with Alexa Stirling. A three-time U.S. Women's Amateur champion, she was the first national titleholder to emerge from East Lake and one of the first to deal with his ferocious temper while he was playing golf.

Bobby and Mary Jones, the closest thing Atlanta had to royalty, at an Atlanta Athletic Club dinner, 1924 or 1925.

Bobby Jones's only golf instructor, Stewart Maiden, whose advice was simple and direct: "Hit the ball hard and it will land somewhere."

O. B. Keeler (left), who devoted much of his career to traveling with and writing about Jones, checks some of Jones's hardware in 1926 at East Lake.

Bobby Jones is carried off by a delirious crowd at St. Andrews—Bernard Darwin called it "a black and seething mass"—after defending his British Open championship in 1927. For a few anxious moments, his safety was in doubt.

Bobby Jones and Chick Evans shake hands after Jones won the 1927 U.S. Amateur at the Minikahda Club in Minneapolis. Their smiles belie their animosity toward each other.

Bobby Jones and his father, Robert P. Jones, known to his friends as the Colonel. The two men could not have been less alike or loved each other more.

Bobby Jones in a New York ticker-tape parade in 1930. He is the only person to have two such celebrations in his honor.

Bobby Jones (center) and Eugene Homans at moment of Jones winning the Grand Slam. After Homans missed his putt, he walked over to Jones and shook his hand, conceding the match.

Bobby Jones with the four Grand Slam trophies. They represent one of the greatest achievements in all of sports.

Bobby Jones receiving the Freedom of the City award at St. Andrews in 1958. He was the second American to receive the award. The first was Benjamin Franklin.

PART II

The Grand Slam

13

Impregnable Quadrilaterals, Then and Now

On June 12, 1870, J. Lee Richmond, pitching for a team from Worcester, Massachusetts, beat Cleveland without allowing a batter to reach base. It was the first time such a thing had happened in professional baseball, and though much was made of Richmond's feat in the accounts of the game, there was no useful shorthand to characterize it. The term "perfect game" did not enter baseball's lexicon until years later.

Bobby Jones's victories in the 1930 British and U.S. Amateurs and Opens similarly caught sportswriters unaware. Not until Jones won the tournaments in Britain, and returned home to his second ticker-tape parade in New York, did more than one or two of golf's keenest observers seem to realize what he was up to. Win all four of the game's most important national championships in one year? The thought simply had never occurred to anyone.

After Jones won the four tournaments, George Trevor of the *New York Sun* wrote that Jones had stormed the "impregnable quadrilateral" of golf, a phrase that appealed to some of his more literary-minded colleagues. But it was O. B. Keeler who gave the feat the name by which it would be remembered. Sometime between the British and the U.S. Opens, perhaps on the boat trip home, Keeler borrowed a term from contract bridge and said Jones was attempting to win the Grand Slam.

Though the phrase caught on quickly enough to be used while Jones was competing in the 1930 American championships—it occasionally appeared in newspaper headlines and articles surrounded by quotation marks—it became a relic soon afterward. Because the trip across the ocean was so expensive and time-consuming, few golfers bothered to compete in all four tournaments in one year. And the decline of amateur golf after Jones's feat occurred so rapidly that before long, only professionals were serious contenders in Open competition. Jones had no sooner won the Grand Slam, therefore, than it became clear that the feat would never be repeated. As applied to golf, the term fell into disuse until, thirty years later, Arnold Palmer brought it back almost literally overnight.

After winning the Masters and the U.S. Open in 1960, Palmer, the most popular golfer of his era, was traveling to his first British Open with a sportswriter friend, Bob Drum. What a shame it was, Drum lamented, that the rise of professional golf had killed off the Grand Slam.

"Well," Palmer said casually, "why don't we create a new Grand Slam?"

In his autobiography, *A Golfer's Life*, Palmer says Drum "gave me one of his famous contrarian glares that made him look like a cross between an annoyed college dean and a sleeping bear someone had foolishly kicked awake."

"What the hell are you talking about?" Drum said.

"What would be wrong with a professional Grand Slam involving the Masters, both Open championships, and the PGA championship?" Palmer said.

Drum snorted derisively, but as soon as he arrived at St. Andrews he explained the idea to his sportswriting colleagues, who embraced it. Palmer finished second to Kel Nagle of Australia in the British Open, but the concept of the Grand Slam was reborn in a radically new way. For three decades after Jones's retirement, it had been a legendary feat beyond the reach of any modern golfer. For the rest of the twentieth century and into the twenty-first, it was a holy grail any winner of the Masters could aspire to but none could achieve.

The only golfers who repeated Palmer's feat of winning the first two tournaments on the yearly schedule were Jack Nicklaus, who won the Masters and U.S. Open in 1972 but lost the British Open by a stroke to

Lee Trevino; and Tiger Woods, who lost his chance when he shot 81 in the third round of the 2002 British Open, which was won by Ernie Els.

As the years went by, golf journalists and historians noted how close Ben Hogan had come to winning Palmer's version of the Grand Slam seven years before he invented it. Hogan won the Masters, U.S. Open, and British Open in 1953, but could not have competed in the PGA championship even if he had wanted to. That tournament took place as he was practicing for the British Open thousands of miles away.

At some point, the idea of a "career" Grand Slam gained currency, one that designated those golfers who had won each of its modern components at some point during their careers. Only Hogan, Nicklaus, Woods, Gary Player, and, again reaching back to a time before the new Grand Slam existed, Gene Sarazen qualified.

The Grand Slam is one of sport's towering monuments—in 1944, sportswriters voted it the "outstanding sports achievement of all time," with Jones outpolling Babe Ruth, 2½ to 1—and its revival represents golf's most lasting tribute to Jones. The quest begins each year with the tournament he inaugurated on the golf course he helped build and is an annual reminder that he is the only man ever to accomplish the feat in either of its guises.

But as talk of the Grand Slam became a permanent rite of spring, Jones was having none of it. It was, he wrote to Charles Price in 1967, a creature of professionals and television people. And it was phony.

14

"Your Boy Is Just Too Good"

By the time Jones arrived in Britain in 1930, his determination to try to win golf's four biggest prizes had already begun paying dividends. For the first time in his life, he began a serious training regimen and lost twenty pounds.

Jones had always been skeptical about golfers who worked out, insisting it only developed "a set of muscles other than the golfing muscles. I never took any other athletic exercise in my life." The best exercise for golf, he liked to say, was golfing. And as for his battle with his weight, he thought it best to enter a tournament "with a few extra pounds available as a sort of nerve cushion."

In a sense, this was easy for Jones to say. While other golfers had to contend with one physical deficiency or another, it was almost as if he had been built to play golf.

"I do not believe that any golfer who has ever lived has had his strength," Chick Evans wrote before the 1930 U.S. Amateur. "There is something remarkable about his enormous strength, a physique that could carry him unharmed through the terrific strains of championships. Large strong hands, wrists of iron, shoulder muscles of great strength and pliability, and the cleverest skill in the use of them, and not a clumsy muscle in his whole body."

But with so much at stake this year, Jones was not counting on his natural advantages alone. After finishing work at his law office, he would go to the deserted Atlanta Theater and play a game called "Doug," which he had learned from Douglas Fairbanks, whom he had met in Los Angeles. A cross between tennis and badminton, Doug featured long rallies and constant running. In just a few months following the Christmas holidays, he told an interviewer, the weight had come right off.

But Jones's real commitment to the season was shown when he began it. He had not played in an important tour event prior to a major tournament since 1927, when he won the Southern Open at East Lake. In 1930, for the first time in ten years, he played in two.

Virtually every good touring pro of the era played in the Savannah Open late in February, and in the Southern Open in Augusta a month later. The field at Savannah included Bobby Cruickshank, Bill Mehlhorn, Harry Cooper, Johnny Farrell, Al Espinosa, Joe Turnesa, and an exciting young player from Springfield, Missouri, named Horton Smith, who, at age twenty-one, had won seven professional tour events the year before. Walter Hagen, off on an exhibition tour of the Far East and Australia, was one of the few top players missing.

Jones and Horton Smith roomed together in Augusta, and Smith's youth did not prevent him from offering the world's greatest golfer a tip about his short-iron play. Try cocking your wrists a little more than normal at the beginning of the downward stroke, he told Jones. "Almost miraculously, this barely perceptible movement seemed to assure that I would strike the ball a crisply descending blow," Jones wrote later. "It is a fact that from Augusta onward during the 1930 season, my pitching was better than it had ever been before."

Smith also offered Jones something more substantial than mere advice: a golf club with two radically new features. One was a wide concave face—all previous clubs had flat striking areas—that dug under the ball and scooped it out of the sand. The other was a fin projecting back from the base to prevent it from sinking too deeply into the ground beneath the ball. Smith, who constantly tinkered with his clubs, had bought the patent from Edward Kerr MacClain, an inventor in Houston, Texas.

"I call it a sand wedge," Smith, who also was practicing with radically new clubs that contained a steel shaft, told Jones. "It's the niftiest antidote for bunkers you ever saw."

In an era before the machine manufacture of matched sets of clubs—and before the rule restricting the number of clubs a golfer could carry to fourteen—Jones, like most golfers, always was experimenting. "It was the custom of the 1920s," noted golf writer Roger Ganem, "to give every different-type club or new version of existing shapes close scrutiny because one never knew where the miracle club was going to be found."

By this time, most of Jones's clubs were made by Tom Stewart of St. Andrews, but he never gave up searching for others. "In my own crude and purely instinctive way," he said, "I had assembled, all unknown to myself, a perfectly coordinated set of clubs." He stuck the odd-looking new club in his bag among the twenty he would take with him to Britain. It might come in handy in the months ahead. Who knew?

Jones played well at Savannah, shooting 67 in the first round and setting a course record with a third-round 65. But he shot 40 on the front nine of the second round and lost to Smith by a stroke. A month later, the field met again at Augusta, where they were joined by Gene Sarazen, and where Jones played his best golf of 1930.

Jones beat Sarazen, his conqueror in the 1922 U.S. Open at Skokie, by 27 strokes over the two difficult Augusta courses that were used in the tournament. He beat Johnny Farrell, who had won their playoff for the 1928 Open at Olympia Fields, by 16. He beat Bobby Cruickshank by 29 strokes, Al Espinosa by 28, and Joe Turnesa by 15. The golfer who came closest to Jones was the one who had just beaten him, Horton Smith. He lost by 13 strokes.

At one point in the final round, Jones led the field by 18 shots and lay down under a tree when play was backed up at the 16th hole. Ty Cobb, who lived in Augusta and had been following Jones with Grantland Rice, encouraged him to get up and swing a club to keep warm, but Jones laughed him off. Jones shot 5-5-6 on the last three holes, which, despite his double-digit lead, infuriated the hypercompetitive Cobb.

"Did you see what that boy did?" Cobb, who had retired from baseball two years earlier, told reporters. "How can a man expect to keep his poise and his fitness when he lies down on the ground for twenty minutes? If a ballplayer of mine did something corresponding to that in a tight game, I'd fine him."

Jones went to Cobb's house afterward for a drink, where he took more abuse. "I got the dressing-down of my life," he said. "It was not Ty's idea just to win, but to win by the most you could."

Rice had a somewhat more sanguine view of what Jones had accomplished. "He is taking this next trip more seriously than he has ever taken any other, his main objective being the British amateur championship, the one prize he has as yet to win," Rice wrote. "I have never seen him hitting his tee shots as far and true as he did all through the Augusta show."

Even Jones curbed his customary modesty long enough to admit to Keeler, "I was hitting the shots as well as I ever hope to hit them."

Most enthusiastic of all was Cruickshank, who told Keeler, "Your boy is just too good. His play in this tournament is the finest thing I have ever seen. Do you want a prediction? Here's one. He'll go over to Britain and win the amateur and the open, and then he'll come back to America and win the open and the amateur. He cannot be stopped this year."

Cruickshank was so convinced, in fact, that he wired $100 to his father-in-law in Edinburgh, where he got 50–1 odds on Jones winning his next four tournaments. A month later, Jones and Mary boarded the *Mauretania*, which was bound for Cherbourg, Plymouth, and Southampton.

15

The British Amateur: "They Ought to Burn Him at the Stake"

A tourist walking from the headquarters of the Royal and Ancient Golf Club at St. Andrews past the 18th green and down the road to the left of the fairway encounters a sign that says, "Danger—Golf in Progress." This is a warning golfers of every ability from all over the world gladly accept as a challenge when they make their pilgrimage to the castle of the kingdom of golf. The lure is as strong today as it was in the heyday of Bobby Jones, just as it was as compelling then as it was hundreds of years before.

St. Andrews was not the birthplace of golf, nor the first town to organize a golf club. The Honourable Company of Edinburgh Golfers was formed at Leith, outside the Scottish capital, in 1744, ten years before twenty-two men, "being admirers of the ancient and healthful exercise of the Golf," created the Society of St. Andrews Golfers, which later became the Royal and Ancient.

But well before the creation of these and other clubs, St. Andrews had laid a claim to the game no one could challenge. Golf was first mentioned in a charter granted to John Hamilton, the archbishop of St. Andrews, in 1552—it gave him the right to raise rabbits on a portion of the links—but there is some indication that it had taken hold as early as the beginning of the fifteenth century.

In *The Story of the R&A*, J. B. Salmond notes that numerous diaries of students at the University of St. Andrews dating back to the sixteenth century spoke of golf. "The links are close by," Arthur Johnston, the physician to Charles I, wrote in 1642; "'tis here Youth wearied with studies finds recreation, and gathers a new stock of strength."

Robert Blair, a St. Andrews minister in the seventeenth century, used golf as an object lesson in his sermons, comparing "the Union of the Kirk to its Sacred Head as that of the staff and the head of a driving club. Faith was the whipping, Love the glue." Local doctors, on the other hand, were said to object to golf because they were afraid the exercise it afforded might reduce their income.

Soon the small university town—even today it can be walked from top to bottom in ten minutes—had become the game's international headquarters. The R&A, which built a large clubhouse overlooking the adjoining first tee and 18th green, was the sport's arbiter and St. Andrews its most famous and historic course.

Originally 11 holes out and 11 holes back along the same track on a narrow, gorse-infested patch of land, St. Andrews required golfers to aim at its holes from two directions, a dangerous enterprise made only a little safer by a rule giving precedence to incoming players. Eventually the fairways were widened a bit and, in 1832, two flags were placed on each of the large greens. But a more lasting change had come earlier, in 1764, when the first and last two holes were taken out of play because they were not considered very interesting. Overnight, the course became 18 holes long, and the universal standard for the game was set permanently in place.

Along with being responsible for the rules of golf, the R&A had to cope with running a golf club. This led it to adopt one provision in the nineteenth century allowing John Low, an elderly member, to ride his horse between shots, and another imposing a fine of 5 shillings on anyone bringing a dog into the clubhouse. A twentieth-century proposal by an American member that "no well-mannered dog shall be forbidden entrance to the clubhouse" was rejected. And as late as 1975, when the British Ladies' Championship was played on the Old Course and its players and officials were allowed the hospitality of the clubhouse, two members resigned in protest.

One aspect of progress the R&A could not deter was the railroad that, beginning in 1846, brought large numbers of golfers from all over Britain to St. Andrews and turned "the retired place of learning and ecclesiastical leisure" into a popular destination for every class. The Old Course, which was later joined by adjacent layouts along St. Andrews Bay, was on public land, so golf there was no longer the sole province of local residents and the wealthy.

By the time the 1930 British Amateur championship was played at St. Andrews, the game had changed in ways that could not have been imagined by its original practitioners. And while St. Andrews also had been altered by time and the elements—the gorse was cut back, the configuration of some of the bunkers had changed—there was little about the world's most historic golf course that would not have been familiar to those who had played there in all the centuries that had come before.

•   •   •

Even before Jones arrived in St. Andrews, it was clear that 1930 would be like no year he had ever known.

The crossing on the *Mauretania* was festive—along with the U.S. Walker Cup team, the passenger list included Douglas Fairbanks, Maurice Chevalier, and Harry Lauder—and the interest in Jones's return to Britain for the first time since 1927 was so great that the country's golf writers did not wait for him to arrive. Led by George Greenwood of the *Daily Telegraph*, a number of journalists sailed out into the harbor at Plymouth an hour before daylight and climbed a rickety gangplank to the ship. When Jones awoke, he invited them to his stateroom where, wearing a silk dressing gown over his pajamas, he chatted amiably for half an hour.

"Everybody is agog to see him," wrote Darwin, in an article commissioned by the *Atlanta Constitution*, perhaps as a way of countering Keeler's reports from the scene in the *Journal*. "People come to me with unutterable pathos in their voices and ask me whether I could not persuade him to go and play on their particular course. Never, I think, has the tremendous tide of his popularity surged and roared here as it is going to do this time."

Jones got a glimpse of the chaos this fascination would create before the Amateur began. The Walker Cup matches were played at Royal St. George's in Sandwich, where an estimated ten thousand spectators saw the American team, captained by Jones, win its sixth consecutive competition in circumstances that were all but out of control.

In an era before fairways were routinely roped off, marshals were simply unable to restrain spectators intent on running from one spot to the next, especially when almost all of them were following one man. The British fans, willing to risk being trampled and hit by golf balls, took to standing around in clusters, hoping shots would fall among them. Time after time, the contestants hit spectators—Roger Wethered did so on three holes in a row during a match—occasionally with comic results. Oscar Willing of the American team hit a member of the gallery in the chest with a ball that was headed for the rough but bounded to a good lie instead. Jones's teammate George Voight hit a portly gentleman trotting across the 18th fairway.

Roland Mackenzie of the British team hit a ball into a crowd off the same fairway and said, "I hope I have not killed anyone. That ball was traveling." The man he struck was unhurt, but the ball could not be found.

"Where did it hit you?" a marker asked.

"Here," the man said, pointing to his side. "Wait, here it is. It's in my jacket pocket."

Even the Prince of Wales, who had flown to Sandwich, willingly braved these precarious conditions. Splendidly dressed in a plus-four suit of chocolate, red, and beige checks, brown and beige stockings, a brown and white checked cap, and carrying a red and white checked umbrella, he pushed his way through the crowd like a commoner, seeking a good vantage point from which to watch. His subjects appeared to take no notice.

The Americans easily retained the cup, winning seven of the eight matches over two days, as the insatiable curiosity surrounding their team and its captain continued unabated. "It has been said," noted one correspondent as the golfers prepared to go to St. Andrews, "that the majority of golfing enthusiasts crowding this ancient cinque ports town have come not to see the Americans play the British in the Walker Cup matches, but to see the Americans play golf."

The best single round of golf Jones played during the British Amateur, and among the best he played in any of the four major tournaments in

1930, was the first one. And a good thing. Anything less, and his quest for the Grand Slam might well have ended as it began, at the hands of a golfer no one outside his hometown of Nottingham seemed to have heard of.

"His opponent," Darwin wrote in the *Times*, "is S. Roper of Woolaton Park, a player hitherto unknown to fame who has now the opportunity of gaining it once and for all. Were he some mute inglorious slater or a plumber from Carnoustie or Monifieth he might frighten the champion; as it is I shall make so bold to assume a victorious Jones."

Sidney Roper was not a slater or a plumber, but he had been a coal miner in one of the Nottinghamshire collieries that, at their peak, provided Britain with twenty-five million tons of coal a year.

"Everybody went down the pit," says Roper's great-nephew Geoffrey Parr, and Roper was no exception. At age thirteen, he first descended a mine called Shonky in Bulwell with his father and uncle. "They would be on their knees the whole time because a lot of these shafts were only about three feet high," says Roper's nephew Stan. "It was strictly pick-and-shovel stuff."

Roper's father managed to save enough to leave the mines and open a liquor store, while his uncle worked underground for more than fifty years before retiring in the 1950s. For Roper, born in 1903 and growing up without an education in economically depressed Britain after World War I, a life spent on his hands and knees underground seemed all but inevitable.

Until he discovered golf.

Roper began as a caddy at the Bulwell Forest Golf Club and demonstrated such a natural aptitude for the game that one of the members decided to put him to use.

"He used to get picked up by a young man in a Rolls-Royce, who would take him to courses around Nottinghamshire," says Roper's great-nephew Stephen. "They'd play for money and he would beat them with his pit boots on. They were the only boots he owned."

Before long, Roper was working as a clerk. Had his mutually beneficial relationship with the man in the Rolls-Royce resulted in a job? No one in Roper's surviving family is sure, but he was out of the mines for good. While still in his teens, he won the first of four Nottinghamshire Amateur championships, which made him a local celebrity and gained him a uniquely British membership at Bulwell Forest.

As far back as the 1880s, the country's working-class golfers, frustrated at being shut off from their local golf courses, which until the 1920s were all private, had banded together and gained admission as "artisans." The concept was first championed by J. H. Taylor, a former greenskeeper who went on to win five British Opens and who believed golf should be available to everyone, regardless of class or financial status.

Artisan golfers, who paid far less than full club members and occasionally did some minor maintenance work, usually had their own meeting room, often in the caddiemaster's quarters or the chauffeurs' room but always well away from the gentlemen's clubhouse. They were allowed to play only at specified hours, usually in the early mornings or late afternoons.

Taylor's system was adopted at many British clubs—not always without complaints from the members—and continues to exist today, when many who qualify as "artisans" drive to their local golf courses in Mercedes or BMWs and have higher incomes than some full-paying members. It might be an anachronism, Sir Michael Bonallack, a former captain of the R&A, told the writer James Cusick, "but it's a part of golf I would not like to see lost."

Roper's fellow artisans at Bulwell Forest included miners, railway men, painters, plasterers, plumbers, joiners, and laborers. The irony was that in the 1960s, when many of the doctors, lawyers, and professional men had moved away, it was the artisans who saved the club.

"There weren't more than a dozen of them left," Stan Roper says. "So our committee put it to their committee: 'Why should we have two separate arrangements?'"

A few of the remaining gentlemen members resigned when it was decided to accept the artisans, but most had to agree with the Bulwell Forest secretary, who, as the club's last class barrier fell, said, "We are all artisans now."

When Jones was told he had nothing to fear from Roper, he had no reason not to believe it. One of Jones's few British friends who claimed to have seen him play predicted he would not shoot better than five on any hole at St. Andrews.

As if to add to the pressure Roper was under, the starting time of the match was delayed half an hour because eight earlier pairings had resulted in playoffs and backed up the field. Nor had Roper ever seen anything like the thousands who stormed the course that afternoon at the Notts County championships. It was, Keeler said, the biggest gallery for the first round of a tournament he had ever seen.

But Jones, who liked to size up his opponents before they played, saw something in Roper's demeanor as they shook hands that intrigued him. He may have been an unknown competitor from an obscure club, but he had an even, steady gaze and seemed quite composed. In short, Jones thought, not just a competitor but a golfer as well.

Jones began the match as if he meant to end it early. He made a birdie putt of more than twenty feet at the first hole, parred the second, and, after playing a delicate pitch out of a bunker within two feet at the third, birdied that one as well. The fact that Roper also was playing well, with fours on the first three holes—if his birdie putt at the second had not hung on the lip, he would have won it—did not seem to matter.

At the fourth hole, Jones faltered for the first time. His tee shot glanced off a small mound and into the Cottage Bunker, a wide depression off to the left that also comes into play on the 15th hole coming back down the far side of the course. Jones stepped down into the bunker for his second shot—"Please don't make a picture just now," he asked an amateur photographer who seemed determined to follow him—and saw that it could have been worse. Instead of being buried in the sand, his ball was perched on top. Also, the ball was well back in the bunker, which gave him plenty of room to clear the lip and shoot for the green, 140 yards away. Jones asked his caddy for his 7-iron.

The shot flew out of the bunker, rose in a high arc, descended steeply, and landed just beyond a small rise at the front of the green. Released from its backspin, the ball rolled slowly and then more slowly still, toward the hole. Finally, as if it were a perfectly judged putt, it slipped softly into the cup without touching the pin.

A tremendous roar went up from down the fairway as Jones emerged from the bunker. "Good heavens, have I?" he said when told he had holed out one of the most spectacular shots of his career, for an eagle.

"I came eighty-five hundred miles to see this championship and that shot is worth five times the trip," the father of an American player told Keeler. "They ought to burn him at the stake. He's a witch."

In the first four holes, Jones had made two birdies and an eagle. "He simply jumped into his stride as if he would span the course in seven-league boots," wrote the correspondent for the *Scotsman*.

It was time for Roper to fold now. He had needed only four strokes on each of the first four holes, yet he had lost three of them. His role as a footnote in golfing history—the first man to lose a Grand Slam match to Bobby Jones—was inevitable. But as Jones climbed out of the Cottage Bunker, Roper merely looked across at him and smiled. Then he parred the hole.

Roper matched Jones's fabulous shot with one he would always consider the greatest of *his* life, at the fifth, where he hit a long 3-wood within twelve feet of the flag. And when Jones missed a makeable putt, Roper thought his chance to turn the tide was at hand. But his own putt lipped out, a great disappointment, and they halved the hole.

Roper won his first hole of the match, the sixth, when Jones three-putted, and the par-3 8th as well when the wind carried Jones's tee shot off line and his sixty-foot putt settled in behind Roper's ball. Jones tried to negotiate the stymie by chipping over Roper's ball but failed. As they entered the back nine, Jones's four-hole lead was down to two. The opponent he had been told would need a minimum of five strokes on every hole had made nine straight fours.

"Does he know who he's playing against?" Jones wondered aloud to nobody in particular.

Jones's lead was back up to four after his tee shot at the difficult par-3 11th landed two feet from the hole, and a huge drive at the 12th put him in position to make a nine-foot putt. But when he drove from bunker to bunker at the 13th, Roper had one last chance to get back into the match. It ended when he missed a three-foot putt, allowing Jones to halve the hole.

Though Roper made one final statement by winning the 14th with two strong shots into the wind and an approach within a foot of the hole, the match was as good as over. It ended at 16, where Jones had one final stroke of luck when his ball banged into some railings, which prevented it from going out of bounds. Roper, surrendering at last, three-putted for his only five of the day after 15 consecutive fours.

In defeat, Roper gained the attention, and the respect, he had never known before. Jones had "never worked harder, suffered more or played more brilliantly," wrote Darwin, while Roper "died the gamest of deaths."

"It struck me very forcibly that any other opponent but Jones would have been beaten handsomely," Greenwood wrote, "and he himself would have passed out of the championship if his golf had not been of a superlative order."

Jones had no quarrel with these assessments. "Did you ever see a chap stick the way he did?" Jones, who had needed only sixty shots to play the 16 holes, asked Keeler when they met in Jones's room in the Grand Hotel. "They told me he was not so hot, but I can tell you one thing. If he had been two degrees hotter, I could not have handled him."

Roper returned home to a hero's welcome and could not resist romanticizing his moment of glory. What had he thought as he approached the first tee? Not to be ruffled, he said. "To play for all I am worth." For after all, he told reporters, "I am an Englishman."

If the match had gone only a little longer, he said, he would have won. "I was wearing him down. Jones was cutting his shots and when a golfer of his class does that you know you're going to get to him. It was my first taste of the big stuff, but it is not going to be my last."

But it was.

Down through the years, the story circulated among Roper's family and friends that Jones had been so impressed by his play that he encouraged him to try his luck in the United States. Jones might have said this in passing, but it would have been a brief conversation because Roper left St. Andrews the day after their match, and they never met again. In any case, Roper was in no position to act on the idea.

"There were hard times in the early 1930s, terrible poverty everywhere," says Harry Johnson, a pupil of Roper's who learned his lessons well enough to win the Notts County Amateur himself. "His buddies said, 'Look, you're making a few bob, has Bobby Jones guaranteed you any money?' And the story came back that he hadn't. I felt terribly sorry for the guy."

And so Roper stayed in Nottingham, where he played out of Woolaton Park and quickly got into trouble with the professional golf establishment. Disdaining the standard five-year apprenticeship during which a budding club pro was expected to learn the fine points of course maintenance and club repair—and to turn over a percentage of his income to the head professional—Roper signed a contract with a manufacturer of golf clubs and set up shop on his own.

"Sid refused because he was already making money," Johnson says. "He had complete sets of clubs in his locker, which he would sell to members and give lessons. This caused the head professional a certain amount of angst."

In the end, Roper was forced out and moved his operation to a building in Nottingham's historic Lace Market, where he set up a golf school in the basement and charged five shillings a lesson. There, with just enough space for a few golf clubs and a net to hit a ball into, Roper would sit on a stool wearing a trilby hat and giving instructions.

"It was a dungeon really," says Johnson. "He loved golf—he would have loved teaching on a golf course—and there he was stuck in a cellar. In those days, to go for a lesson was very undignified. To even practice was looked upon with scorn. You were supposed to go out and play and enjoy it. That was the British attitude about learning to play the game. We all went surreptitiously. We didn't want our pros to know we were going to see him."

After closing his shop for the day, Roper would adjourn to a nearby pub, where he would hold court and tell stories, such as the one about the time he was about to play an important shot in a tournament when out of nowhere a vendor suddenly appeared pushing a cart with a pile of oranges and asked if he would like to buy one. "I told him to kindly go away," Roper replied, "or words to that effect." Roper also would imitate with great accuracy, and a fair amount of cruelty, the swings of the various golfers to whom he had given lessons.

But despite his disappointments and his reduced circumstances, Roper had something useful to impart, something that kept alive, if only in his own mind and those of his pupils, the one great match of his life.

"Sometimes, I would sit on his stool and get him to swing," Johnson says. "That would be my lesson—I'd go out there and try to remember what he'd done. He taught one basic thing, that the golf swing is very simple. And he would prove it when he would stand there, address the ball and swing the club perfectly in slow motion. The way he swung the club was just like Bobby Jones."

In 1958, when Jones made a final emotional return to St. Andrews, he received, among a number of greetings from Britain's most famous golfers, a short telegram from Roper:

BEST WISHES, GOOD LUCK, GOOD HEALTH.

"I sincerely appreciate your thought," Jones wrote back, adding that he had thought many times of their match. "If I had not been very lucky to get that fast start, there would not have been any Grand Slam. It makes me shiver a little bit still to think of it."

Before the Amateur began, the R&A took the all but unprecedented step of issuing a flyer asking spectators to assist the marshals in their attempts to ensure fair play for the competitors. It did not help. Golf fans, holidaymakers, and the just plain curious flooded St. Andrews from all over Scotland. It was the 1927 British Open all over again, only more so.

During Jones's match with Roper, noted the *Scotsman*, "It was an affair charged with the big occasion atmosphere, super-charged when the American began his 'fireworks,' galloping spectators, and thunder of feet on the fairways, and the shouting of perspiring stewards. The moment the strokes were struck the crowd headed pell-mell along the course; the click of club on ball seemed to open invisible gates and release the human flood in which men, women and children ran as if for dear life, and the red gowns of University students ballooned in the breeze."

Eric Fiddian, who played a few holes ahead of Jones several times, recalled how difficult it was to compete in this atmosphere—for Jones and for everybody else. "The crowds were so enormous they came forward several holes to get in place so they could see him come by," Fiddian says. "They had no regard for anybody else at all. They would walk across the green while we were putting because all they were thinking about was getting a place either on the side of the green or the side of the tee."

"On other courses, stewards emit a constant and plaintive cry of 'Round the greens please,'" wrote Darwin. "At St. Andrews, the spectators march right over them, horse, foot and artillery. When they are watching play in the fifteenth, they would certainly tread right in the third hole if a steward did not stand over it with arms outspread in the attitude of one saying, 'Kill me, but spare the hole.' Sometimes they do not spare it."

"It is grotesque that a championship should be ruined for fully ninety percent of the players," complained a writer for the British magazine *Golf Monthly*. "We declare emphatically that large numbers of golfers who took part in the Amateur Championship were not accorded a fair chance. They are strong words, but the truth admits of no debate."

At times during the tournament, a few observers even expressed the unthinkable: St. Andrews, its narrow fairways unable to handle such large crowds, might no longer be suitable for championship golf.

The most difficult area for the golfers to negotiate was the narrow peninsula leading from the Eden Estuary, which contains the 8th and 9th holes leading out and the 10th and 11th coming back. Playing with Tony Torrance, a well-known British amateur, Fiddian stood on the 11th tee, where all they could see was the flag sticking up above the crowd in the middle of the green.

"What are we going to do?" Fiddian asked Torrance after a long wait.

"Well, we'll have to play," Torrance said.

"Of course, we had to hit somebody," Fiddian says. "Fortunately, nobody was hurt."

Over the years, the dozens of times spectators were hit by golf balls during the 1930 British Amateur would fade into memory until they were forgotten. With one exception.

After beating Roper, Jones spent a day off sightseeing in Edinburgh with Mary, and when they returned to St. Andrews he found completely different weather from what he had left behind, and a completely different opponent.

Cowan Shankland grew up in one of the first houses built near St. George's Hill Golf Club in Surrey, where his father was a member and that Darwin called one of the prettiest courses in England. Shankland joined the club at the tender age of nine and further developed his love of golf at Rossall, one of England's most exclusive boarding schools. He remained a member of the St. George's Hill for seventy-three years and a director for forty-nine. A stockbroker who lived a classic life of British privilege, Shankland test drove his friend W. O Bentley's new luxury automobiles; played high-stakes poker on Saturday afternoons; was an excellent shot; and, with his wife, Peggy, adjourned to Scotland every summer for salmon fishing on the Ness.

Shankland's good fortune against Jones was to catch him on a bad day. Shankland's bad luck was not being able to take advantage of it. Teeing off just after 8:00 A.M., the two men played through a cold west wind fierce enough to blow sand from the bunkers, and to have many of the spectators wearing woolen mittens and seeking shelter behind the dunes whenever there was a lull in play.

Jones, wearing two sweaters and blowing on his hands to keep them warm, needed forty strokes to navigate the front nine. The change in the speed and direction of the wind made St. Andrews a much harder course to play than two days earlier, he thought, but when Sid Roper got word of the match back home in Nottingham he could not help but wonder what might have happened had Jones shot 40 instead of 33 in the first half of *their* match. Even with this advantage, however, Shankland could not stay with Jones and lost, 4 and 3. The stage was set for the most anticipated match of the tournament that afternoon—Jones against Cyril Tolley, the defending Amateur champion.

The last time Jones had played Tolley at St. Andrews was in the 1926 Walker Cup, where Jones won, 12 and 11. It was the worst defeat of Tolley's career and is still the second-greatest margin in the history of the event's singles competition. But that match had been over 36 holes, while every round of the Amateur until the final would be 18. Though Jones no longer feared 18-hole matches the way he once did, he had to face reality. Any golfer could get hot—or cold—for one round, he thought, and Tolley was the most dangerous man he could possibly play over 18 holes at St. Andrews.

A tall, heavy bear of a man, Tolley was one of Britain's longest hitters—he drove the 350-yard 18th green at St. Andrews twice in one tournament—who also possessed a delicate touch on and around the greens. Jones admired his flair for the spectacular and thought he played the game like Hagen—"in the grand manner." And if Tolley's talent were not enough, he also was a national hero in more ways than one.

Playing in his first Amateur in 1920, Tolley leaped onto the golfing stage, and into legend, when he outlasted Robert Gardner in a match that went to a 37th hole, thereby preventing the tournament from being won by an American-born player for the first time. The story was often told that before making his long winning putt on the extra hole, Tolley had handed his caddy a £5 note, as if to guarantee that the match was about to end. Tolley never denied it, and those who played against him certainly thought it possible. "He was known for his gamesmanship," Fiddian remembers. "He would putt and walk off the green, leaving his opponent to wonder where he was going. It would unnerve them."

The British press and public were thrilled to their patriotic bones by Tolley's victory over Gardner and could not help but cast it in the light of recent events. "Every putt and every drive made by Mr. Tolley symbolized the vitality of British manhood, that vitality to which at bottom Germany owes her defeat," wrote the correspondent for the *Evening Standard*.

The fact that Tolley had actually fought in World War I burnished his victory to an even finer gloss, although his experiences were more out of *Hogan's Heroes* than *All Quiet on the Western Front*.

In 1917, Tolley was captured during a tank battle at Bourlon Wood in northern France and counted himself fortunate to be sent to one of Germany's showplace prisoner-of-war camps in Heidelberg. "I received very good treatment," he wrote. "We played tennis, hockey and rugger, had a cinema twice a week, a billiard room, and a theatre, where the English put on a show one week and the French one every alternate week."

Tolley's one regret was not having a chance to play on a six-hole golf course set up in the camp by a British army major. In the afternoons, a German officer would parade about, and the prisoners would try to hit him with a ball. The fact that nobody connected, he wrote, "rather points to the players being a little erratic."

Repatriated after the Armistice, Tolley went straight to the golf course and played his first round on Christmas Day. A few weeks later, he lost a tournament to Darwin and then entered Oxford, where he and Roger Wethered became the college team's mainstays and two of Britain's brightest young stars.

Several years after the 1930 British Amateur, the British mystery writer Gerard Fairley set a story in St. Andrews in which a murderer walks down the street unapprehended, blood dripping from his hands. His clean getaway is made possible by the fact that the entire population of the town is at the Old Course watching Bobby Jones play Cyril Tolley.

Though Darwin said the moments before the match began reminded him of "the lull before the storm in which men speak instinctively in whispers," the crowd did not remain decorous for long. A half holiday in the region, along with anticipation of the match, had brought what Darwin called an enormous rabble to St. Andrews, and the course simply could not handle it. Play often had to be held up as Jones and Tolley sat waiting for the stewards to try to make a path on the fairways or to clear the greens. They did their best, noted the *St. Andrews Citizen*, but they were like a broom trying to sweep away the Atlantic.

As for the other golfers playing that afternoon, they were on their own. "My opponent and I constantly got tangled up in their gallery," Fiddian remembers. "At the 16th, I had to stand guard over my drive to prevent the ball from being trampled into the ground." "The insignificant wretches who were trying to play their own insignificant matches played through, round or over a mob," Darwin wrote.

The only benefit anyone could see in this huge crowd was its occasional use as a windscreen for the players. The day had grown a little warmer since the chilly morning round, but the wind continued blowing out to sea with such force that neither man could be sure where his shots were headed. When Jones and Tolley hit with the wind behind them, the ball often flew over the green. Shots into the wind were blown back onto the fairway. The wind also had dried the greens, which had been scuffed up by other competitors and spectators to a glasslike quickness.

This was not a test of golf, Jones thought, but of resourcefulness and maneuvering. "I think we both have found something of the aesthetic in golf," he wrote, "but we would have none of it that day. I know I felt the same exaltation and desperate urgency I should expect to feel in a battle with broadswords or cudgels."

Jones took a quick lead when Tolley topped his initial drive into the road that crosses the 1st and 18th fairways. But Jones three-putted the second hole, and what Darwin called "a dogfight on a magnificent scale" was on. Fighting the wind, the crowd, and the pressure that wound tighter and tighter with each hole, they played a match that for drama, confusion, and thrust and parry back and forth has seldom been equaled.

Jones took the lead twice on the front nine and three times on the back, but Tolley battled back to tie him on the next hole every time. Tolley gained his only advantage at the fourth hole and kept it until Jones tied at the seventh. But though they were never more than a single hole apart, Jones could not escape the fear that he was losing. "All the way I had the uneasy conviction that he was hitting the ball better than I was," he said.

Tolley was certainly hitting it farther. He was longer off the tee on virtually every hole, never more so than at the 512-yard 14th, where he outdrove Jones by 100 yards and hit a 2-wood within six feet of the flag. When Jones's second shot was well short, he conceded Tolley an eagle that tied the match again.

But for every fine shot the two men hit, another went off line, or over the green, or into the crowd. Tolley said he hit spectators with his ball five times, while Jones did so with eight shots. George Greenwood counted half a dozen instances of Jones hitting people—Darwin said he saw three or four—while the *New York Times* and the Associated Press listed a number of examples of Jones hitting spectators: off someone's head and onto the 4th green; into the crowd and back out on the 5th fairway; off a member of the gallery and into the gorse at 9.

Jones took the lead for the fifth time with a birdie at 15, but Tolley again outdrove him by a long distance at the 16th, where Jones's tee shot landed in the Principal's Nose Bunker, in the middle of the fairway. Jones recovered, but missed a six-foot putt, and the match was tied once more. By the time they arrived at 17, St. Andrews' famous Road Hole, the crowd was immense and the golfers' nerves all but shot.

"We went through another match at the 16th without knowing they were playing," Tolley said. "It was the kind of match in which each player plays himself so completely out that at the end the only feeling to which he is sensitive is one of utter exhaustion," Jones wrote.

The wind had picked up at 17, and many in the crowd rushed around the corner of the dogleg hole to find a vantage point. Soon they were packed dozens deep out onto the road behind the green that gives the hole its name and backed up against a stone wall that marks the limit of the course. The windows and balconies of the buildings across the road were jammed, one observer noted, as if a royal parade were passing by.

Mindful of the wind, both men took care to place their drives out in the fairway, well to the left of the railway shed marking the right-hand turn to the green that golfers occasionally tried to shoot over in an attempt to shave distance off the hole's 461 yards. The balls bounded through the running crowds, with Tolley once again outdistancing Jones.

Standing in the crowd with Alister Mackenzie, Keeler had little doubt that Jones would do what he always did on his second shot at the Road Hole: lay up with an iron to the right of the green, then try to pitch close and get down in one putt. Jones had long since learned to take this cautious approach at St. Andrews—he had done so in all four rounds of the 1927 British Open—and for good reason. If he aimed for the hole and was short, the ball could land in the gaping Road Bunker built into the side of the hill in front of the green. If he hit his ball too hard, the ball could go over the green and onto the road.

But Keeler and Mackenzie were startled to see Jones climb a fairway mound and wave at the stewards down the course. Move the spectators back from behind the green, he gestured. He was going to hit in the direction where the crowd was standing—toward a swale in an open space *beyond* the green—and hope the ball would roll back down toward the hole.

Two things dictated Jones's change in strategy—the hard greens and the high winds that might carry his usual shot to the right out onto the road. He had never heard of anyone intentionally playing past the Road Bunker to the left, but he thought it made sense under the circumstances. He waited for the crowd to move from the green and the area beyond.

But the crowd did not budge. No amount of pushing or cajoling by the stewards could dislodge the spectators from their hard-won spots that gave such an excellent view of the action. After waiting for several minutes, there was nothing for Jones to do but what he and Tolley had done all day, and what so many other golfers had done throughout the tournament: hit the ball and hope for the best. Jones took his 4-iron and swung.

From the instant the ball took flight, Keeler could see that Jones had hit it too hard and too far to the right. The pressure had gotten to him, he thought. Jones's only question as he nervously watched the flight of the ball was how much he had overswung and how far it would carry past the green. The ball bounced high off the hard surface of the green straight at the crowd, where it struck a raincoat dangling from a spectator's arm and fell to the edge, some ten yards from the hole. It was a colossal piece of luck.

"But for the obliging spectator," wrote Greenwood, "the ball must surely have dived on to the road beyond, where anything could have happened." Other observers said the ball was headed not toward the road, but onto the 18th fairway. All agreed, however, it would have gone well past the green, and Jones would have been in big trouble.

"A line from an old romantic novel hopped into my head," Keeler wrote as he saw the ball come to rest on the green: 'Men call it fate!'"

In the years to come, the legend would grow that Jones had intentionally hit the ball into the crowd as a way of keeping it from going over the green. In 1957, an eyewitness named Harry Andrews wrote in the *Glasgow Sunday Express* that Jones had seen Tolley's second shot land in a good position in front of the green and asked his caddy, "Can I trust the crowd?"

"Man," came the reply, "they canna move."

There are several problems with this account. The first is that Tolley outdrove Jones off the 17th tee, so Jones was the first to hit a second shot. The second is that Andrews says Jones's shot wound up twelve feet from the flag, whereas the closest contemporary account had it three times as far away.

"That was very definitely not the case," Jones wrote of Andrews's accusation. "I should never have been so heedless of the possibility of inflicting injury upon a spectator."

Andrews's story is finally undone by the fact that Tolley's second shot landed not in a good position but a bad one. Stunned by Jones's good fortune, Tolley attempted to clear the bunker and land his ball on the green near Jones's. It was a desperation move, Jones thought, something only to be attempted from Tolley's distant position on the fairway when the match was on the line.

Worried about hitting into the road beyond the green, Tolley flinched, and the ball landed just short of the Road Bunker. He had lost his gamble and now had to hit a shot hard enough to climb over the steep bunker yet gently enough so it would not bounce off the unforgiving green, which sloped downhill, toward the road. Keeler thought the match was as good as over. No man alive, he was sure, could clear the bunker and land close enough to the hole to get down in one putt. "In the road likely—never near the flag."

He was mistaken. Standing in front of the bunker and looking at the fluttering flag above, Tolley eased a 5-iron over the top of the hill with no room to spare. The ball rolled slowly down and came to rest inches from the hole. It was, Tolley would always say, the best shot he ever hit in his life.

Jones was dumbstruck. Never, he wrote, had he seen Tolley's shot surpassed for exquisitely beautiful execution. He would carry the memory to his grave. With one shot, the match had turned completely around. From being an almost certain winner, Jones, whose first putt rolled some eight feet from the cup, was now in danger of losing the hole. But he made the putt, and Tolley his tap-in. The match remained tied. All but limp with the pressure after as tense a hole as Jones had ever played, the two men went to 18, where more agony awaited.

Jones's tee shot was off to the left—Darwin says he hit another spectator—and his second landed twenty-five feet past the hole. Tolley played within half that distance and, after Jones's putt came up short, found himself putting for the match. Thinking of Tolley's penchant for heroics, and his long putt that beat Robert Gardner in their playoff at the 1923 Amateur, Jones went through "the most agonizing moments of that entire year. I fully expected him to hole this one and there was nothing I could do about it."

Tolley missed.

After 18 holes, the match was tied in every conceivable way. Jones had won six holes, Tolley had won six, and six had been halved.

Both men had shot 75. The crowd fled down the first fairway for the playoff.

Tolley outdrove Jones, but his second shot flew off line to the left. His chip to the green landed seven feet below the hole, where Jones's second shot also lay, ten feet from the cup. Jones saw his chance and quickly seized it. It was not as important for him to sink the putt, he realized, as it was not to overrun the hole. If he could keep his ball between Tolley's and the cup, the Englishman would be stymied. Putting carefully, he left his ball a few inches short, directly in Tolley's path.

Though the stymie was not finally eliminated from the rule book until the 1950s, golfers had hated it for centuries. It was unfair, those who agitated against it maintained, that a player should be able to win a tournament by blocking his opponent's path to the hole. But the guardians of golf, who defended the stymie as an integral part of the game, could not be moved, especially since the alternative was lifting the ball, an abomination that could lead to such outrages as "surreptitious cleaning" and "inaccurate misplacement."

"Golf over a perfectly level space, with no rough, no hazards, no trees and no stymies would be little more than knocking the ball around," one editorialist noted. Darwin, calling himself "a true blue Tory," was all in favor of retaining it. So was Jones, who objected to its removal from the game until the end of his life.

Down on his hands and knees, Tolley spoke with his caddy, then stood up and took the only course open to him: try to chip a shot over Jones's ball. He did not have a chance. A match for the ages had ended with Tolley forced to attempt an impossible trick shot and failing.

"I am sorry, Cyril," Jones said as Tolley shook his hand. "That was a bad, a cruel, finish. The gods were with me."

"I left myself open by loose play," Tolley said. "It is the fortune of war."

For all that he championed the stymie, Jones could not help but regret that his thrilling match with Tolley had ended anticlimactically. "I'm sorry it ended in a stymie," he wrote, "but I fancy it's just as well that it did. It was as hard a match as I ever played in. The great battle had ended and the release from tension was almost unbearable. I was neither exalted nor elated, just very, very tired."

In 1950, Cyril Tolley, age fifty-four, returned to the British Amateur at St. Andrews. Though he could no longer drive any of the greens at the Old Course where he and Jones had created such excitement twenty years earlier, he was still a compelling figure as he strolled the familiar fairways, a pipe in his mouth and a contented smile on his face. He also was capable of winning through to the semifinals, where he gave the powerful young American golfer Frank Stranahan, who would go on to win his second Amateur title, an excellent match before finally losing.

Jones had two more easy matches before making the final, and two in which, once again, he came agonizingly close to losing.

In his fifth-round match against George Watt, a clerk in a Dundee jute mill who seldom played in competition anywhere but at the magnificent triumvirate of links near his home—St. Andrews, Carnoustie, and Monifieth—Jones shot six threes in a row from the 6th through the 11th greens and won, 7 and 6. "People often ask me how I felt," Watt said in an interview years later. "I'll tell you. I felt I was being slaughtered."

For twenty-year-old Eric Fiddian, who had won Britain's Boys' Championship in 1927, the highlight of his quarter-final match with Jones came on the first green. After teeing off, Jones was swallowed up by the crowd, and when Fiddian reached the green with two shots, he saw his ball lying not far from Jones's. Fiddian was then startled to hear his caddy say, "He's played three, sir."

Jones had mishit his tee shot into the mud of the Swilcan Burn and, rather than try to pitch out, had taken a drop at the cost of a stroke. Both men two-putted, and the referee loudly announced, "Mr. Fiddian, one-up."

Fiddian would have many fine experiences in golf in the years to come, including a trip to Brookline for the 1932 Walker Cup, but that moment would remain vivid in his memory seventy-three years later. "It doesn't sound like much now," Fiddian says, "but at that moment it was quite something, wasn't it? One-up on Bobby Jones. Imagine."

The moment did not last long, as Fiddian hit into a bunker at the second hole and Jones tied the match. By the time they made the turn he was four-up and, though Fiddian played him shot for shot thereafter, and even won another hole, Jones coasted to a 4 and 3 victory.

Jones's victories over Harrison Johnston in the sixth round and George Voight in the semifinal were far more complicated.

Against Johnston, who as a nineteen-year-old doughboy had gone to France where he had been gassed on the battlefield, and whose career had been crowned by his victory in the 1929 U.S. Amateur, Jones was coasting along nicely and leading by four holes with five to play. "No one could blame me, I think, for feeling fairly comfortable at this stage," he wrote. Nor could anyone blame the spectators for drifting away to other matches and leaving behind a clearer view of the action than in previous days for those who remained.

"I see you girls have not begun fighting yet," Keeler told Mary Jones and Betty Johnston when he saw them sitting together early in the match and watching their husbands play.

"Why, we're going to Paris as soon as this cruel war is over," Betty Johnston said.

But over the closing holes, the match quickly heated up. Johnston hit a long second shot close to the flag at 14, and Jones missed a four-foot putt at the 15th. His four-hole lead was down to two with three holes to play.

Johnston kept the match alive with a nine-foot putt for a half at the 16th and, needing to win the final two holes to have a chance to tie, had no choice but to aim for the Road Hole green from the fairway. His shot landed some ten feet from the cup, and he won the hole. "There was no possible answer to such a thrust," Darwin wrote. Jones came to the 18th leading by one.

Hearing the news, the crowd raced for a vantage point at the home green, and several spectators fell into the Swilcan Burn.

Johnston's second shot ran to the upper left-hand corner of the green, about thirty yards from the pin. Jones all but duplicated it, his ball landing a few yards closer to the pin.

Johnston kept the pressure on by sending his putt dead to the hole, and Jones's touch suddenly deserted him. His approach curled up eight feet short of victory.

Standing on the balcony of the Grand Hotel, George Von Elm told Francis Ouimet, "Bobby has holed hundreds of putts like that one. He will pop that in."

Jones was not so sure. Facing what he would later call the longest eight-foot putt he had ever seen, and taking Johnston's great charge over the previous five holes into account, Jones was certain that if the match went to a playoff, he would lose. "You know how it is when a chap gets his tail up," he told Keeler afterward. "He can do anything and you can't stop him."

Jones's putt negotiated the break of the green perfectly and dropped into the center of the cup. He had never been happier to see one fall in his life.

The huge crowd that gathered to see Jones play George Voight in the semifinal on the afternoon of Friday, May 30, got a glimpse of what was in store at the 1st hole when, after Voight sank a twenty-five-foot downhill putt for a birdie, Jones responded with a fifteen-footer of his own.

Voight, one of the finest American amateurs of the time—he had won his Walker Cup singles match 10 and 8 earlier in the month—entered the match thoroughly satisfied with the way he was playing in the tournament. Jones came to the first tee drunk.

Despite his easy victory over Fiddian in the morning round, Jones was terribly nervous about the last 18-hole match standing between him and the final of the one major tournament he had never won. He also was still desperately tired. Perhaps a glass of sherry during the long lunch break would help, he told Mary. He dared not risk anything stronger. They went to the sitting room on the second floor of the Grand Hotel overlooking the 18th green and sipped their drinks.

"I could not have made a greater mistake," Jones wrote. "Wine flushed my face and caused me to be very keenly aware that my eyes were the slightest bit out of focus. I began to get panicky as the starting time approached and the condition continued. I have never gone into a match with as much fear."

Jones's ability to hold his liquor had always awed his contemporaries. "He had a water glass of corn whiskey and he polished it off between rounds," Harry Cooper said of playing with him at the Masters. "But he was always the same. You never knew he'd had a drink. How he did it, I don't know."

"He loved that stuff," said Toney Penna, who once drove up from Pensacola, Florida, with a jug of bootleg corn whiskey he had been told Jones particularly liked. "When I brought that out there, hell, I could have bought Bobby Jones for five cents. He'd just sip it like he was sipping a soda."

Jones never saw the harm. "Playing an exhibition match," he wrote, "I eat—and drink—whatever I please between rounds and seem none the worse for it." Once, he said, he was served "five or six pleasant-tasting cocktails" between rounds of an exhibition and was reeling when he got back to the course. He shot a 66.

His match against Voight was no exhibition, of course, but still, one drink? There was only one explanation: Jones was a nervous wreck.

The effects of the drink lasted through the first half of the match, and it was Jones's putting, which had never been more reliable all week than against Fiddian in the morning round, that suffered most. He missed a five-foot putt at the 5th hole; a three-footer at the 7th; and another, from five feet, at the 8th. "No one of them would have been criminal, but his aggregate of misses was decidedly criminal," Darwin wrote. "If Jones had lost, and, upon my word, I doubt if he deserved to win, he would have had his putting to thank." Still, Jones was out-driving Voight and managed to win two holes. They made the turn tied with one-over-par 37s. It could have been worse.

At the par-3 11th, Jones hit his tee shot over the green, took a bogey, and trailed Voight for the first time. At 13, where Jones's second shot was short of the green, the crowd gasped as his pitch to the hole traveled only ten yards. "Surely we weren't seeing straight," Guy C. Campbell wrote in the *New York Times*.

For the first time in the tournament, Jones was trailing an opponent by two holes—only Tolley and Fiddian had led by one—and there were just five holes left to play. "I resolved to swallow my medicine, whatever it might be," Jones wrote.

As the players approached the 14th tee, Ouimet, who was in the gallery, noticed that the wind, which had been unusually calm all afternoon, had blown in from the sea across the course. But with the crowd pressed in tightly around the tee, Voight could not feel the change. He played what he hoped would be a safe shot to the right, only to see the ball drift over a stone wall to his right, as if it were a balloon, and land out of bounds. Saved for the second time in the tournament by the crowd, Jones hit his tee shot well to the left and won the hole.

"Never was a gift so unexpected nor so eagerly accepted," Jones wrote. "With that one stroke I was hauled back into the golf game."

Voight drove into the Principal's Nose Bunker on the 16th fairway, and though he made a great recovery within twenty feet of the hole, his putt rolled around the lip of the cup. The match was tied.

The crowd raced to the 17th, where Jones laid up short of the Road Bunker while Voight boldly went for the green and made the front edge, many yards short of the hole. Jones's approach was good, landing twelve feet from the hole, but Voight seized the advantage when his long approach crawled up to the lip of the hole. "As fine a runup as ever was played or ever will be," Darwin wrote. "Stone dead."

And there Jones was, facing a twelve-foot putt to end all twelve-foot putts. Make it and the match would remain tied. Miss it and he would trail by a hole with one remaining. Jones walked around behind the ball, judging every angle. He's taking a long time, Ouimet thought. No customary quick squint and a putt for him now. He's not going to make it, Voight thought. He can't.

What was it? Jones wondered as he assessed the feeling that came over him. Was it the many crucial situations he had faced so far in the tournament? Was it the fact that he had come out ahead in every one of them? It didn't matter. All he knew was that he could see the path from the ball to the cup as plainly as if it had been marked on the green with a piece of chalk. He knew it for a certainty. The putt was going into the hole.

Never a doubt, Voight thought ruefully as the ball found the center of the cup. The crowd roared and raced up the 18th fairway.

Both tee shots were good, and then Jones got one more lucky break. Voight found himself without the club he wanted for his second shot. A 5-iron was too much club, he thought, but he had no 6-iron or 7-iron in his bag. An 8-iron would have to do.

Voight's shot was short, landing on the lower slope of the green and rolling back down to the Valley of Sin at the bottom, some eighty feet away. Jones's second shot, by contrast, was brilliant, landing six feet from the flag. The crowd rushed past him to surround the green and applaud him on to the final.

Even when Voight made another excellent approach shot, to within three feet, the match appeared over. A victory shout began to swell in the crowd as Jones's putt crept closer and closer to the hole. But it turned into a gasp when the ball stopped on the rim of the cup, one turn short of dropping in. Voight still had a chance to maintain the tie.

I don't want to be here, Voight thought as he judged the short putt he needed to send the match to a playoff. Well, I can't just stand here looking at it—that will just make me more nervous. One more quick look and then I'm hitting it.

The ball rolled around the lip of the cup and stayed out. Voight threw his arm around Jones's shoulders seconds before they were engulfed by the cheering crowd.

Roger Wethered never had a chance.

With victory now within reach, and competing over 36 holes, at last Jones could relax and enjoy the match he had been waiting for. A match in which he could just play his game and wait for his opponent to self-destruct.

Which Wethered did soon enough. Though he played well for nine holes—both men needed only thirty-five shots in the first half of the morning round—his driving quickly deserted him. Jones won five of the first seven holes on the back nine and led by four as they broke for lunch.

But for a missed four-foot putt on the Road Hole, Jones would have been the first golfer ever to play a tournament round at St. Andrews without a five on his scorecard. He was playing at his automatic best—drive, pitch, putt dead to the hole. The end was just a matter of time.

Jones was hardly surprised. For one thing, he had beaten Wethered 9 and 8 in their Walker Cup singles match earlier in the month. And though Wethered, along with Tolley, was one of the great names in British golf—he had won the Amateur in 1923—Jones could never understand his casual approach to the game.

In 1921, the year of Jones's calamitous withdrawal from the British Open at St. Andrews, Wethered had quite surprisingly tied Jock Hutchison after four rounds to force a playoff. Jones could hardly believe his ears when he heard Wethered telling friends he was thinking of defaulting the title because he had agreed to play in a village cricket match back home.

"Our arguments finally prevailed," Jones said, "but remembering the little session convinced me that Roger thought golf championships were very nice things, but it was plain that he did not want to win them so badly as I did. I honestly felt that Roger himself had very little hope of winning. I was not even certain that he cared."

Jones was more impressed by Roger's sister, with whom he played in a foursome shortly before the Amateur began. Joyce Wethered was a four-time winner of the British Ladies' Championship, and her game all but mesmerized him. "She did not half miss one shot," Jones said. "I have no hesitancy in saying she is the best golfer I have ever seen." Others, Darwin among them, agreed. Joyce Wethered, it was said, had the most nearly perfect swing in all of golf.

As for her powers of concentration, the story was told of a championship match between Wethered and Cecil Leitch during which a train whistle hooted out across the course just as she was addressing a crucial putt. Asked afterward how she had been able to concentrate, Wethered asked, "What train?"

For Roger Wethered, by contrast, golf was more of an intellectual exercise. When he and Joyce were youngsters in Surrey, he would pore through books in the library of their father, the golf writer and course architect H. N. Wethered, looking in the index for such subjects as "Putting, slice in: how to avoid."

"Oh, Joyce, you will never play golf. You won't study the game,"

Roger would tell his sister, who felt the chastisement was rather severe for an eleven-year-old girl.

The audience for the morning round had been barely manageable, but as the Saturday touring buses, trains, and cars rolled into town, a crowd estimated at fifteen thousand, the largest in St. Andrews history, jammed the Old Course for the final holes.

But it was a sparkling day and, since there was an air of inevitability rather than excitement, the spectators were a bit more subdued than previously in the tournament. Baby carriages, elderly spectators, and entire families were in Jones's entourage, including one father who, in his excitement, raced down the course holding an infant upside down.

Jones's victory lap did not take long to complete. Wethered won the first hole on a stymie, but Jones immediately returned the favor. He won the seventh and eighth as well and led by six holes at the turn.

The end came at 12, where, as the crowd held its breath, Jones sent his first putt inches from the hole. Wethered missed a three-footer and quickly walked over to Jones, his hand extended in congratulations.

The gallery was there with him.

The pent-up emotion of an afternoon of relative calm gave way to pandemonium as spectators rushed to the green, bent on getting near, or touching, Bobby Jones. One man standing at the edge of a bunker was pushed into the sand and trampled by the eager crowd. For a moment it appeared that Jones might be knocked around himself.

"Francis, please look after Roger," Jones called out to Ouimet, who, along with Von Elm, had served as marshals. Ouimet was more concerned for his friend's safety and tried to help protect him. Four large Scottish policemen pushed their way through the crowd and joined hands to form a barrier around Jones. He looks like a dangerous prisoner, George Greenwood thought as the officers moved off down the course with their precious cargo in tow.

It was a scene never before witnessed at St. Andrews. The policemen surrounding Jones slowly began forcing their way through the crowd in a jubilant march down the entire length of the golf course. Cheered all the way, the party made its way down the 18th fairway as

Jones looked up to the second-floor balcony of the Grand Hotel where Mary stood waving.

Back home in Atlanta, Jones's friend Chick Ridley, who had gone to the offices of the *Atlanta Journal* at dawn to read the hole-by-hole accounts of the tournament arriving by telegraph—"I couldn't sleep anyway," he said—called Jones's father with the news.

"I'm mighty happy, that's all I can say," the Colonel would say later as clerks and stenographers at his law office cheered. Special editions of the paper appeared on the streets, and customers cheered the newsboys who carried them.

At East Lake, caddies shouted out the news from hole to hole, while in New York, Stewart Maiden said, "It's great that the boy has now won all the major titles there are, but it's sad in a way, too, for there's nothing left for him to win."

From Tokyo, where he was barnstorming, Walter Hagen cabled that he was "highly elated that Bobby finally crashed through and rounded out a collection of crowns such as no other golfer had ever acquired."

NBC contacted Keeler and asked him to do the first transatlantic broadcast of a sporting event—the upcoming British Open—from the BBC's studios in Liverpool. Darwin agreed to perform the same service for his countrymen.

Before accepting the trophy, Jones met with reporters in his suite. Without exception, they noted how tired he looked. "He was pale and worn, and his usually immaculately brushed hair was tousled," wrote Fred Pignon in *Golf Monthly*. "The smile which seems to play forever about his features had gone, and the face looked lined and seared now after the weeks of strain and triumph had come."

A few minutes later, Jones stepped out on the balcony of the R&A clubhouse for an awards ceremony that was amplified so it could be heard by the huge crowd that had gathered down the length of the first and 18th fairways, and those standing in the windows of the neighboring houses and hotels. He had never worked harder to win a tournament, Jones said, or suffered more.

Jones would never change that assessment. The 1930 British Amateur was a tournament like no other: 140-yard eagles from the fairway, missed 3-foot putts, balls being hit into the crowd that saved him, sensational back-against-the-wall shots by his opponents, whom he would then go on to beat anyway.

Somehow Jones found a way to write a short article for the Bell Syndicate in which he put a pleasant face on his week-long ordeal. "Isn't it great to think I'll have nothing to do tomorrow," he said.

His words to Keeler were more revealing.

"I'm awfully, awfully tired," he said as he prepared to move on to the British Open. "I don't care what happens now."

16

The British Open:
Great Men of Hoylake

In the second half of the eighteenth century, as many as three-quarters of the ships carrying African slaves from Europe to America left from Liverpool. In all, about 1.5 million slaves began the final leg of their bitter journey from its docks.

"All of the great old Liverpool families were more or less steeped in the slave trade," an author wrote under the pseudonym "Dicky Sam" in 1884. Many of these wealthy merchants built their mansions across the Mersey River in a small fishing village on the Irish Sea named Hoylake.

Hoylake remained a bedroom community for the Liverpool elite until after World War II, when many of the great houses were torn down, or converted into apartments or retirement centers. Today the town is an unprepossessing home to many elderly people that, except for a lively Friday night bar scene along Market Street, sends its younger residents to Liverpool to find their fun.

In 1849, the Liverpool Royal Hunt Club held flat races and steeplechases along the sea on open land that also served as a rabbit warren. Twenty years later, the *Liverpool Courier* reported that "the usual quietude of Hoylake was broken by two events out of the ordinary common run of amusements. These were amateur horse and pony races, and, what is likely to prove of much more abiding interest, the Scottish national game of golf was played."

The golf course and the racetrack shared the grounds for seven years, and in 1885 the Royal Liverpool Golf Club, by now headquartered at Hoylake, held an informal tournament open to all amateur golfers in England and Scotland. It was so successful that the Royal and Ancient staged the first official British Amateur championship at St. Andrews the following year.

Hoylake produced three of the country's finest golfers: John Ball, who won eight Amateur titles; Harold Hilton, who won four British Opens, two British Amateurs, and a U.S. Amateur; and Jack Graham, by common consent the best British golfer to die in World War I. Bernard Darwin called them the great men of Hoylake.

While the club's annual Spring Meeting in the 1870s brought together the best of the country's professional and amateur golfers for a week of spirited competition and great conviviality, to many minds there was something off-putting about the course itself. The flat plot of land stretching out to the sea seemed unappealing even to local residents when it was first marked out for golf. Jack Morris, who became the club's first professional in 1869 and remained on the job for sixty years, noted that "the rabbits did all the green-keeping and except on Saturday nobody came there to disturb them."

Once, looking out over an empty golf course and seeing some human figures far off in the distance, Morris told John Ball, "They don't look like golfers."

"Dang it!" Ball replied. "Who would come here *except* to play golf?"

As late as 1951, Patric Dickinson, who had been poetry editor for the BBC, wrote of Hoylake, "It is depressing to find on seeing it for the first time that it is utterly flat and dreary to look at, and for all the infinite subtleties to be discovered it remains rather formidably unattractive." Playing Hoylake, Dickinson said, was "a three-hour sermon in a gaunt building, all white-washed walls and black-clad sinners."

Even Darwin, who played at Hoylake for more than half a century, admitted that the course looked "dull and rather mean" and that "to the superficial eye Hoylake with its ugly red villas may not be a place of beauty." Still, Darwin called himself a Hoylake patriot who loved "every cop of it and every breeze that blows across it." Anyone who dislikes the course, he wrote, "has effectually written himself down as an ass."

The one thing no one could deny Hoylake was its place in history. The rules of amateur golf were codified there, and the course has hosted more than a score of British Open and Amateur championships. Today, its ivy-covered clubhouse, a three-story building with jutting eaves and multiple chimney pots, contains so many portraits of Hoylake's greatest sons, and so many of their medals, cups, balls, and clubs, it could easily pass as a golf museum.

Over the years, Hoylake partisans became so protective of its traditions that when it fell into disrepair after World War I, they greeted plans to modernize it with horror. "Shouts rent the air!" wrote club historian Guy B. Farrar. "'Old Hoylake' was being desecrated, natural features were being removed, and holes that had become old friends were being replaced by hateful examples of modern course architecture."

Some remnants of Old Hoylake would always remain, however, as the field for the 1930 British Open discovered when it arrived in June. Local Rule Number 1, according to the tournament's official program, allowed the removal of any ball landing in a rabbit hole, at the cost of one stroke.

In the end, the pull Hoylake exerts on those who consider it the capital of English golf becomes a matter not of old versus new, of physical beauty or of competitive subtleties, but of memory.

"Whatever anyone may say," Darwin wrote, "Hoylake can look lovely, when you are out practising all by yourself somewhere near the sand-hills, when the summer dusk is coming on and the lights are beginning to twinkle in the houses."

.   .   .

George Greenwood was the first to print it.

"I am persuaded that Bobby Jones has in view the biggest coup ever dreamed of in golf—the winning of four national championships, two British and two American," Greenwood wrote in the *Daily Telegraph* on the day the qualifying rounds for the British Open began. "It is an incredibly ambitious scheme, one that if associated with the name of any other golfer would be laughed to scorn. But in the case of an outstanding genius such as Jones anything seems possible."

Not to Jones it didn't. As the Open approached, he was feeling distinctly out of sorts. All of a sudden he had no idea how and where to hit the ball. The trouble, he said, was not in his hands but in his head. He had never felt less self-confident at the beginning of a tournament.

Jones shot a lackluster 73 in his qualifying round at the nearby Wallasey course and a 77 at Hoylake the following day. The latter, he said, was the worst round of golf he had ever played in Britain. It left him buried in twentieth place among the qualifiers. Let others declare the Open was Jones against the field. Let the British bookmakers install him at the ridiculously low odds of 4–1. Jones did not like the way he felt, did not like the way he was playing, and did not much care for Hoylake, either.

"Singularly lacking in subtleties," Jones wrote of the course where he had shot an embarrassing 86 against E. A. Hamlet and lost the British Amateur to Allan Graham nine years earlier. "The whole course is there for the player to see, and I should think that the first time around he ought to know as much about it as he could ever learn."

The only thing that did please Jones was being back in Britain after his trip to Paris with Mary and Harrison and Betty Johnston. After all that rich French food, he thought as the boat steamed back across the English Channel, it would be good to get back to cold mutton and boiled potatoes.

Working in Jones's favor was that the field for the Open was not especially strong. Walter Hagen, Gene Sarazen, Tommy Armour, and Johnny Farrell had not made the trip. The top American amateurs, Johnston and George Voight, had gone home after the Walker Cup. George Von Elm stayed behind but shot 81 in the first round. Cyril Tolley eliminated himself with an 84.

That left only a handful of golfers with a realistic chance of winning, all of them professionals. From the United States there were Leo Diegel, Jim Barnes, Horton Smith, and Macdonald Smith, all mainstays of the PGA tour. From Britain there were Fred Robson, Archie Compston, Henry Cotton, Abe Mitchell, and perhaps one or two others. And whatever Jones's misgivings about Hoylake, it was to his advantage to play on a course that was built for long hitters and did not easily surrender low scores. If he could hit the ball consistently in the fairway and make his putts, there was no reason why he should not win.

The gallery promised to be less of a problem, too, as it would be restrained to some extent at least in the traditional Hoylake manner, with squads of blue-shirted fishermen, many of them bearded old men, stretching coils of rope down the course. He would love to see them imported to America, Keeler wrote. "I was not trampled, knocked down or gored and the competitors got a square deal."

The fishermen could not keep the crowds from running from hole to hole, though, and Jones, who had taken the galleries at St. Andrews in stride, finally lost his hard-won composure. During his qualifying round at Wallasey, he called out to ask spectators not to cross the green. Several times early in the first round, he backed off his swing and glared at people making noise or taking pictures.

"Ladies and gentlemen, will you *please* stand still till both of us have holed out," Jones cried out after bogeying the first hole of the tournament as his playing partner, Raymond Oppenheimer, stood over a three-foot putt while the crowd fled to the second fairway. The spectacle of Jones snapping at the crowd was one more indication of the state of his nerves.

Jones drove poorly at the start and lost two strokes in the first three holes, which were among the easiest on the course. Then, without warning, he was Bobby Jones again. His drives flew straight down the fairway; his approach shots found the green; and his putts dropped, at least the short ones. "You could cover the ball and the hole with a derby hat," Keeler wrote of Jones's approach putts— which was one way of saying that his longer birdie attempts were not quite dropping.

Finishing just in time to beat a thunderstorm that drenched the field behind him, Jones posted six threes and a score of 70, which tied him with Henry Cotton and Macdonald Smith for the lead. Cotton, a twenty-three-year-old professional who had taken up golf as a schoolboy when, as a punishment, he had been forbidden to play cricket, performed brilliantly in the rain before faltering on the final holes. Smith, a popular Carnoustie native who had immigrated to the United States years earlier, brought the crowds running by shooting 33 on the front nine until he, too, faded.

Back at his hotel in Liverpool, Jones was startled to pick up an afternoon paper and discover he had come within a shot of the course record. But for a five-footer that teetered on the edge of the cup at the 15th hole and refused to fall, he would have tied it. Considering his state of mind and his shaky start, he had played well.

But more trouble was waiting on the opening holes of the second round the following day. A hooked second shot at the first led to a bogey. Then, rather than lay up from a lie in the rough 250 yards from the second hole, Jones went for the green and wound up in thick, high grass. Hacking out, he was lucky to get away with a second bogey. It was the worst error in judgment he had ever seen him make, Greenwood thought. "I cannot for the life of me get past them," Jones said later of his second straight failure over the first three undemanding holes, where he was now four over par in two days. "The dreadful thing is I have to play them twice tomorrow."

But once again Jones righted himself, made the turn at 37, and came in with a 72. It was a battle all the way, though, as he needed to make long putt after long putt to keep his score from getting away from him. "It was one of the hardest rounds I ever had to play," he said. "I hope it is over and done with."

Cotton and Macdonald Smith had not fared as well. The Englishman hooked drive after drive, shot a 79, and was effectively out of the tournament. In the years to come, he would win three British Opens; battle his country's golf establishment over its shabby treatment of professionals; become a distinguished golf journalist; and, a few days before he died in 1987, be awarded a knighthood. Smith shot 77 and was five strokes behind Jones going into the 36-hole final day of the tournament. The only golfers at all close to him at the start of the round who had played well were Robson and Horton Smith, who were one and three shots, respectively, behind him. The tournament was Jones's to win.

Friday morning was sunny and windless. With the greens softened up after two days of rain and the players able to shoot straight at the flags, Hoylake was playing at its most benign. But not for Jones. After getting a lucky bounce off a wall of turf—a Hoylake eccentricity known as a cop—and managing to save his par, Jones pitched into a bunker fronting the second green for a bogey, then out of bounds at the third for another. His three-round total for the first three holes was now six over par.

But once again, Jones settled down for the remainder of the front
nine and made the turn at 37. By the time he came to the 14th hole
for the difficult finishing stretch that had treated him so kindly in the
first two rounds, a 71 or a 72, and a comfortable lead going into the
final round, seemed well within reach.

And then he heard the noise—a series of huge roars coming from
well behind him on the golf course, where Archie Compston was
making his move.

"You could trace the blond giant's progress about the links by the
blasts of cheering that swept like a hurricane across the dunes and
burst like a bombshell over the clubhouse," Keeler wrote of Compston. A British writer seconded the motion. Archie Compston, thirty-
seven years old and six-foot-five, was playing like a frenzied giant.

Compston had teed off half an hour behind Jones and, with
birdies on the 2nd, 3rd, and 4th holes, had quickly made up five shots.
With the shouts of the crowd ringing in his ears, he and Jones were
suddenly tied. Even when Compston drove under a gorse bush at the
5th and took a double bogey, his momentum was halted only briefly.
He got one stroke back at the 8th, began the back nine with three
threes and a two, and took the lead.

Jones, in the meantime, began hitting bunkers and missing putts.
The closing holes, which had saved his previous rounds, were now
exacting their revenge. With four fives in the final five holes, the 71 or
72 he had been hoping for became a 74. He went to the clubhouse to
watch Compston finish his round. It was not an encouraging sight.
Driving with precision and knocking in putt after putt, Compston was
playing like a man possessed and feeding off the crowd, which was as
delighted as it was surprised.

"I can still see the awesome figure made by Compston toward the
finish of his round," Jones wrote. He was "truly striding after the ball
as though he could hardly wait to vent his fury upon it. As I saw him
sweep past the sixteenth green, I had the feeling that spectators, tee
boxes, benches even, might be swirled up in his wake."

By now, rumors had reached the clubhouse that even the most
hopeful British observers could scarcely believe. But they were true
enough: Compston had come to the 16th five shots under par. A
birdie at that par-5 hole, which was certainly not out of the question,
would put him in position to break the course record by *four shots*!

Even when Compston bogeyed the 16th after hitting his second shot out of bounds and stabbing at a two-foot putt that missed, he was in high spirits. "Never mind, I wanted to be two up on the little man, but I shall be one up," he said. He parred the last two holes and pushed through the cheering crowd to the clubhouse. "To those who do not know Hoylake," wrote Greenwood, "I can only describe it as a staggering performance."

He had never seen a happier man in his life, thought Jones, who had given up six shots and the lead to a man who, with a 68, had broken the Hoylake record by two strokes. Compston continued accepting congratulations as Jones returned to the course to begin his final round.

Archie Compston was as Bunyanesque a figure as British golf ever produced. Tall tales of his exploits on and off the golf course abounded, and the stories that were verifiable were just as outlandish as those that were probably apocryphal.

Born in Staffordshire, where he signed on as an assistant to a club pro at age sixteen, Compston went on to win a number of tournaments and become a member of four British Ryder Cup teams. But the crowning moment of his career, one that raised him to mythic proportions in Britain, came in 1928 when he beat Walter Hagen in a 72-hole match-play challenge at Moor Park Golf Club north of London for a purse of £750. Hagen, who had not played much for several months and had just arrived from New York on the *Aquitania*, trailed by 14 shots after the first day and lost by the astonishing score of 18 and 17. It was, he said, the worst beating of his life.

The British public was thrilled by Compston's victory—"Hagen Submerged!" "Hagen's Ghost Is Laid!" "Hagen Takes His Physic!" were some of the headlines—and the *Morning Post* wrote, "It is an event that must be dear and refreshing to a British golfer's heart, which for a long time has been uncheered by any challenge to American ascendancy."

Hagen was equally impressed by the way Compston profited from the victory. There were so many newspaper and magazine advertisements featuring his conqueror's face that the man who pioneered self-promotion in golf could only marvel at how he was making money from "the manufacturers of practically everything he wore, every bit of equipment he used, and everything he ate, drank, smoked, or glanced at in passing."

For many years, Compston was the professional at Coombe Hill Golf Club south of London, an exclusive course that attracted politicians from David Lloyd George to Winston Churchill; members of the royal family; show-business celebrities; and later, while preparing for D-Day, General Dwight D. Eisenhower. For safety reasons, the commander of the Allied forces played only four holes.

Though some members of the club objected to Compston's irascible nature and his insistence on enjoying the comforts of the clubhouse, others delighted in them.

"I could piss further than that, Your Highness," Compston told the Prince of Wales after observing the royal tee shot. The prince roared with laughter and made Compston his personal coach. In his history of Coombe Hill, golf writer Donald Zec says the two men made several trips to the Continent together and took a Mediterranean cruise during which they hit some three thousand golf balls into the sea.

Compston thought nothing of insulting the rest of Coombe Hill's affluent clientele as well. Approached by a member for lessons, he might examine the contents of his golf bag, then yell to his clubmaker in the next room, "George, show this gentleman a proper set of golf clubs." Once, says Henry Longhurst, the Marchioness of Northampton became so exasperated with Compston's truculence she jabbed him on the shin with her 8-iron. "Now you hit a golf ball," Compston shouted at her.

At Coombe Hill, golf was occasionally accompanied by high-stakes gambling, and Compston was happy to oblige. He would provoke members by betting them they could not break 90, and he often had dozens of bets going at the same time. He would then go out to the 8th hole to see how his bets were coming along and up the ante of those that looked most promising.

These wagers earned Compston thousands of pounds a year and attracted the attention of Inland Revenue, which levied a tax. Compston went to court, said he had been betting his own money and that the income tax people certainly would not pay *him* if he lost, and won the case. Once more, the press and the public were delighted by his victory over a supposedly superior force.

But beneath Compston's bravado there was a sentimental streak that was revealed in a letter he wrote to the father of a boy applying for an unpaid job as his assistant at Coombe Hill. Zec calls it "a literary gem which Charles Dickens might well have relished," and it is hard to quarrel with that assessment:

> You must impress upon this boy when he comes here that he will not be allowed to smoke, have anything to do with any girl or take any intoxication. He must on no account talk to the caddies or mix with any low-grade individual. He must not go loafing about the streets at night and will have to go to bed at 9 o'clock. He will hear a lot of swearing on the golf course but he must not cultivate that habit on any account.
>
> You must impress upon him the great importance of a bowel action every day. If I want him to carry my clubs and get up at seven o'clock in the morning before breakfast to practise a certain shot he will have to jump to it and no excuses.

Compston was surely recalling his own days as an apprentice in Staffordshire as he wrote these words, for as much as he enjoyed working in golf's high-rent district he was always mindful of the distance between himself and his employers. Longhurst, who was the captain of the Cambridge golf team the first time they met, recalled how, after losing a match at Coombe Hill, he and his teammates encountered Compston watching them while sitting on the fender of a car.

"You're just a bunch of lousy golfers," Compston said. "I could beat any three of you."

The morning sunshine at Hoylake gave way to black clouds and produced a sprinkle of rain as the final round of the tournament began. A fine setting for a murder, Keeler thought darkly, or an upset in the Open. Wearing an extra sweater and with rain gear at the ready, Jones approached the tee, where he heard stewards warn the crowd lining the fairway all the way down to the green not to run or applaud until all the putts had been holed.

Except for Compston and Jones, there appeared to be only two golfers with a reasonable chance of winning as the round began: Leo Diegel and Jim Barnes.

Diegel had played the front nine brilliantly in the morning, needing only thirty-three shots, before faltering and coming in with a 71, to finish three shots off Compston's lead. "With the start I had it should have been the best round of my life," Diegel said ruefully. Barnes, Jones's conqueror in the 1921 U.S. Open, had shot 72 and was five behind Compston, but quickly played himself out of contention with a 38 on the front nine of the fourth round en route to a 77. Fred Robson, who had trailed Jones by only a stroke at the start of the third round, was no longer a factor after a 78. Macdonald and Horton Smith, who were seven and eight shots off the pace respectively, also appeared too far back to contend.

Jones teed off thirty minutes ahead of Compston and, after an uneventful par at the 1st hole, seemed destined for early-round troubles again. His high drive at the 2nd went off line toward heavy rough on the right side of the fairway, and Jones watched nervously as the ball flew in the direction of a gallery steward wearing a red skullcap—and hit him in the head!

What must that fellow's head be made of? Jones wondered as the ball ricocheted forty yards farther to the right, across the 15th fairway, and into a bunker fronting the 14th green, which was comfortably close to the 2nd hole. Instead of a difficult shot out of the rough, Jones now had a clean lie in the sand—another great stroke of luck involving a spectator, although this time it was a lone man who had saved him rather than someone in a large crowd.

Jones blasted a long shot out of the bunker that, considering the circumstances, looked as good to him as his eagle from the fairway against Roper in the British Amateur. The ball rolled within twenty feet of the hole, and he made the birdie putt. A par at the third and he was safely past the opening three holes, which had caused him so much trouble for three days now, at last. Jones proceeded comfortably through the next few holes, and a score of par for the front nine—or even one under if he could birdie the long 8th—seemed within reach. Surely, Compston wasn't going to shoot *another* 68, Jones thought. He liked his chances.

Compston returned to the course just as he had left it—the picture of confidence, laughing and chatting with the excited British fans. At the first tee, he posed for pictures as if he were off to play a jolly exhibition rather than the final round of the British Open. When he was applauded by the crowd, he clapped for them in return.

And then he fell apart.

His iron shot to the first green was short, and he missed a putt for par no longer than his putter. "I shall always believe that if Compston had holed the thirty-inch putt for a par at the first hole, he might have settled his vast stride into a championship round," wrote Keeler. "He looked at the ball like a man dazed when it stayed out." Darwin agreed. "Perhaps that began the rot," he wrote of Compston's opening bogey. "At any rate, it was terrible rot."

Compston had no one to blame but himself. For all his experience and golf-course savvy, he had one glaring failure as a competitive golfer: impatience.

At the 1926 British Open at Royal Lytham and St. Anne's, he was six shots off the lead at the beginning of the final round, but a fine start put him back within shouting distance of Jones and Al Watrous. At the 12th hole, Compston hit his tee shot into an area that appeared to be out of bounds and was told to wait for a ruling. He played the ball instead and was disqualified from the tournament.

Now, four years later, he committed another beginner's mistake. Keyed up from the excitement of his morning round and unable to relax for a few moments, he went to the practice tee adjacent to the first fairway and began hitting balls. Driver after driver, iron after iron, Compston hit some fifty practice shots in all. For a man who had just played 18 holes of intensely competitive golf and had 18 remaining, it was a supremely foolish thing to do.

"To us it looked as if he was doing the hitting as an outlet for sheer joy," said an unsigned column in the British magazine *Golf Monthly*. "Though a giant in frame, Compston is a cheerful, over-grown boy. A little judicious advice before that fatal final round might have made the championship sure for Britain."

At the second hole, Compston shanked his second shot and took a six. By now, word of Jones's good start had come back to Compston, and he realized his lead was gone. One hooked shot followed another, and the result, Darwin wrote, was "a long and gloomy row of fives." Compston played the front nine in 43 and finished with 82, 14 shots worse than his morning round. His poorest previous score in two rounds of Open qualifying and three of competition was 74. A 75 in the final round would have made him the champion. Instead, Compston left the course with a rare distinction: he had won his greatest victory against Walter Hagen and suffered his most galling defeat to Bobby Jones.

Jones came to the 8th hole in excellent shape. With Compston out of the picture—though he would not learn of this for another hole or two—and no other contenders making an early move, he needed only to continue shooting par to run away with the tournament. The 8th was an excellent place to begin staking his claim. An unprepossessing, 482-yard par-5 that stretched along the front edge of the course, it contained no turns, no bunkers, no hazards. In Jones's mind it was a par-4, and indeed he had birdied the hole in each of the first three rounds.

A bit of wind blew up as Jones stood at the tee, but not enough to keep him from going for the green in two. Even when his second shot fell short and rolled down a slight slope about fifteen yards from the green, there was nothing to worry about. A decent pitch would put him close enough to the hole for a birdie. And if he did need two putts, his par was secure.

Trying to get the ball just onto the edge of the green and hoping it would roll down to the hole, Jones woefully underhit his chip shot. It hopped feebly up the slope and stopped well short of the green. Nervous now, Jones changed clubs and chipped again. "Short," a number of spectators said quietly as the ball landed ten feet from the hole. But at least it was on the green.

This is getting a bit thick, thought Keeler, who had a flashback to the 7th hole at Winged Foot the year before, where Jones had begun throwing away his three-shot lead in the U.S. Open with a seven at the 8th hole. But that was a far more difficult hole surrounded by bunkers. For Jones to be near the green after two shots and still be faced with a long putt for a five made no sense.

Jones's par putt slid a foot past the hole. Angry and disgusted, he walked up to the ball and, rather than take a moment to line it up, petulantly stabbed at it.

And missed.

Trembling, he made his tap-in for a seven, the highest score he had ever taken on a hole during competition on a British golf course.

Unbelievable, Keeler thought as he added up the carnage: Jones had needed five shots from within fifteen yards of the green. Then he remembered something Joyce Wethered had said as she was ending her tournament career: competitive golf was a game not worth the candle.

It was, Darwin wrote, the most ridiculous and tragic of all sevens. "A nice old lady with a croquet mallet could get a five" and now "it seemed that this loss of an iron self-control for just one minute had thrown away the championship."

Jones could only agree. "If ever a person could be made groggy by a blow entailing no physical consequences," he wrote, "I had been made so by that seven. I will play that hole over a thousand times in my dreams. I thought everything was done for."

He had done it again.

Just as he had in 1923 at Inwood, where he had blown a three-shot lead over Bobby Cruickshank with three holes to play.

Just as he had in 1927 at St. Andrews, where he had led the British Open by three shots at the start of the final round and made three fives in the first five holes.

Just as he had in 1928 at Olympia Fields, where he had a three-shot lead at the start of the final round of the U.S. Open, birdied two of the first six holes, and lost to Johnny Farrell.

Just as he had in 1929 at Winged Foot, where he had blown a five-shot lead over Al Espinosa with six holes to play.

It was his greatest shortcoming as a golfer, and Jones could never quite come to terms with it.

"Whatever lack others may have seen in me," he wrote, "the one I felt most was the absolute inability to continue smoothly and with authority to wrap up a championship after I had won command of it."

During his career, Jones had harnessed his temper, perfected every part of his game, and developed a competitive attitude second to none. But give him the lead in the closing stages of a golf tournament and he could almost count on getting into trouble.

Thirty years after he retired, Jones was still grappling with this failing, still wondering why, of all the championships he ever won, it was the 1926 U.S. Open at Scioto, where he had trailed by four shots with nine holes to play, that had caused him the fewest qualms. "The significant thing to me," he wrote in *Golf Is My Game*, "was that at no time during this round did I feel the fear that I have known while leading the field."

Jones's memory was being kind to him. His knees had been shaking as he played the final hole at Scioto, and he had burst into tears in front of his mother afterward. But there was no doubt he always felt more comfortable when he was trailing the field than leading it, and his attempt to explain this riddle is not entirely convincing.

When he was well ahead, he wrote, he "became fearful of making myself look ridiculous by kicking things away. I began to be conscious of my swing and began trying to make too certain of avoiding a disastrous mistake. . . . The fellow who is fighting a close fight is a little better off. The fight is still on for him and he has no consciousness that he will feel like a fool if he fails."

It is difficult to imagine a golfer with Jones's self-confidence worrying about how he looked to others, but that is the best he could come up with. Whatever the reason for his failing, Jones's record is all the more remarkable for the fact that he lacked the one trait that sets so many of sport's greatest champions apart: a killer instinct.

Though Jones was badly shaken by his disaster at the 8th hole, he had the presence of mind to fashion a response. What he needed to do now, he realized, was simple. Finish his round and get off the golf course. Not worry about his score, not worry about anybody *else's* score, not worry about attacking or defending or winning or losing. Just play golf, nothing else. What was it Harry Vardon once said? "No matter what happens, keep on hitting the ball." That was what he had to do now.

He stepped up to the 9th tee, hit one solid shot, then another, and made his par. *That's* the way to face misfortune, Darwin thought. And when a birdie putt from fifteen feet lipped out at the 10th, Jones appeared to have survived the trauma. He was two shots over par, Compston was finished, and there appeared to be no other serious challenges. As long as he made no more foolish mistakes, he should be fine.

And then the wheels came off.

After badly misjudging the speed of the 11th green—the ball ran ten feet past the hole, and he missed coming back—Jones could feel the wind come up. Suddenly he could not find the fairway or the hole.

He hit into the rough at the 12th hole, into a bunker at the 13th, into the rough with his second shot at the 14th, into the rough with his second and *third* shots at the 15th. Only a nice recovery at 12 for par, a beautiful pitch and a five-foot birdie putt at 14, and a chip dead to the hole at 15 that prevented a double bogey kept him from losing more than one stroke during this stretch.

Facing Hoylake's tough finishing holes—the British liked to think they were the most difficult of any championship course in the world—Jones was now three over par and looking at a 76. Could he be sure he had not given Leo Diegel and Macdonald Smith an opening? He could not. He had to try for a birdie at the par-5 16th, a troublesome 532-yard dogleg to the right where the green was fronted by bunkers on both sides.

Jones's tee shot was down the middle, but when he tried to reach the green by hitting a 2-wood as hard as he could, the ball swung a bit to the left and rolled down into the bunker at the left front corner. Worse yet, it landed very close to the back wall of the steep hole. A normal chip shot out of the sand was all but impossible. The only way Jones could get at the ball was by putting his right foot almost on top of the bank behind him. With no room for a backswing, he had to strike a sharply descending blow just behind the ball and hope to drive it out of the bunker and toward the hole, about twenty-five yards across the green. There was only one possibility.

"My sand wedge, please," he told his caddy. "That extra-heavy niblick with the steel fin."

Since he had come to Britain, Jones had used the odd-looking new club Horton Smith had given him in Augusta that spring only twice— once to get out of the gorse at St. Andrews, and once for a routine shot earlier in the Open. It was dangerous to use a club he had so little experience with for such an important shot, Jones thought, but he had no choice.

The gallery whispered quizzically at the sight of the sand iron. What on earth was that? That fin projecting out from the rear, thought George Trevor of the *New York Sun*, looks like the spur on the leg of a gamecock. A few rays of sun peeked through the clouds and flashed off the head of the club as Jones drove it down behind the ball.

"Up came the ball, floating in a geyser of sand, flopping on the green like a tired frog, rolling, rolling," Keeler wrote. It reached the cup, circled the rim and, as the crowd shrieked, settled three inches from the hole. It was, Jones would say later, one of the best shots he ever hit.

The British Open had no sooner ended when the attention Jones brought to the MacClain sand wedge led to protests. Surely, such a radical club had to be illegal, observers suggested. Overnight, shots from the sand had been made too easy for unskilled players. And the danger was spreading. A number of pros were already using the wedge, and Horton Smith had assigned the patent to Walter Hagen's clubmaking company, which sold the club for $12 and could not keep it in stock. The U.S. Golf Association had ruled clubs illegal in the past, some of its officials noted. It must now act again.

In January 1931, after some dispute within its ranks, the U.S.G.A. agreed. The wedge would be banned not because of its radical fin, but rather its concave face. "Repeated tests proved conclusively that from grass a ball could strike the club face at two different points at the same time," the U.S.G.A. said. Hit the ball twice with a single stroke, in other words, which is clearly against the rules.

The ruling had two immediate effects, one practical and one historical. Manufacturers reacted by producing a sand wedge with a straight face of the type that remains in use today. And Jones had played a key shot in one of the most important tournaments of his life with a club that would soon be ruled illegal.

After his birdie at 16, Jones needed to make a twelve-foot putt to par the 17th, and he got it. With abject relief, he saw his second shot at the final hole come to rest fifteen feet from the cup. Two putts later, he came off the course bewildered and exhausted with a 75. His two-round total for the day, which he had begun leading the tournament by a stroke, was five shots over par. His face, Greenwood thought, was gray as stone.

Helped by several policemen, Jones made his way through the crowd to the secretary's room in the clubhouse, sank into a chair, and poured himself a drink. "I have never had such a terrible time in my life," he told a few reporters.

"When are you going to quit this sort of foolishness?" asked Keeler before going back out onto the course to see if anybody behind him was mounting a threat.

"Pretty soon, I think," Jones said. "There's no game worth these last three days. This tournament has taken more out of me than any other I ever played in."

After a while, Jones got up and roamed restlessly around the small room, holding his drink firmly in both hands. Finally he walked over to the window to see if he could get a glimpse of Leo Diegel coming in.

The winner of the PGA championship the two previous years, Diegel was one of the tour's hardiest pros. From 1919 to 1929 he was ranked among the top ten golfers in the United States, and he was much in demand as a private instructor for many wealthy men, among them Hollywood studio bosses Joe Schenk and Adolph Zukor. But although Diegel won thirty tour events and was a member of seven Ryder Cup teams, he was best known for two quirks in his game: his unorthodox putting style, and the national championships that always seemed to be slipping from his grasp.

On the putting green, Diegel was a sight to behold—crouched over, his chin almost touching his club, elbows jutting straight out to the side. "Diegeling," it was called, and when he had some success during a Ryder Cup, Darwin said, "hundreds of British golfers were assiduously conjugating the verb 'to diegel' and trying to attain what they believed to be his pose."

Diegel's near misses in major tournaments began with his first U.S. Open, at Inverness in 1920, when he shot a 77 on the final round and lost to Ted Ray by a stroke. "Poor Diegel! he could never quite take what the gods gave him," Darwin wrote of this and other close calls in U.S. and British Opens. His nickname on the tour was "third-round Diegel."

Playing well behind Jones, Diegel trailed by two shots at the start of the final round, and when he needed 38 strokes to get to the turn, he seemed to have eliminated himself from contention again. But he birdied the 12th hole as Jones struggled home, and suddenly Diegel trailed by just one shot. With two par-5 holes remaining, he was still alive.

Diegel needed three shots to reach the green at the long 14th, parred 15, and that left it up to the 16th, which had been Jones's salvation. He hit his tee shot into a bunker, three-putted when he finally reached the green, and that was that. A par at 17 left him to try the impossible—an eagle from the fairway on the final hole to force a tie. His approach shot landed at the front edge of the green, rolled within twelve feet of the cup, and stopped.

"Hard luck, Diegel!" the spectators shouted as he came off the green.

"There are too many bunkers on that course for me," Diegel said, smiling all the way to the clubhouse.

Last in was Macdonald Smith, who also needed an eagle at 18 to tie. His long shot landed on the green, bounced in front of the cup, and ran past.

Upstairs, in the secretary's room, Jones took one hand off his glass.

"Seeing him nearly past speech," Darwin wrote, "I thought that the time had come for him to call a halt. Golf had always taken a prodigious toll and now I thought it had taken too great a one. The time to go, even at twenty-eight, was fast approaching."

17

The U.S. Open: "The Lord Must Have Had His Arms Around Me"

In the winter of 1909, fifteen members of the Bryn Mawr Golf Club in Minneapolis met in a restaurant to discuss an increasingly vexing problem: the construction of new homes on their golf course was threatening its existence. "Every month they build a house somewhere on one of the holes, and we have to change the course," one of the unhappy golfers said. It was time to look for a new place to play, preferably out of the growing city.

After several more meetings, the group dwindled to six men who, after a careful search, settled on three farms that occupied 146 acres north of the town. The land was a perfect combination of woods and meadows, had plenty of water, and one further attraction that made it all but irresistible: it was only twenty-five minutes from downtown Minneapolis by streetcar. The members of the newly formed Interlachen Country Club put down a deposit of $1,000.

A further payment of $12,000 was due a few months later, and as the six men went about raising the money, a complication arose: one of the farmers had discovered the identity of the buyers and their intentions. Sensing he might have a well-heeled partnership over a barrel, he let it be known that if payment were not received on time, the price would go up. Desperately seeking to reach their goal, the members prevailed upon Calvin G. Goodrich, the president of the Twin City Rapid Transit Company, which owned the streetcar line.

Perhaps thinking ahead to future riders carrying golf clubs, he pledged $5,000 without collateral.

As the deadline approached, the Interlachen members were confronted with one more problem: the payment was to be made in gold or gold certificates, and no local bank could supply them with $12,000 in paper. The only solution was to put together a combination of certificates and gold bullion for delivery in person.

Late on a February afternoon, two Interlachen committee members, G. B. Bickelhaupt and R. J. Powell, boarded the streetcar, rode out to the stop nearest the farmhouse, and walked through the snow carrying a bag of gold. Their host, attended by several rough-looking farmhands, nearly fainted when he saw the money and realized that his dream of further riches would go unfulfilled. But surely the two men did not expect him to keep all that gold in his farmhouse overnight, the farmer said. They returned to town, where Bickelhaupt sat up guarding the bag with a shotgun until the banks opened in the morning.

Ground was broken at Interlachen the following month, and memberships were offered to all adult male residents of Hennepin County for an annual fee of $50. William Watson designed the course, which was opened in July 1911, but it was completely rebuilt eight years later by Donald Ross, the most celebrated golf course architect of the day.

From the beginning, Interlachen offered far more than golf. The British model of a golf course and a members-only clubhouse was not at all what the club's founders had in mind. Interlachen was meant to be a club where members and their families could gather for lunch, dinner, and good fellowship. Soon there were informal "maid's-night-off" suppers on Thursday, Saturday night dances, and Sunday evening tea. Chicken dinners were served not just on Sunday but every night of the week for the bargain price of $1.50. Members' wives, who were allowed on the course only on Fridays, played bridge and mah-jongg. Teenagers were invited to "come out to the club for a private dance with our phonograph, no charge." The only proviso was that they "must come early and go home early."

"Interlachen is more than a golf-playing club," noted a report by the entertainment committee in 1925. "It is a real Country Club. Next to our homes, Interlachen should represent the social center of our members."

In the years ahead, it would go to great lengths to achieve that goal, and Harry James, Woody Herman, Jimmy Dorsey, and Guy Lombardo would bring their bands to play for the club's Saturday night dances.

The fame of Ross's layout quickly spread, and Interlachen became an important tournament venue in 1914, when Jim Barnes won the Western Open by a stroke over a young Scottish immigrant named Willie Kidd. Six years later, Kidd became the head professional and remained so until 1958, when he was succeeded by his son, Bill, who retired in 1993. Together, father and son worked at Interlachen for seventy-three years.

The greatest golfer the club ever produced was a red-haired young girl who preferred football but, when her father gave her younger brother a junior membership, cried until she received one, too. Patty Berg went on to win twenty-nine amateur tournaments, fifty-five more as a professional, and a charter membership in the Ladies' Professional Golf Association Hall of Fame.

Over the years, a number of homes have been built on Interlachen's grounds—all carefully located so as not to interfere with any but the most errant shots—but the most lavish structure remains its massive fifty-eight-thousand-square-foot clubhouse. It contains a Patty Berg Room, a Willie Kidd Pub, and original drawings by Donald Ross as well as quotations by Ross that have been carved into the walls.

The one theme most in evidence, however—in the trophy cases, in a stained-glass portrait at the entrance to the men's locker room, in dozens of framed newspaper clippings, and in a painting of one of the most legendary shots ever struck in golf—is a celebration of the 1930 U.S. Open and the man who won it.

.   .   .

On the final day of the 1930 U.S. Open, thieves entered the hotel room of Harry Cooper, broke into a wardrobe trunk, and took most of the clothes he and his wife had brought with them. The Coopers had asked for it, police noted, because they had left the door open in the vain hope that just a bit of air might cool the room while they were at the golf course.

Nobody in the Midwest could remember a hotter spell. Scores of people died as temperatures rose above a hundred throughout the region. Seventeen deaths were reported in the Twin Cities during the week of the U.S Open, including that of C. V. Kerkove, a fifty-year-old man who left behind a suicide note saying he could no longer stand the heat.

The shores of the area's lakes were packed with tens of thousands of people seeking relief. Fire hydrants were opened, pleas to conserve water were issued, mail delivery was called off, and Minneapolis mayor W. F. Kunze issued an order allowing policemen to remove their uniform jackets as long as they were wearing a clean shirt. One man called police to ask if he would be arrested if he were seen on the streets wearing pants that reached only to his knees. "There's no law against it," police captain George Hillstrom told him. "Go ahead if you've got the courage."

At Interlachen, the golfers were feeling the heat, too, and it left them, and their clothes, dripping with sweat to a point beyond embarrassment. The "awning stripes of their stylish shorts" were clearly visible, wrote Ed Danforth in the *Atlanta Constitution*. "These men of golf dress well even to the foundation garments."

Chick Evans was so dizzy he could not see his ball during his swing, and he nearly withdrew from the tournament. Tommy Armour sent his caddy back to the clubhouse for ice he wrapped in a handkerchief and applied to his neck. Horton Smith had a friend walk in front of him waving a large towel in the hope of stirring up a breeze. Cyril Tolley carried several bath towels, but remained all but blinded by perspiration.

"I have to putt between drops," said Tolley, who said he longed for a breeze off the North Sea back home. A woman spectator said the big Englishman looked like an iceman who had carried a hundred pounds of ice up five flights of stairs and found the lady of the house not in.

"I never thought I was going to finish," said Walter Hagen, just back from a lengthy barnstorming tour of the Far East with a trunkful of gifts for friends, after playing the first round of the tournament. "After nine holes, I didn't know whether I was on foot or horseback. I wish I had on one of my Japanese kimonos."

Bobby Jones, whose neck was so severely sunburned after two practice rounds that he wore a bandanna oozing with ointment as the tournament began, had a similar thought. "I think we're justified to play in pajamas," said Jones. "I never felt such heat since I was born." He would lose seventeen pounds before the end of the week.

The day before the tournament began, Jones was able to cool off a bit by fishing on Lake Minnetonka with his friend Harrison Johnston, the reigning U.S. Amateur champion and a Minneapolis resident. Jones was hit by the full blast of the heat the following afternoon, however. He came off the course with the pocket of his white knickers stained red from some tees he had been carrying and, when he was unable to undo the sodden knot of his red foulard tie, Keeler cut it off with a pocketknife. It was promptly snatched up as a souvenir.

"This championship will go to the man with the thickest skull," said Charlie Hall, a long-hitting pro from Birmingham, Alabama.

"Maybe it did at that," Jones said.

The heat did little to stifle the air of excitement at Interlachen, however. Jones's triumphs in Britain had brought thousands of spectators to the course, some in cars from distant cities and many more on the streetcar. By the time the tournament began, there were few hotel rooms available anywhere in the area. Shortly after the first day of play began, organizers ran out of tickets, which were priced at $3 for a daily admission and $7.50 for the week.

Temporary wooden buildings sprang up around the course to house the press, sell refreshments, and allow a Red Cross doctor to treat spectators overcome by heat prostration. The only thing missing to complete the county-fair setting, one observer noted, was a band.

Long lines stood outside the clubhouse grillroom where, it was noted with some disapproval, prices had been raised for the tournament. A cheese sandwich cost 50 cents, coffee and pie 20 cents, near beer 35 cents, ice cream a dime. "None get off cheaply," a local reporter wrote. "Fans dug deep for the privilege of watching Bobby Jones."

One structure that drew a great deal of attention was a large scoreboard erected near the clubhouse that offered up-to-date information provided by runners from around the course. The scoreboard was presided over by James Preston, the head of the press gallery for the U.S. Senate.

Deputy sheriffs and the National Guard helped local police direct traffic coming to Interlachen, while marshals attempted to control the crowds on the course by extending fishing poles and uncoiling lengths of rope where the golfers were standing. Nothing could keep people from running between shots, but at least there was some order while the contestants were actually hitting them.

One surprise was that perhaps half the huge gallery was made up of women. The *St. Paul Dispatch* sent out a fashion writer, Lois P. Hatton, who noted "the intense heat took curt liberties" with the wardrobes on display. She had never seen so much linen and sheer cotton, Hatton wrote, though "the gayly colored dresses soon wilted and men were besieged for handkerchiefs for delicate low-necked frocks."

The large press corps from around the country that descended on Minneapolis was one more indication of the fascination with Jones's quest, which had now reached the United States. Some ninety newsmen were housed in a screened-in shed near the first tee, where they were supplied with typewriters, telegraph machines, and telephones, and where they were scorched by the heat. "It is hotter than a turpentine camp," wrote Danforth. "The place will no doubt be destroyed by spontaneous origin along about noon Friday and quite rightly, too."

The most intrepid members of the press were seven New York reporters, including that rarest of journalistic creatures, a woman sportswriter. Nan O'Reilly of the *New York Evening News* was in a group that flew in on a seaplane that was forced down onto Lake Ontario by an oil leak. "I thought our end had come," O'Reilly said of the wind and waves that buffeted the small plane. Luckily, a Coast Guard ship came to their rescue, and they continued their journey without further incident.

Newsreel camera trucks from Hearst Metrotone, Pathé, and Paramount Sound News also were on hand for the Open, but a greater curiosity was the well-known sports broadcaster Ted Husing, who walked the course carrying a large microphone with a bulky radio transmitter strapped to his back.

There had been radio broadcasts from golf tournaments before— Darwin and Keeler had both spoken over the air at the end of each day's competition in the British Open—and even a few attempts at live coverage. But this was the first time the whole country could listen in. In touch with his base in the press building by shortwave, and aided by reports from Boy Scouts bringing in scores from around the course, Husing's broadcasts were carried by the CBS network to the thirteen million American households that owned radios.

Husing's reports were further enhanced by a number of the Open contestants who agreed to say a few words—Hagen, Johnny Farrell, and Gene Sarazen among them. But there were a few programming glitches that showed the new technology was still a work in progress. On the final day of the tournament, the broadcast was delayed by live coverage of Kentucky Derby winner Gallant Fox's victory in the Arlington Classic in Chicago. By the time Husing came on the air, the winner had finished his round.

One last sign of the excitement surrounding the Open appeared when it was announced that a ring of "dips" had relieved spectators of as much as $1,000. The fact that golf fans were crowded close together, police said, made it easier for the pickpockets to avoid detection. It would be particularly simple, they warned, for thieves to operate undetected in the huge gallery surrounding Bobby Jones.

Jones was in a good mood when he arrived in Minneapolis. He and Mary had remained in Britain for a week after his victory at Hoylake, where he appeared in several exhibitions, sailed home on the *Europa*, and, no longer quite so much to his astonishment, received another hero's welcome in New York. So many people had come in from Atlanta on the Bobby Jones Special this time, and they had been joined by so many reporters, that it took two city boats, the *Macom* and the *Mandalay*, to welcome him into the harbor.

Jones, who amused himself taking pictures with a new movie camera of the city fireboat spouting water in his honor, was jovial with reporters, and a little coy. Retire? It was true he had said he would not return to Britain in 1931—"I have to work sometimes—but as for my retirement there's nothing in that report."

"Suppose you win all four this year?" he was asked. "Will you quit then?"

"I have given no thought to winning all four," Jones said. "I wonder where all these rumors come from."

The Colonel, his wife holding his arm tightly in the middle of the confusion, wept shamelessly at the reception, and even Mary exchanged a few words with reporters. She had had the time of her life in Britain, she said, although she had been worn to a shred every time another match at the British Amateur went down to the final green.

With his family in tow, Jones took another ride through cheering crowds in lower Manhattan as ticker tape came showering down. He remains the only person ever to have two such parades in his honor, a fact that did not impress a New York policeman sweltering in his heavy uniform while trying to get the march started.

"What's the parade for?" someone asked.

"Oh, some goddammed golf player," he responded.

Once again, Jimmy Walker greeted Jones at City Hall and noted that Admiral Richard Byrd had recently received a parade for his exploration of the North and South Poles. Jones had united two poles as well, Walker told a nationwide radio audience: the world's best golfer was being welcomed by the world's worst. Jones laughed, spoke gracefully in return, and made ready for another banquet at the Vanderbilt.

After not having played in so long, Jones felt a little off his game at Interlachen. But he was scoring well in practice and not truly concerned. He and his young Walker Cup teammate Doug Moe even rode scooters and the Ferris wheel at a local amusement park after their round. "I had the best time since I was a kid," Jones said.

With Mary having gone home to look after the children following her extended absence—she was also pregnant with their third child—Jones enjoyed the company of his mother and the Colonel, who both gave interviews to a press corps looking for something new to say about the man whose name was on the nation's lips.

She had not been feeling well, his mother said, but "I haven't seen him since before he went to England so I just had to come along. Yesterday and today are the first two days I've been out of bed. I mean to spend most of the next week in bed."

Jones's caddy, a lucky seventeen-year-old named Donovan Dale, whose name had been picked out of a hat, also found himself giving interviews. Jones was a swell guy, Dale reported, but not very talkative. All he said during his first practice round was "What's your name?" and "Where's the water?" Dale reported. He was signed to write a column for the Associated Press and soon was predicting victory and referring to Jones as "we."

The field for the Open was widely considered to be the finest the tournament had ever seen. Virtually every top professional in the country and most of the top amateurs were on hand. But beyond the sheer numbers of excellent golfers, the entry list was notable for something else as well. It was a virtual history of Jones's career.

Nearly all of his great moments on the golf course through the years had come at the expense of someone who had come to Interlachen. His most bitter defeats were represented, too.

Jock Hutchison, the winner of the 1921 British Open at St. Andrews, where Jones had picked up his card, was there. Tommy Armour, his partner in the Florida matches during the winter of 1925–1926 that had helped Jones prepare for five years without equal in the history of golf, was there as well.

The victims of some of his most heroic shots, most stirring comebacks, and greatest escapes were there: Al Watrous, Al Espinosa, Joe Turnesa, Cyril Tolley, Harrison Johnston, George Voight, Leo Diegel, and Macdonald and Horton Smith. Among the few missing were Francis Ouimet and Bobby Cruickshank, who had failed to qualify for the tournament but was halfway to winning his bet on Jones.

Men who had beaten him in big matches were there: Walter Hagen, Gene Sarazen, Johnny Farrell, Jim Barnes, Willie Hunter, Willie Macfarlane, Johnny Goodman, George Von Elm, and Chick Evans. Other opponents he had met many times, such as Bill Mehlhorn and Harry Cooper, were there, along with four future U.S. Open champions: Billy Burke, Olin Dutra, Ralph Guldahl, and Craig Wood.

It was as if Jones's entire past, and some promising younger golfers as well, had shown up to pay him homage, and to try to gain lasting recognition as the one who halted his sweep through golf's four major championships. None of them underestimated the task.

"Here is the greatest field ever assembled on any golf course," Hagen told Grantland Rice. "Here you have the survivors of twelve hundred entries. And yet it is the field against one man—Bobby Jones. Nothing like this has ever happened in golf."

What Hagen did not say was how badly he wanted to step out of that field and beat Jones. Joe Kirkwood, with whom he had just returned after barnstorming in the Far East for two months, was not so reticent. "Walter has been dying to win this tournament for years," Kirkwood said. "It has become an obsession with him. He feels that the British championships he won are so much ancient history and have no value now to him professionally. He is thirty-eight years old and imagines that time is flying."

Keeler was among those who thought Hagen might be Jones's most dangerous foe. "When that old boy makes up his mind to do something, he's going to come mighty close to doing it," he wrote. "Walter Hagen is the greatest competitive spirit in sport."

If there was one thing that gave Hagen and the others hope, it was that Jones had played so erratically in the British Open. "Bobby will have to play a better long game here than he did at Hoylake," said Horton Smith in one of the newspaper articles he had been commissioned to write during the tournament. If he got into Interlachen's punishing rough, Smith said, he might be in trouble.

Bob Harlow, who managed both Hagen and Smith, let it be known he had bet $2,000 that one of his clients would win the tournament. Sarazen and Diegel announced they were playing well, too. U.S. Golf Association officials were so impressed by the strength of the field that they ordered six thousand tickets printed for a 36-hole playoff on Sunday.

The thermometer in the shade of the clubhouse read 101 degrees as Jones and Jock Hutchison arrived at the first tee at 9:45 A.M. on July 10. The heat did nothing to deter a gallery of twenty-five hundred people, and the start had to be delayed fifteen minutes while pictures were taken and the fairway was cleared.

Hutchison spent the time entertaining the crowd. First he did a little dance and then, discovering a discarded tee, he pretended to look for more. Now forty-six years old, the Scotsman, who had immigrated to the United States and returned home to become the first American citizen to win a British Open, knew he had no chance. "I am afraid my game won't do Bobby a bit of good," Hutchison said. "I have found everything but the fairway."

From the beginning, Jones's plan was clear. He would play conservatively, try to stay out of trouble, and take the chance that none of his competitors would run away from the field in the stultifying heat. It was a good idea, Keeler thought, as he saw Jones barely outdriving Hutchison off the tee, refusing to gamble the few times he landed in the rough, and hitting even his long putts delicately lest they run past the hole.

With two Atlanta friends, Chick Ridley and Charley Cox, providing a buffer from the crowds and carrying half-pint bottles of water, Jones's strategy worked to perfection. He shot a 71 that only a few putts hanging on the lip of the cup kept from being even better. He finished the day one shot behind Armour and Macdonald Smith, with Hagen, Horton Smith, and Cooper just behind him, in a group at 72. And he survived the heat. "For the first time in my life, I found myself in an important competition with only one instinct and desire—to get the round over as quickly as possible," Jones wrote. "It was terrible out there."

But despite his bedraggled condition and his soaked knickers, Jones had no complaints. He could even take a moment to grin when, at the 12th hole, he caught the sheepish Ridley drinking some of his precious water. "We started pretty well," Donovan Dale, who had nearly passed out from the heat himself, wrote in his newspaper diary. "I mean Bobby Jones did."

In England the following morning, Bernard Darwin also was in a good humor as he read the morning paper. A 71 was good but not alarmingly so, he thought. Nobody knew better than he how much trouble Jones could make for himself when he had the lead.

Jones teed off at 12:50 P.M. on Friday, which allowed the gallery to take its time getting to the course and to marvel over the first newspaper photographs of an infant named Charles A. Lindbergh Jr. By the time Jones did begin, he found himself sharing his gallery with one of his chief competitors, Horton Smith, who was playing just ahead of him. The handsome twenty-two-year-old sensation of the professional tour was the object of much attention on and off the golf course.

"Have you no bad habits, Mr. Smith?" asked a hostess at a party who had been told he did not smoke, drink, take coffee or tea, or keep late hours.

"Well," he said, "sometimes I'm short on my long putts."

Smith and Jones were both under par in the early going, which had the fans running back and forth trying to get a glimpse of both men. At the ninth hole leading back into the clubhouse they had their reward.

Smith's second shot at the par-5 485-yard hole was sensational, a long wood from the fairway that cleared a pond in front of the green and rolled within twenty feet of the cup. When he made the putt for an eagle that gave him a one-shot lead over Jones, a huge roar went up from the crowd spread out on the long, rolling lawn overlooking the 9th and 18th greens.

Next up was Jones, and he immediately found himself in trouble. His drive sailed too far to the right and landed in a difficult lie near a clump of trees next to the gallery ropes. Hemmed in by spectators as he stepped up to the ball with his 3-wood, Jones felt as if he were playing next to a human fence.

Jones took his stance when, without warning, a spectator stepped out in front of him and started across the fairway. Jones stepped back as a marshal called out a plea for no one to move, then addressed the ball once again. At the top of his backswing, Jones's peripheral vision caught another sudden movement in the gallery—two little girls making a break for it. He flinched, chopped at the ball, and, as the audience groaned, skulled it low and flat toward the pond....

Before the tournament began, Bill Mehlhorn had taken his first look at the ninth hole—the bend to the right, the bunkers in front of the green, the pond full of plants and turtles—and said, "That's certainly a great-looking hole. Somebody's going to lose the championship there."

Or win it.

... The ball caromed off the water twenty yards short of the bank, skipped once, then again, and, as the crowd shrieked in disbelief, hopped out onto the slope of the bank thirty yards short of the green.

A boy with a flat stone could not have performed the trick more neatly.

In itself, Jones's shot was not all that remarkable. Several golfers skipped balls across the pond during the Open. Al Espinosa did it twice, once in the same round as Jones.

"If I stood here with five balls and a low-lofted club—a 3-wood or a 3-iron—I could do it two or three times," says Jock Olson, the head professional at Interlachen today. "A lot of members try to do it just so they can say they have something in common with Bobby Jones. Of course, they use old balls."

And, of course, they don't attempt the shot with thousands of people watching and the U.S. Open on the line.

Before the day was out, Jones's stroke was being referred to as the lily-pad shot, which implied that the ball had bounced off a plant on its way out of the pond. Jones always would say that no lily pad was involved, that the ball struck only water, but that is not at all certain.

Today the pond is devoid of vegetation thanks to a fountain in the center that keeps the water constantly churning. A few turtles climbing on rocks near the edge are the only signs of life. But in 1930 there was no fountain, and a short film of the Open at the Minnesota Historical Society shows a great deal of plant life in the area where Jones's ball landed. Clearly it was the ball's flat trajectory and lack of spin that propelled it out of the water, but it may well have glanced off a plant en route. The best description of the shot might have come the following day in Donovan Dale's newspaper diary.

"It skipped through the lily pads like nobody's business," Dale wrote. "It reminded me of skipping a rock down on the crick."

The shot saved Jones from disaster. Had the ball gone into the water, he would have been penalized a stroke and would have had to hit another ball from the bank of the pond. He was looking at a 6 or a 7 on the hole, he said. Instead, he hit his third shot dead to the hole and escaped with a birdie 4.

"The Lord must have had his arms around me," Jones said.

Watching the entire episode from the 10th tee was Horton Smith, whose eagle moments earlier was now forgotten, and who immediately understood the import of what had happened. "When I saw that topped shot come off the water," he wrote, "I knew nobody else had a chance to win the tournament. The far shore must have looked to

Jones like the shores of North America looked to Christopher Columbus. That stroke will ever be talked about by golfers. It approached the dignity of a miracle and was as pleasing to Jones as any miracle could be."

"That's the way it goes in championships," said Keeler. "If your name is up, the ball will walk on water for you."

But the tournament was not over yet. Nor was Jones's round.

A bogey at the 12th hole and a double bogey at the 15th raised his score on the back nine to 39, for a total of 73. Including his practice sessions, it was his worst round at Interlachen, and it left him in a tie for second place, two shots behind Horton Smith, who, after his blazing 33 on the front nine, had come in with a 70.

"I played like an old woman on the back nine," said Jones, who was particularly angry at himself for hitting his ball near a tree and over the green at 15 and then compounding the damage by missing a three-foot putt. Still, he had to admit that after the miracle at 9, he could hardly complain.

Many of the tournament's biggest names were effectively out of the running after the second day. Sarazen, Diegel, Barnes, Mehlhorn, and other top pros had either wilted in the heat or succumbed to Interlachen's tight fairways and unforgiving rough. After hitting three successive shots into the sand at 17, Jock Hutchison picked up his ball and withdrew. He did not want to delay Jones's round any further, he said.

Hagen also looked spent. Though he was only five shots off the lead after a round of 75, he had needed forty shots on the back nine and become increasingly frustrated. As his gallery deserted him to watch others play, Hagen began tapping in his bogeys left-handed.

As for the top amateurs, only Jones remained. Cyril Tolley and Minnesota's favorite son, Jimmy Johnston, did not make the cut, while Chick Evans, who had spent two days listening to the cheers for Jones off in the distance, barely did. "The announcer asks my score rather softly and sympathetically," Evans wrote of his rounds of 81-75. "The crowd listens pityingly, with a sure sense of 'he used to be a good player.'"

In England, Darwin read the afternoon paper with a sense of foreboding. Horton Smith, he told himself, was a very impressive golfer to be given a two-stroke lead. "I must admit," Darwin wrote, "that at that point my faith in Bobby came near to faltering a little."

Jones, however, was not concerned. He was just off the pace, right where he wanted to be. "It's a pretty good position to be in," he said. "I'll let the other fellow do the worrying."

By the time the bulk of the field arrived at Interlachen for the 36-hole final day, the tournament appeared to be over. Teeing off at 9:15 A.M., Jones played one of the great rounds of his life, a course-record 68 that was his best score ever in an American championship.

Abandoning his caution of the two previous days in his attempt to catch Horton Smith, Jones blasted his drives down the fairway, out-driving his playing partner, Joe Turnesa, by ten to twenty yards on every hole. Jones's approach game also was close to perfection as time after time his shots landed near the hole. Grantland Rice counted three from 90 to 100 yards away that stopped within a foot, and Turnesa could only marvel at such precision as he and Jones fought through the huge gallery of ten thousand people or more.

He's giving himself a birdie chance on every hole, Turnesa thought. Amazing. In all, Jones had ten one-putt holes, his longest a ten-footer at No. 1, in a round that included six birdies. Not even bogeys on the final two holes could diminish the impact of the round or keep Jones from reaching for an analogy from another sport to describe his feeling of dominance.

"I felt as I think a good halfback must feel when he bursts through a line of scrimmage and finds the safety man pulled out of position, sees an open field ahead of him, and feels confident that he has the speed to reach the goal," he wrote.

The competition thought so, too.

With a later tee time, Horton Smith stood on the practice green as Jones putted out at the 9th hole while the gallery roared its approval. He had not even teed off yet, but his lead was already gone. "The champion, it seems, had been toying with the first nine holes while the rest of us were deciding between sauerkraut juice or orange juice," Smith wrote. "I could hear the newsboys shouting it out on Peachtree

Street and selling their papers as fast as the presses could turn them out: 'Jones is out in 33.'"

As the word of Jones's round spread, one disgusted pro said to Hagen, "I think I'll turn amateur."

"Boy, you're not good enough," Hagen replied.

Neither was he. Ten strokes off the lead following a third-round score of 76, Hagen saw his gallery scatter and his enthusiasm disappear. In the afternoon he was accompanied by his young son, who imitated his father's putting stroke with an umbrella he had brought home from Japan. Hagen's final-round score of 80 left him in a tie for seventeenth place and earned him $47.50 for his week's work.

His putting stroke was shot, Hagen told Chick Evans, who, twice having failed to break 80, could only commiserate. Though Hagen would compete at a high level for the next five years and continue to be a fan favorite wherever he went, his last chance to win a major national championship had come and gone.

By noon, the heat had broken. A reading of 82 degrees, down from only a few hours earlier, promised a comfortable setting for the inevitable—a victory march in the U.S. Open by the greatest golfer in the world.

Jones could hardly have asked for more. Cooper, who had played three solid rounds—72, 72, 73—was the only man in the field within five shots of his three-round score of 212. Horton Smith had shot par on the front nine in the morning to pull within a shot of the lead, but then lost his putting stroke and came back in 40 for a 76, which left him six shots off the pace. Macdonald Smith was seven back, at 219. They were all fine golfers, with many victories and years of major tournament experience, but make up half a dozen shots on Bobby Jones in the last round of a major championship? It hardly seemed possible.

"I hope I can last," said Macdonald Smith, who was feeling all of his forty-two years. "I'm certainly tired."

Jones did it again.

At the second hole, he missed a three-foot putt. At the par-3 3rd, his tee shot went into a bunker and, after missing a two-footer, he three-putted for a double bogey. His closest competitors had yet to take the course, and already they had gained three strokes.

In an instant, all the confidence Jones had displayed in the morning disappeared. Back to his conservative strategy of the first two days, he was only barely outdriving Turnesa now, sometimes not at all. One more time, Jones had turned a triumphal procession into a forced march.

He's pressing, Turnesa thought as he saw Jones struggle with his approach shots. Balls he would normally hit straight at the hole were coming up short. What tension he must be under. He was still hitting the ball fairly straight, though. You never know.

Jones blamed shifts in the wind for his misfortune—the huge crowd kept him from judging the changes, he told Keeler—and really he was not playing that badly. But nobody could have blamed him for thinking something else as the round continued: give him the lead and he was guaranteed to get into trouble.

At the 9th hole, the site of his lily-pad miracle the day before, Jones's problems turned comical. Misjudging the wind, he hit his second shot over the pond, the green, the crowd, and the golf course itself. The ball landed on a practice green where golfers preparing for their rounds looked up, startled, thinking someone was playing a joke on them. Two ropes had to be removed before Jones could hit his third shot, an 8-iron that cut a divot into the putting green and sent the ball skidding to a stop fifteen feet from the hole. He managed to hole out in two putts to save his par and made the turn with a two-over-par 38.

"Now if I had been that halfback in an open field," Jones wrote, "I stumbled so many times before I got to the goal line that I am sure my coach would have made me turn in my uniform before taking himself off to the hospital to recover from a heart attack."

Jones steadied a bit with three straight pars to begin the back nine, and then the first reports on his opponents began coming in. They were not encouraging. Cooper and Horton Smith had played the front side in even-par 36 to close within three and four shots, respectively, while Macdonald Smith had shot 34 to reduce his gap from seven shots to three.

Jones's response to this news was disastrous—a windblown tee shot at the 13th hole into a greenside bunker, a failed attempt to get out, and two putts. It was his second double bogey of the afternoon at a par-3 hole. His lead was down to one.

And then, without warning, his approach game righted itself.

At the 444-yard 14th hole, his 4-iron landed fifteen feet from the hole, and the gallery shouted as his birdie putt looked good from the moment he struck it. His second shot at 15 was closer yet, though he missed an eight-foot birdie putt. His approach at 16 was best of all, landing just four feet from the hole for his second birdie in three holes.

With his lead back up to three shots, Jones was even par for the back nine and looking at a 74 if he could par in. Macdonald Smith would have to play the final nine holes in 33 shots to force a tie; Horton Smith and Harry Cooper would need 32s. Good luck to them. It was all nicely settled, Jones thought as he approached the 17th hole. Wasn't it?

A visitor to Interlachen today stands at the 17th tee, peers down the fairway in the direction of the green, and thinks there must be some mistake. A 225-yard par-3? A driver off the tee for all but the most accomplished of members? Isn't that stretching things a bit?

"Turn around," says Jock Olson, and he points to some trees at the top of a hill off in the distance. "*That's* where the tee was in 1930."

At 262 yards, the 17th at Interlachen was the longest par-3 in U.S. Open history and perhaps the longest in the world. With marshland fronting a lake off to the right, bunkers on either side of the green, and trees hiding the speed and direction of the wind, it was an almost certain bogey for any golfer whose tee shot did not make the green.

Jones had done well to play the hole in 3-4-4 in the tournament thus far, though he rued the fact that his bogey that morning was the first to appear on his card. If ever there was a time to play cautiously, to hit the ball carefully down the middle, with the tournament in hand and the end in sight, this was the time for Jones. Instead, he tried to guide the ball close to the trees on the right, became tangled up in his swing, and watched the ball slice crazily off toward the swamp. It banged into a tree and disappeared.

Fans, caddies, and officials came on the run and began stomping through the marshland—some up to their ankles—in search of the ball. Had it bounced right or left? Had it landed in the swamp or flown off somewhere else? And what would happen if it could not be found?

Finally, a ball was discovered buried in mud and heavy swamp grass. Fans and officials, relieved that the tournament could go on, rushed over for a look. Jones held them up.

"I think we'd better make sure that's my ball," he said quietly, and he reached down into the mud, pulled out the ball, and held it up. It was not.

What to do? The rules governing a lost ball are clear, and the penalty is severe: a player loses both stroke and distance. Jones would have to return to the tee, where anything could happen. A simple par would now become a double bogey. A 6, or even a 7, was certainly possible.

It never came to that. Refereeing Jones and Turnesa was U.S. Golf Association secretary Prescott Bush, who ruled that the ball was not officially lost at all. Before the tournament began, Bush announced, the swamp had been ruled a parallel water hazard. This meant Jones could take a drop on the fairway. Rather than return to the tee 262 yards from the hole, he would be only 50 yards short of the green.

The ruling caused a sensation. Before the day was out, one writer would compare it to Gene Tunney's controversial "long count" decision over Jack Dempsey three years earlier, and a number of the pros would be up in arms.

A parallel water hazard? Since when? They had never been informed of such a ruling. And how could anyone be sure the ball had landed in the swamp in the first place? How did they know it was not lying undetected somewhere in the heavy rough instead? Or perhaps an eager fan had pocketed the ball as a souvenir. If this was not a lost ball, what was?

"Nobody saw the ball splash," Harry Cooper, who finished fourth in the tournament, remembered of these discussions more than half a century later. "So he said. So they said. I don't know."

For years there had been talk among Jones's competitors that he received favorable treatment from tournament officials—the best starting times, the most generous rulings. One story related by Cooper had to do with the 1929 U.S. Open at Winged Foot.

"Horton Smith told me—and he wouldn't tell me a lie—that

Bobby Jones's ball was in the rough on the 12th hole," Cooper said. "There'd been quite a bit of rain and the rough was kind of muddy, and a lady apparently had stepped in a pile with her high heels, and Jones's ball stopped in that hole. And Mr. Ramsay [U.S.G.A. vice president Herbert Ramsay] picked up the ball and handed it to him and he says, 'You get that drop, Mr. Jones.' Horton said he was standing right there at the time. Now there was nothing that said 'ground under repair' or anything of that kind."

At Interlachen, it was Sarazen who was most adamant that an injustice had been done to the rest of the field. It was "just another of those regrettable incidents that have slightly tarnished Bobby's record," he said.

"I am sorry that his victory, great as it was, should be tainted by the decision made by the United States Golf Association," he later wrote in a newspaper column. "It seems to me that Jones, who in the eyes of the public is a good sport, should have gone back to the tee and made another drive. There is no doubt in the minds of many who witnessed the unfortunate incident that the ball was lost. The rules of golf weren't made to be interpreted on presumption."

Some members of the U.S.G.A. were furious at this criticism. In Los Angeles, Everett Seaver, a member of the executive committee, said Sarazen should be banned from future tournaments. But despite the uproar, Jones did not address the issue then or at any time in the future. Nor does he seem to have been asked directly about it. Prescott Bush was not questioned, either, and it was not a subject he often talked about.

"I never heard him discuss that ruling," says his son, former president George H. W. Bush, who, until he was asked about it in 2004, was unaware of any controversy concerning Jones's play on the 17th hole.

Reprieved, Jones easily got down in three strokes for his third double bogey on a par-3 hole. He had needed fifteen strokes on the shortest holes on the course instead of nine, and his lead over Macdonald Smith, who had been seven strokes behind at the start of the round and was playing steady par golf behind him, was down to one shot.

.   .   .

Still unsettled by his narrow escape, Jones hit a tentative tee shot at 18 and then an approach that barely made it to the front of the green. His ball was 40 feet short of the hole and would have to travel up one steep rise, across a small plateau, and then up again. Not a good shot, Turnesa thought. Normally he would have knocked that three-iron easily onto the green. The strain is getting to him.

The excited gallery rushed past the marshals and out onto the fairway, stormed up the course past the golfers, and merged with the thousands waiting on the grassy slopes behind the green that led to the clubhouse. Some fans climbed on chairs to get a view but were pushed off as police moved the crowd back. Others climbed the rungs of photographers' ladders, while a few brave souls found perches on the clubhouse roof and the Interlachen water tower.

More to get away from the crowd and calm down than to check his lie, Jones emerged from the gallery and walked up to the green. He looked, one observer thought, like an actor approaching an empty stage. As Jones climbed the hill to the flag and went through the motions of looking things over, the applause was deafening.

Just get it close, Jones told himself after he walked back down the hill and stood over his ball. He could feel every muscle quivering. No sense waiting any longer. The crowd fell silent as he gave the ball a sharp smack. It climbed up the first rise of the green, out into the sunlight, and toward the second hill. This is taking a long time, Turnesa thought. The ball continued rolling.

Six feet short of the hole, it broke for the cup, and Jones knew he had it. There were no words for the feeling he had as the ball fell into the cup and the waves of sound from the vast circle of people crashed over him.

Walking up the 15th fairway, Macdonald Smith could hear the noise coming from the direction of the clubhouse. Some excited members of the gallery, realizing he was the last man left with a chance to catch Jones, ran back out on the course, and the word quickly spread. Jones's birdie at 18 had brought him in with a 75 and a final score of 287. Smith would need two birdies on the final four holes to tie.

An eighteen-foot putt at 15 hung on the lip. A fifteen-footer at 16 also just missed. At the 17th, Smith's tee shot was short of the green, and his chip missed by four feet. Now he needed an impossible eagle from the fairway to tie Jones—just as he had needed one on the 72nd hole of the British Open less than a month before.

He had no chance. It was over.

Upstairs in the clubhouse, Keeler approached Jones, put both hands on his shoulders, asked the same question he had asked at Hoylake, and received the same reply.

"Bobby, when are you going to quit this damned foolishness?"

"I don't know, but pretty soon. I'm awfully sick of it."

In truth, Jones did know. He had had enough. Nothing could be worth this any longer. All he wanted to do was go home. One more tournament and then he was done—*finis*.

The victory ceremony boomed out of radios onto Atlanta's streets and sidewalks. Several dozen of Jones's friends, his father-in-law among them, had gathered in the city room of the *Atlanta Journal* to follow the two rounds hole by hole on the Associated Press wire and shouted in jubilation.

Newsboys crying "Extra! Jones Wins!" carried freshly printed papers through the business district. At East Lake, members seeking refuge from the hottest day on record, 103 degrees, gathered around a radio to listen. Sitting at home, Mary heard the radio reports, too. Three-year-old Robert Tyre Jones III announced he was anxious to see his father to show him he had learned how to whistle.

The great crowd sat on the hillside to observe the ceremonies on the practice putting green below. A semicircle of chairs was arranged in clear view of the divot Jones had taken when he so badly misplayed the 9th hole.

"It's just a little practice ceremony," U.S.G.A. president Findlay S. Douglas told Jones as they stood before the microphones of four nationwide radio hookups and the newsreel cameras. He was, Jones replied, exceedingly lucky to have won.

Macdonald Smith stepped forward to accept the first-place prize money, $1,000, the winner could not accept. He had finished second to Jones by two strokes in two Opens in barely a month. During his career, Smith had several close calls—he once lost a U.S. Open playoff to his brother, Alex—and though he won sixty tournaments, twenty-four of them on the PGA tour, he never became a national champion.

"We've all tried hard to corner the elusive Mr. Jones," said Horton Smith, who also had finished exactly as far behind Jones, five strokes, as he had in the British Open. "But we haven't succeeded."

Watching from the top of the hill was Chick Evans, for whom the tournament had been a disaster—a final score of 315, which placed him twenty-eight strokes behind Jones. "I hope you find your dear mother better," he said when he came over to shake his old adversary's hand. "I owe everything to mine."

After the ceremony, Keeler emerged from the clubhouse shower and saw Jones speaking with other members of the press corps that had come from around the country to witness his fourth U.S. Open victory and his third national championship of the year.

"What are you going to do when you retire?" a reporter asked.

Jones turned to Keeler and said, "You'd better tell them, O. B. You know."

Keeler did know. Though there was something—*something*—that would keep Jones from saying the words out loud, and that would make his public comments on the subject maddeningly contradictory during the next few months, he knew it was all coming to an end.

Wrapped in a towel, Keeler climbed on a bench and quoted some verses from "The South Country" by the French-born British writer Hilaire Belloc that he and Jones both knew by heart:

> If I ever become a rich man,
> Or if ever I grow to be old,
> I will build a house with a deep thatch
> To shelter me from the cold.
> I will hold my house in the high wood
> Within a walk of the sea,
> And the men that were boys when I was a boy
> Shall sit and drink with me.

.   .   .

In England the following morning, Darwin arrived for breakfast early and let out a howl when he could not find the Sunday paper. It was quickly produced, and he tore it open to read a full account of Jones's third round. A 68? Well, surely, that meant he had won . . . wait, here was the final result on an adjoining page, barely squeezed in before the paper had gone to press. There was no description of the match beyond the name of the winner, but that was enough.

"Breakfast seemed very good indeed," he wrote, "and I could wait with placidity bordering on indifference for further details on Monday."

A few days later, Grantland Rice sat down to write an article for his magazine the *American Golfer*. It appeared under the title "Last Stop—Merion."

18

Homecoming

Planes flew over the parade route. A police escort, with the chief himself in front, led the way. The 122nd Infantry followed with its thirty-six-piece band. A delegation from the Disabled American Veterans, waving and saluting, was next. One hundred Atlanta firemen followed, some riding on one of the department's biggest trucks.

Members of the Chamber of Commerce rode by, followed by the Junior Chamber, all dressed for golf, who walked. Every civic organization in town was represented—Rotarians, Kiwanians, Lions, and Civitans—along with a thousand Georgia Tech students and alumni, led by football coach W. A. Alexander.

The American Legion drum and bugle corps marched, as did soldiers in olive drab, representatives of many city businesses, the Atlanta Women's Club, and a delegation from the Georgia Power Company, which, in accordance with a mayoral proclamation, had been given the afternoon off. The Atlanta Crackers baseball team, accompanied by its board of directors, waved from cars along the route. The players had been scheduled to march in honor of their world-famous vice president, but at the last moment they elected to ride.

Toward the rear of the parade welcoming Bobby Jones back to Atlanta, and marching to tunes played by the Colored Elks band, were three hundred black caddies from several municipal and private golf clubs carrying signs that said "Welcome Home, Mr. Bobby," and, in the East Lake contingent, "Us, too, Mr. Bob."

The sign that delighted the huge crowd the most, noted the *Constitution*, "was one carried by the boys from the Capital City Country Club that read: 'Welcome Home, Mr. Bob. You Sho' Brought Back the Bacon.'"

There had never been anything like it, longtime Atlantans agreed. They could only guess at the actual numbers of the turnout: 100,000? 150,000? More? Something approaching half the population of the city, in any event. Charles Lindbergh had not drawn nearly as many people when he had visited the city. The Georgia Tech team that won the 1929 Rose Bowl had been greeted enthusiastically, to be sure—it had outdrawn Lindbergh, too—but this was different.

The only larger outpouring in the history of Atlanta had come on November 11, 1918, when World War I ended. But that was a night of worldwide celebration that was marred locally by drunkenness, fights, and the cracking of heads by MPs. This, by contrast, was a day when Atlanta would welcome home one of its own, a native son whose exploits had become news the world over.

Even before the U.S. Open was played, plans for a celebration were under way, inspired to some extent by Jones's second ticker-tape parade in New York a few weeks before. "Whereas, Atlanta's admiration and affection for Bobby are far beyond the enthusiasm of New York, hearty and tumultuous as that was," Mayor I. N. Ragsdale said in his official proclamation declaring July 14, 1930, a civic holiday. The fact that Jones had added his victory at Interlachen to his triumphs in Britain merely put the celebration over the top.

Live descriptions of the parade were broadcast from microphones installed at the Capital City Club and the First National Bank along the route, where blasts of carnival horns competed with police whistles. By the time the final car in the procession turned from Harris Street onto Peachtree, so much confetti had floated down from office buildings it could barely move.

The car traveled slowly as police on motorcycles raced their engines and veered toward the curb, trying without much success to move people back. Perched on the rolled-up convertible top, the man of the hour waved to the crowd while Mary, serene and beautiful in a white summer dress, sat with the Colonel and the mayor on the backseat below him.

At last the entourage arrived at City Hall, where three generations of Jones men—Robert T., Robert P., and Robert T. Jones Jr.—posed for pictures. Several times, police lines had to be deployed to prevent the welcoming party and noted guests from being overwhelmed by excitable spectators.

The mayor presented Jones with a gold key that the mayor said "will open not only the gates of the city but the hearts of all its citizens as well. When you left here two months ago in quest of golfdom's highest honors, the hearts of Atlanta followed you, and with it went all our confidence. We looked forward to some such a scene as this, but even this cannot tell you all the admiration we have for your character and achievements."

Jones spoke for several minutes—a record for him, one reporter wrote. The welcome, he said, "has fairly taken my breath away. I appreciate all the things you have done for me, more than I can tell you. And I just want to say you don't think any more of me than I do of you."

And then he was gone, off to lunch at the Atlanta Athletic Club, where he was the guest of honor. His next round of golf, he said, would be with his father and a few friends at East Lake. The U.S. Amateur was still more than two months off. He would worry about that tomorrow.

Though the day had been exciting and memorable, some thought its import went beyond the moment itself. The celebration had not been for Atlanta's favorite son alone, but for the city, too, and what it was on its way to becoming.

"Atlanta saw itself in a mirror—a living mirror of multitudes—and today, perhaps for the first time, knew that it was a big city, a true metropolis," wrote William O. Key Jr. in the *Constitution*; "the thrilling scene of reality justifies the oft-heard contention that this town of ours is the New York of the South."

From California, Will Rogers sent a telegram to the *Journal* that ran on the front page the following day:

"Atlanta no more than gets cleaned up from one Bobby Jones celebration till another comes along. You can easily exist in Atlanta by eating only at Jones testimonial dinners. . . . So find a spot on Stone Mountain for Bobby. Had he lived in the days of Jeff Davis, Stonewall Jackson and Robert E. Lee, he would have done to Grant and Sherman what he did to Hagen, Diegel and Sarazen.

"And just think, ten years ago all Atlanta had was Coca-Cola."

19

The U.S. Amateur: "Into the Land of My Dreams"

On December 16, 1865, sixteen men gathered in Lower Merion Township near Philadelphia to sign a document founding the Merion Cricket Club. The president of the new organization, Archibald R. Montgomery, it was explained in a footnote, was unable to add his signature because "while on duty at the funeral of President Lincoln on April 22, 1865, the premature discharge of a saluting cannon caused the loss of his right arm."

Cricket was introduced to America in Philadelphia, and the game remained popular for many years at the new club, which entertained a number of teams from around the world and once drew ten thousand spectators for an international match. But in 1879, a new sport came to Merion patterned after one that had recently gained a good deal of attention in Wimbledon, England. "With the first white line drawn on the cricket pitch," says Desmond Tolhurst in *Golf at Merion*, his 1989 history of the club, "cricket at Merion was doomed."

Golf did not join tennis at Merion until 1896, when a farm in Haverford was rented from the Pennsylvania Railroad and where a nine-hole course was laid out and its three-story farmhouse converted into a clubhouse. The game quickly became so popular that by 1900 a new clubhouse was built and enough adjoining land was donated by shipping magnate and Merion member Clement A. Griscom for nine more holes.

The club grew to become an important part of life in and around Merion, even taking over the public livery service in 1906 and earning enough money to buy four horses with harnesses and three buses. The following year, nearly twelve thousand people rode the buses for free. Then disaster struck in the form of a new rubber-cored golf ball, which was changing the nature of the game in the United States and England by allowing golfers of even limited ability an additional twenty-five to thirty yards off the tee. Shorter courses such as Merion, which had been designed for the old gutta percha ball, were rapidly becoming obsolete.

With no more land available for expansion at its present site, the newly formed Merion Cricket Club Golf Association bought 120 acres south of the Philadelphia and Western Railroad tracks on both sides of Ardmore Avenue in 1910. The club then packed off one of its members, Hugh Wilson, to Scotland and England to get ideas for a golf course to be built on the property.

Wilson, who had been captain of the Princeton golf team and had joined his brother's insurance firm, knew nothing about designing a golf course, but he returned seven months later laden with notes, surveyors' maps, drawings, and ideas. He proceeded to create Merion's East Course (in response to members' requests, he built the West Course, a mile away, two years later), drawing inspiration from many of the British courses he had seen. It was widely acclaimed a masterpiece.

Along with its tight fairways and blind landing areas that required delicacy of touch and careful thought as well as distance, Merion possessed idiosyncrasies that made it unique. Originally, golfers had to hit their shots on the 10th, 11th, and 12th holes across Ardmore Avenue, which was then a seldom-traveled country road. Some years later, these holes were reconfigured to be played on one side of the street or the other, though an element of danger continued to exist. Club lore has it that when a man who had driven in the Indianapolis 500 was denied membership, golfers crossing Ardmore Avenue sometimes found themselves dodging his speeding car.

Merion also is noted for the wicker baskets perched atop its flagsticks, another idea Wilson brought home from Britain. Their exact origin was shrouded in mystery until 1989 when, Tolhurst notes, a

British golf historian provided a drawing of Harry Vardon lining up a putt in the first formal match between England and Scotland, at Prestwick in 1903. A caddy is holding Vardon's bag of clubs and a flag-stick with a wicker basket on top.

Merion first gained national attention in 1916 when Chick Evans won the U.S. Amateur to complete his unprecedented double, which began with his victory in the U.S. Open. But the course faced great difficulties immediately afterward. World War I, which forced it to be closed for a time, claimed the lives of thirteen members and required the services of most of the grounds crew. They were replaced by local women, who kept the East Course in excellent condition.

The coming of Prohibition also was harmful, as it cut off a signifi-cant source of Merion's income at the clubhouse restaurant and bar. On June 28, 1919, two days before the Noble Experiment took effect, the club built up its cash reserves by auctioning off its remaining sup-ply of liquor. The receipts were less than hoped for because a large portion of these liquid assets was consumed by the members before the sale.

By the time the U.S. Amateur returned in 1930, Merion was on the verge of hard times once again. The crash of the stock market and the Depression caused a steep decline in the membership rolls and maintenance budget, the mortgage went into default, and the fee for caddies was set at 85 cents per round. It would not be until well after World War II that Merion would regain its financial footing and solid-ify its position as one of the premier golf courses in the United States, one that, like a relatively new course in Augusta, Georgia, counted many members who lived great distances away and seldom visited.

But none of this was on the minds of the American public that September when, after a stop at the White House, where he received a pep talk from Herbert Hoover, Bobby Jones returned to the golf course where he had played in his first national championship four-teen years before.

.   .   .

When Jones arrived at Broad Street Station in Philadelphia on September 17, 1930, his stomach hurt, his shoulder ached, his nerves were on edge, and he was desperately tired. After playing in three tournaments on two continents within six weeks, the long break between the U.S. Open and the Amateur should have been a godsend. But it also made for an enforced period that allowed the pressure to build and the old anxieties to assert themselves.

The weekend before he left for Merion, Jones felt sharp pains in his stomach and was taken to the hospital, where appendicitis was suspected. It turned out to be an attack of nerves. Playing before five thousand people the next day in an exhibition at East Lake for the benefit of the Army's 82nd Division, which had trained in Georgia before fighting in France in World War I, he shot 70.

The ten-week layoff also gave Jones more than enough time to brood about his long-held belief in fate.

"Look out, mister!" a voice shouted as he walked along the sidewalk between his office and the Atlanta Athletic Club one day.

Jones turned and saw a car climbing the curb and heading straight for him. He jumped out of the way as the car crashed into the space he had just vacated. But for a warning from the only pedestrian on the block, he surely would have been crushed.

Anything could happen, Jones realized. He had better be careful.

All but unrecognized by the crowd at the Philadelphia train station, Jones invited several reporters into his Pullman car for a chat. After accounting for Mary's absence by saying "She's seen enough of golf for one year" (though without mentioning that she was five months pregnant), and saying how much he had always enjoyed playing at Merion, he admitted what was really on his mind.

"Right now, I want some sleep more than anything else."

From the moment Jones stepped onto the course, he could see that never before had there been a U.S. Amateur championship like this one. There were easily four thousand people following him during his first practice round, more than had witnessed the *final* of the 1924 tournament, when he had beaten George Von Elm to win his first amateur title. It was, Keeler thought as he saw Jones trying to navigate a small alley between the fans on Merion's narrow fairways, the largest gallery he had ever seen at a practice round anywhere in the world. The crowds were so huge, in fact, that ticket sales for the first days of practice were cut off. "We feared the players would be seriously handicapped in their preparations for the tournament," said Frank M. Hardt, the chairman of the competition committee.

But if the size of the crowd caught officials by surprise, so did its makeup. There were the regular tournament patrons, to be sure—wearing fashionable summer clothes and sitting at tables under lawn umbrellas, sipping drinks, chatting, and waiting for the action to begin. But others, many of whom had clearly never been to a golf course before, had come to the course, lured as much by the magnitude of the event and the anticipation of Jones's impending accomplishment as by the competition itself.

Workmen with their coats over their arms, young people just off work and wanting to get in on the excitement, even entire families paid the admission fee—$1 for the practice sessions, $2 for the opening rounds, $2.50 for the final two days. Others, it was widely suspected, simply walked onto the course somewhere on the perimeter away from the ticket takers.

"More than one father, caddying for momma, carried a baby on his hip," Ed Danforth wrote in the *Atlanta Constitution*. "Men are men in Pennsylvania and women see to it that they prove it. Imagine lugging a baby over 18 holes."

For the first time at any championship, marshals carried poles with signs attached to the tops so the galleries could see the current score. It was a great system for the crowd, Danforth wrote, but it must have been a painful sight for the golfers who were losing. Other marshals wore red armbands and berets, and carried long coils of rope to cordon off the golfers as they took their shots. A hundred state troopers wearing gray shirts, riding breeches with black leggings and Sam Browne belts, and carrying single-action .44 revolvers next to their ammunition belts, also were on hand. They were, it was announced, particularly on the lookout for pickpockets to prevent any repetition of the indignities that had taken place at Interlachen.

The final bit of security was provided by fifty U.S. Marines in full-dress uniform, an unprecedented step for any golf tournament. They were under the command of Lieutenant Whitey Lloyd, a former fullback at the U.S. Naval Academy.

The press corps had arrived in force and set up shop at long wooden tables in an old whitewashed barn that had been built more than a hundred years earlier and later been turned into a dressing room. A scoreboard nailed to a wall was updated with reports delivered over telephone lines installed at the 3rd, 6th, 9th, and 15th holes, and by messengers stationed around the golf course. One of the Philadelphia papers, facing tight deadlines and trying to cram as much of the hole-by-hole action into its afternoon editions as possible, took even more drastic action. Reporters covering some of the biggest matches would hand a page of scribbled notes to runners who would rush them over to Ardmore Avenue and give them to bicycle riders for speedy delivery to the press barn.

The *Philadelphia Evening Bulletin* assigned no fewer than sixteen reporters to cover the tournament, including one who described the dress and deportment of the crowd ("You wonder why the girls in red dresses and hats always make the front line," she wrote), and another whose sole job was to cover Jones away from the golf course. The assignment paid immediate dividends when, covering Jones's arrival at the Barclay Hotel, he saw a bellman drop a large package. The aroma of corn liquor soon filled the lobby.

Jones played poorly in his early practice rounds—a 73 over Merion's short par-70 course the first day, a 78 the next—and was furious. When he hit a ball into the creek guarding the 4th green on the second day, he threw his club to the ground in disgust. Those whose memories extended back to Little Bob's debut in 1916 might have wondered if he was completing the cycle of his career at Merion in more ways than one.

"I don't seem to have too much trouble getting off the tee," Jones said after his first practice round, "but I may just as well have had a baseball bat in my hands when I reached the green."

The course was playing longer and slower than it had when Jones won the Amateur in 1924—rain had softened it up considerably—and that was not to his liking, either. He also was having trouble with his stance, as the ball seemed to be crawling back on him. He just could not get comfortable.

Why should this be happening now? Jones wondered. What could account for these patches of mediocre golf just when things were going so well, when he was playing the one American golf course where he felt most at home and, let's be honest, when he was playing in the one national championship that should be easiest for him to win?

To a friend from New York who lamented that Jones would be too busy for them to spend much time together, he said, "As a matter of fact, I may be watching the others play. If that turns out to be the case, we'll walk around together."

Look at him, Keeler thought as he saw Jones fighting his way around the course for the second time without registering a single birdie. He's nervous as a cat—jumpy, impatient, snappish. It's because he is so alone, Keeler wrote, and he reached for the ultimate metaphor: "No other could have suffered the last night in Gethsemane, and no other can do one single thing for Bobby Jones when he goes to the first tee in Merion on Monday morning."

For one of the few times in his life, Jones was unable to sleep at night during a tournament. No matter how much pressure he had been under through the years, his regular evening regimen had seen him through. He would have two stiff drinks—the first taken while soaking in a hot bath, which was "the finest relaxing combination I know." A good dinner would follow, a few cigarettes, some conversation with Keeler or other friends, and lights out at nine o'clock.

In all the tournaments he had played, Jones could remember only two nights when he had not been able to sleep. One was before his playoff loss to Willie Macfarlane in the 1925 U.S. Open, and that was because of the brutal New England heat. The other was during the 1926 British Amateur at Muirfield, where he sat at the window of his hotel room until almost midnight, contentedly watching cattle in a distant field in the long Scottish twilight. But now he was waking up at midnight, pacing the room, his mind racing as the pressure closed in on him.

The morning after Jones's second practice round, the reporters dogging his footsteps at the Barclay saw him getting into a car with Keeler.

"Just going for a little ride," Jones told them.

"There seem to be some bags of golf clubs in the car with you," one of them said. Jones smiled, and they drove off.

Jess Sweetser, Jones's old friend and adversary who had been avoiding the crush of the crowds at Merion by practicing at Pine Valley, had called to suggest that Jones join him there. Jones jumped at the idea, and he and Keeler drove across the Delaware River to New Jersey where they met Sweetser and Cyril Tolley and played a round with no more than half a dozen people following them. A reporter from the *Evening Bulletin* who managed to track Jones down noted that while putting on the 14th hole, Jones swore at some ducks quacking in a nearby pond.

Away from the crowds, Jones finally managed to relax a bit. By the time the group made the turn, he was playing his game again. He shot 33 on the back nine and celebrated by spending the afternoon at Baker Bowl, watching the St. Louis Cardinals beat the Phillies. Two days later, Jones played his final practice round at Merion and shot 69. "I finally got some putts to drop," he said. "With a little luck, I may qualify."

Luck had nothing to do with it as, after shooting another 69, Jones tied the tournament qualifying record of 142. But for a 5 on the final hole, he would have broken it. The only real excitement came when Jones chipped a piece of the horn inlay in his driver—Merion's head pro, George Sayers, inserted a new one, and Jones pronounced it as good as new—when he frowned in annoyance at a noisy dirigible hovering over the 15th fairway, and when he was asked about a report that he was about to sign a movie contract for $100,000.

"You can say there is nothing to it," Jones said. "Maybe they want me to replace Lon Chaney."

The 1930 U.S. Amateur was a thrilling golf tournament. Each day brought remarkable upsets, amazing shots, and matches so competitive the huge galleries ran all over the course trying to catch up.

Jones figured in none of them.

His early troubles behind him, Jones played some of the most solid match-play golf of his career and never won by fewer than five holes. Nor did he trail any of his opponents by as much as a single hole. But even now, even as he was breezing to the victory that would give him a place in sports history no one else would be able to attain, the one constant of his game remained—his inability to put opponents away when he had them down.

All week long, it seemed, Jones would play well and then poorly, sometimes from hole to hole. Several times he would take big leads and then blow them. Yes, his game was there when he needed it, but why should he be struggling like this? Why couldn't he end the matches sooner, get off the golf course, away from the suffocating crowds, and relax?

"I'm playing rotten and I don't know what to do about it," Jones told Keeler after shooting a 76 in the morning of his third-round match against Fay Coleman. "I simply don't know what's the matter. I feel fine, but I just can't seem to hit the ball right. And I'm putting like a dear old lady." After a visit to the practice tee—What *was* it with his stance all of a sudden? Why was the ball so far back on his right foot?—his game improved in the afternoon, and he won easily.

What made it truly maddening was that after the first day of play, the tournament was his for the taking. Even those whose memories went back to the turn of the century could not recall a greater failure rate by the nation's top amateurs in the early going.

Jones's friend Harrison Johnston, the defending champion, failed to qualify for the 32-man field. So did a host of other former titleholders—Max Marston, Jesse Guilford, Davy Herron, Chick Evans. Cyril Tolley did not make the field either, nor did Chandler Egan, who had been a semifinalist at Pebble Beach the year before. And when the tournament proper began with each competitor playing two 18-hole matches on the first day before the survivors met at 36 holes, the result was the greatest day of upsets in U.S. Amateur history.

Oscar Willing, the runner-up to Johnston in 1929, lost his first-round match. So did Francis Ouimet and Johnny Goodman, who had eliminated Jones at Pebble Beach. George Voight, who had given Jones such a scare in the British Amateur three months earlier, lost his afternoon match, while George Von Elm, who had beaten Jones in the final of the 1926 Amateur, lost an amazing second-round match to Max McCarthy that went 10 extra holes.

McCarthy's feat was all the more remarkable because he had shot a hole-in-one at the 17th hole in qualifying the day before just to get into a sudden-death playoff for one of the final spots in the field. His first day of tournament play had consisted of two playoff holes, a 19-hole victory over Watts Gunn in the morning and his marathon match against Von Elm—49 holes in all.

Only about a hundred people were following McCarthy and Von Elm when the playoff began, but an hour later, after Jones had won his second-round match, more than ten thousand people saw McCarthy, a former intercollegiate champion, drive from the rough to within eight inches of the 28th hole to win. But while the gallery would peel off to watch this and other exciting matches the next few days, there was never any doubt who the main attraction was.

"It was the experience of a lifetime for a young golfer," said Emery Stratton, who was paired with Jones during the qualifying rounds. "But I don't think I'd care to go through the ordeal again while trying to qualify." Stratton did not make the field.

"Say, Mr. Jones will be playing here all week," said J. Wood Platt, a multiple winner of the Philadelphia Amateur championship as he grabbed a member of the gallery who had almost knocked him down trying to catch up to Jones. "Today will be my last. But if you don't mind, I would like to make this one shot."

What a one-man show this is, thought Ouimet. What does that make the rest of us? The chorus? The scenery? By now he was rooting for Jones himself, and he half suspected most of the rest of the field felt the same way. Jones also was frustrated by the long wait at almost every tee. It was, he told Keeler, like playing his first drive eighteen times, not good for anyone's game.

If anybody needed reminding of the biggest barrier standing between Jones and the Grand Slam, Johnny Goodman was living proof of what could happen over 18 holes. "Gee, I only hope to meet him again," said Goodman, who, as Jones's most recent conqueror in a national championship, was a popular interview subject in the days leading up to the tournament. "It's one of the greatest honors a contestant can hope for."

He would get one break at least, Jones thought, as he contemplated playing two 18-hole matches the first day. A semiseeded draw should guarantee he would not play one of the best players left in the tournament in the first round. But it did not.

"Who have you got this morning, Bob?" Sweetser asked him when they met outside the clubhouse.

"Sandy Sommerville."

"Phew, what a guy to get in the first round."

"I know," said Jones and he slipped away unnoticed by the huge crowd that had begun gathering three hours before his 10:00 A.M. tee time, to chip a few practice shots onto the 18th green.

C. Ross Sommerville might have been the least appreciated amateur golfer in the world, Jones thought. A former halfback for the University of Toronto football team who also had been a professional hockey player, he had won the Canadian amateur championship three times—he would win it twice more—and was two years away from winning the American title.

From the beginning, Sommerville showed he was prepared to give Jones everything he could handle if he was not on his game. He parred the first hole; chipped dead to the second for a birdie; and, after hitting a spectator off the third tee and losing the hole, recovered as if nothing had happened. But just as he had been against Sid Roper in his first match at the British Amateur, Jones was at his best, or something close to it. He matched Sommerville hole for hole to keep his one-hole lead until they came to the seventh green and found their balls no more than a foot apart.

What an important putt, Jones thought, as he studied his eight-footer. If he could make it, Sommerville's putt would suddenly become much tougher, and his lead could go to two holes, a lot in an 18-hole match. Miss it and the pressure on Sommerville would be off; he might well even the match, and Jones would be playing for his life.

Jones always would swear he had never worked harder to make a putt. With the green slick, and the slight right-to-left break difficult to read, he needed to be very gentle. As he hit the ball, he thought it might be just a little off line. But his touch was perfect. The ball stopped on the upper edge of the hole and dropped in. It was, Jones thought, the break of the match—and the tournament.

Sommerville's putt traveled the same line but was hit a bit too hard and traveled past the edge of the hole. Jones birdied the next two holes to make the turn 4-up. Five holes later, he sank a three-foot putt to win the match.

As well as Jones played against Sommerville in the morning, that is how poorly he performed against Fred Hoblitzel, another Canadian, that afternoon. Playing in blistering heat, and before crowds that jammed the first fairway from tee to green and lined up across the road hoping to get a glimpse of the upcoming holes, Jones was all over the golf course. He hit his ball out of bounds twice, into traps three times, and needed 41 shots to play the first nine holes, eight more than he had taken only hours earlier against Sommerville.

It did not matter because Hoblitzel, an oil magnate from Toronto, played worse. Even when Jones drove out of bounds at the 8th hole and had to hit a second tee shot, Hoblitzel went from one trap to another and fell farther behind. What a difference, Jones thought, as he walked off the 14th hole a winner for the second time that day. He had needed six more shots than in the morning, yet he had won by the same score, 5 and 4.

The worst was over, Danforth thought, as a squad of Marines escorted Jones off the course. "The 18-hole terror proved nothing this time but a shadow cast by moonlight on the wall," he said.

By the time Jones approached the end of his first 36-hole match of the tournament, he was smiling. If not at the way he was playing, then certainly at the result. Again, he butchered the first half of a match—topping shots into bunkers, three-putting greens, even hitting one tee shot over the spectators—and again it did not matter.

Fay Coleman, a twenty-five-year-old Californian, had played the round of his life during qualifying, a 69 that matched Jones's best effort, but he could not stay with him in the tournament. Even the fact that Coleman did not have to contend with a typical Jones gallery—only a few hundred fans were on hand when they teed off as the rest looked for excitement elsewhere—did not help.

Coleman had five three-putt greens in the first round, and every one of them cost him a win or a half. With the match tied through 15 holes, he could only wonder what sort of pressure he might have applied to Jones had a few of those second putts dropped. Coleman botched the 16th and 17th holes, and Jones led by two at the break.

After raging to Keeler about his play, Jones took out his frustrations on the practice tee—he adjourned to his favored spot near the 18th green, where a crowd showed up to watch—and tried to come to grips with his second bad round in a row. These were not competitive players he was facing. What on earth was the matter with him?

The spectators were back for the afternoon round—more than

five thousand of them, by some estimates—but the excitement was not. The desultory play seemed to match the heavy black clouds that hung over the golf course. Slowly, inexorably, Jones took command of the match as Coleman, finding every bunker on the course, it seemed, lost hole after hole. By the 10th, he trailed by seven holes, and victories on the 11th and 12th only delayed the inevitable. He hit into one final trap at 13 and it was over, a 6 and 5 victory for Jones that ended just as a thunderstorm, accompanied by spectacular bursts of lightning, drenched the gallery.

They were down to the semifinals now, and it was not hard to see that if Jones was going to lose the U.S. Amateur, it was almost certainly going to have to happen here. The other match was between Charles Seaver, an exciting nineteen-year-old player from California, and Eugene Homans, a reed-thin twenty-two-year-old from New Jersey. They had played well in the tournament thus far, but stand up under the pressure of a 36-hole final against Bobby Jones? It was not likely.

No, if anybody was going to stop Jones from winning the Grand Slam, it would have to be Jess Sweetser.

How many times had they done this? How many national amateur championships had they entered together? How many Walker Cup teams had they played on side by side? How often had they spoken over the years? How often had Sweetser made a friendly gesture to Jones—such as the invitation to sneak away to Pine Valley and practice—and how many times had Jones returned the favor?

They were almost exactly the same age, they both had Ivy League credentials (Sweetser won the intercollegiate championship at Yale), they both had won the British and U.S. Amateurs—a rare accomplishment—and they both had business careers and no interest in turning professional. For all the intersecting vectors of their careers, however, Jones and Sweetser had faced each other in a major championship only once before—in the semifinals of the 1922 U.S. Amateur at Brookline, where Sweetser had holed a shot from ninety yards away and won, 8 and 7. It was the worst beating Jones ever took in an amateur championship.

If there was any consolation for Jones's loss that day, it was that Sweetser had been nothing short of brilliant throughout the tournament, cutting a wide swath through some of the game's finest amateurs. After winning his opening match, 10 and 9, he beat Willie Hunter, the reigning British Amateur champion, 7 and 6; Jesse Guilford, the current U.S. Amateur champion, 4 and 3; Jones; and in the final, Chick Evans, 3 and 2. Sweetser almost won again the following year at Flossmoor, where he got to the final and lost to Max Marston in a two-hole playoff.

But Sweetser's greatest triumph came in 1926 at Muirfield when, to the astonishment and delight of the British press and public, he became the first American-born golfer to win the British Amateur. Since it was a Walker Cup year, the United States had brought over a powerful group of players that included Jones, Ouimet, Von Elm, Guilford, and Gunn. But they were all beaten in the early going, leaving Sweetser to carry the U.S. banner alone—which he did despite the fact that he was on the verge of becoming desperately ill.

Though Sweetser denied reports that he had to drag himself to the tee for his first match, he was in the early stages of a particularly violent strain of flu and had considered withdrawing. Only the fact that his first-round opponent had already scratched gave him the last bit of encouragement he needed to play. "Once I hit a few practice shots I felt pretty good," Sweetser told golfer writer Robert Sommers many years later, "and I didn't tire too much until the day the tournament was over. As the week wore on, I got stronger each day. Where I really felt sick was at St. Andrews."

That was where the Walker Cup was played, and though Sweetser won his singles match and his foursome, by then he was a very sick man. He left Britain before his teammates, sailed home under a doctor's care, and spent more than a year recuperating in North Carolina.

By 1928, Sweetser was back and playing well, but although he was selected for several more Walker Cup teams, he never won another championship. He always had been a big, burly man, and some suspected that he never truly regained his previous strength and stamina.

At Merion, Sweetser was the first to admit that he was no longer at the top of his game—"It was the year after the stock market crash and I had been forced to neglect my golf game for business," he wrote—and his early performances proved it.

He had to survive a playoff just to get into the tournament—his first qualifying round was a dreadful 81—and he struggled in the 18-hole matches as well; he outlasted Phillips Finlay, 2 and 1, and needed an extra hole to beat another unseeded golfer, Jack Ahearn, in the afternoon. In his first 36-hole match, Sweetser ended the excitement for Max McCarthy, who may have been exhausted from his adventures of the day before, with a 5 and 4 victory.

If he had any chance at all, Sweetser thought, it would be because of Jones's memory of their earlier match and his own suspicion that for all his success, Jones was never as comfortable at match play as he was at stroke play. If he could win a few of the par-3 holes, which might be the one slight weakness in Jones's game, perhaps he could stay with him.

The overnight rainstorm had left Merion hot and extremely humid, which quickly wilted the clothes of golfers and spectators alike and had them wiping away the sweat. Some members of the gallery, gasping for breath and expecting another uncompetitive match, headed for the clubhouse veranda and cold drinks, but others kept coming through the gates to take their place. Perhaps the match between Seaver and Homans, which began shortly after Jones and Sweetser teed off, might be competitive.

Not long after the round began, it was clear that Sweetser was right about one thing: if they had been counting strokes, he would not have had a chance. Jones had two birdies and three pars on the first five holes. Sweetser, whose first shot found a bunker—so did his second, and he overshot the green with his third—opened with two double bogeys and a bogey. Jones won four of the first five holes and took seven fewer shots. Many in the crowd stayed behind to see how Seaver and Homans were doing.

And then, as Jones and Sweetser moved down the course, each guarded by his own squad of Marines, it happened again.

At the 7th, Jones hit out of bounds. He was 3-up.

At the 9th, he was in a bunker off the tee: 2-up.

At the 10th, he missed a four-foot putt: 1-up.

After shooting two under par for the first six holes, Jones was five over for the next five and fighting for his life.

Jones reversed the momentum briefly at the 11th when he laid Sweetser a stymie, but when Jones missed a three-foot putt at 12, his lead was back down to one. The crowd, immense now that there was some hint of real competition, broke across the road to watch them halve Merion's 125-yard "Tom Thumb" 13th, then galloped across the course to the 14th fairway. It sounded, Danforth thought, like a herd of cattle on the move.

After another half at 14, both men made the 15th green in two, with Sweetser away. His long putt was excellent, stopping some ten inches short. Jones carefully eyed his six-footer and sent it straight at the hole. The cheers echoed throughout the golf course. The tide had broken.

Jones won the 17th and 18th as well to finish the morning round with a four-hole lead. A 73 was nothing to be proud of—not after those two early birdies—but Sweetser, who had shot 79, was simply not a match for him.

Leading by five after the first six holes in the afternoon, Jones won the 7th with a birdie, the 8th when Sweetser's drive smacked a spectator on the left side of the fairway in the jaw, and the 9th with a twenty-foot putt that drew roars from the crowd. Jones was eight up with nine holes to play; there was only one thing left to decide.

Jones hit his drive at the 335-yard 10th hole down the middle, some fifty-five yards short of the green, and watched as Sweetser hit his approach shot thirty feet short of the cup. Jones then applied the coup de grâce, a 7-iron that hit eighteen inches short of the pin, took one small hop on the wet green, and came to rest six inches away.

That made them even for that eagle from the fairway at Brookline, didn't it? Keeler thought. Sweetser's putt for a birdie was wide, and he walked over to Jones and stuck out his hand, conceding the 9 and 8 victory. Surrounded by Marines, they left the green with their arms around each other's shoulders.

"I did want to take the match to the 11th green and let it end 8 and 7," Sweetser told Jones in the locker room. "Then I could have said we're still square. But I couldn't make it. You're 1-up."

"I felt sort of mean at that 10th green, the way that pitch stuck up there," Jones said. "It was like a stab in the back or a shot in the dark."

"It wasn't any shot in the dark, old man. And it certainly ended things."

.   .   .

As an intellectual exercise, the possibility of Eugene Homans competing on equal terms with Jones in the final was at least worth considering. Homans had tied Jones for the qualifying medal at Pebble Beach a year earlier, and in their only previous head-to-head meeting, in the second round of the 1927 Amateur at Minikahda, Jones's winning margin had been a modest 3 and 2.

Though still a young man at twenty-two, Homans was an experienced and polished golfer, and he had played several excellent matches in the early rounds of the tournament. But when he arrived at the first tee just after 10:00 A.M. on Saturday morning, there was nothing about Homans's stature or demeanor to give the slightest indication that he would be a match for Jones.

"Of course, you can imagine how nervous I was," Homans recalled years later, but it did not have to be imagined. He just *looks* so nervous, Charles Seaver thought. He doesn't have a chance.

Still disappointed from his semifinal loss to Homans the day before—he had been up by five holes at one point and never trailed until Homans caught him on the 36th hole—Seaver could sense the lack of tension in the crowd, which was quite unusual for the final day of a championship. It was as if everybody had come to the golf course with the same thought: it's over.

With his thin build, his horn-rimmed glasses, and an almost palpable shyness, Homans was easy prey for golf writers who thought he did not look the part. Professorial-looking, wrote one. Anemic, said another. He looks as if he might be more at home behind a pulpit than on a golf course, offered a third.

Certainly Homans had inherited none of the physical presence of his father, Shep Homans, who had twice been an All-American fullback at Princeton back in the Gay Nineties. He had tried to emulate his father by going out for football at Choate, Homans said, "but coach said I was too heavy for the backfield and too light for the line. Or something like that."

Homans left Princeton because of illness, and though he became a regular on the amateur circuit, none of his contemporaries could quite figure him out. He never seemed to have much to say for himself—his nickname was "Gabby"—and Seaver thought he was a bit of a snob. "It was just the way he acted, like he was better than anybody else," Seaver says. "Typical Princeton."

.   .   .

Dark clouds filled the skies, and though the temperature was in the sixties, a biting wind had led many spectators to dress as if they were at a football game. A number of them carried periscopes, camp stools, chairs, boxes, and even a few stepladders to get whatever glimpse of the action they could.

After waiting several moments at the first tee for the introductions and for the crowd to settle in, Jones looked down at the club in his hand and laughed. He was carrying his putter. His caddy, Howard Rexford, a nineteen-year-old Ardmore resident who had become something of a celebrity after being assigned to Jones, had already started down the fairway, and Jones had to wave him back. Homans was not the only one whose nerves were on edge. Indeed, Jones had been pacing his hotel room and smoking one cigarette after another since early in the morning. He felt so sick to his stomach, he said, it was as if jackrabbits were jumping up and down inside.

The match was over almost as soon as it began. Homans, wild off the tee and troubled by the wind, bogeyed the first five holes, and that was that. "It was as one-sided as the Spanish-American War," wrote Stan Baumgartner in the *Philadelphia Inquirer*, "as flat as a billiard table."

Jones did not play particularly well himself in the early going—he three-putted three greens on the front nine—but came in with a 33 for a decent enough score of 72. He had won nine holes and lost only two; he was seven up with eighteen holes to play. A certain triumph and uniquely historic achievement over his favorite golf course in the land was just hours away.

His father was out there somewhere, lurking behind trees lest his presence somehow become a jinx.

His dearest friends in all of golf—Francis Ouimet, Jimmy Johnston, Jess Sweetser—were in the huge gallery. Sweetser, bless him, had even brought along a periscope, hoping it would allow him to see a little something now and then of what was going on.

In the press barn, the writers who had been following him for years—Keeler, Danforth, Grantland Rice, William D. Richardson of the *New York Times*, Francis Powers of the *Chicago Tribune*—and many others were fussing with their stories, trying to find the right words to sum up the most majestic event they had ever been called on to describe.

Back home in Atlanta, his mother, wife, and children were listening to the reports coming in over the radio telling them the end was near.

It was the moment he had been working toward for four years—working toward his entire life, if you stopped to think about it. It was the pinnacle of his career, a moment no other golfer would ever be able to equal.

So why, *why* couldn't he take just a moment to enjoy it?

Look at him, Rice thought as Jones came in off the golf course. Has he ever looked as tired and spent as this? Seven strokes up, the match in hand, and he only wants one thing: for it all to end.

Jones railed to Keeler once more about his putting; the greens were fine, he said, there was something the matter with *him*. He was right, Keeler thought. There was something the matter, but it had nothing to do with his putting. It was the pressure of finishing the job, of doing what had never been done before.

By 2:00 P.M. the sun had come out, the wind had died down, and the crowds had grown until they covered entire sections of the golf course. Some holes were completely blotted out by the thousands of people who had no hope of seeing a shot struck but simply wanted to be where history was being made. Estimates put the crowd at eighteen thousand, among the largest ever to assemble for a golf tournament. Jones, whose favored practice area at the 18th green had been discovered by now, was surrounded as he took his last few warm-up shots, and the Marines had some difficulty moving him back through the crowd to the first tee.

The first two holes were halved—the crowd groaned when Homans missed a thirty-foot birdie putt at the first—and Jones then overshot the 3rd green and landed in a bunker. For the first time since the British Open, he pulled out the sand wedge Horton Smith had given him that spring.

Homans had the concave-faced club in his bag, too, and had used it to good effect several times against Seaver the day before. "You could drink out of it," Seaver said of the club, which he thought looked like a ladle. "It literally threw the ball out of the sand, and Homans was good with it."

Not as good as Jones. His shot popped out of the bunker and rolled within six inches of the cup. The resulting par gave him an eight-stroke lead, and after Homans landed in a trap on the 4th, he gained one more.

Standing on a hillside a quarter of a mile away, the Colonel saw the crowd surrounding the small figure on the fourth green.

"How's the match now?" he asked a spectator who had just trotted up from that direction.

"Eight up," came the reply. "When he makes this putt, it will be nine."

"Nine up and fourteen to go," Jones's father said to himself and then he softly began to sing: "There's a long, long trail a-winding into the land of my dreams."

Jones did not win another hole. His drives found the rough, his approach shots landed in bunkers, his putts refused to drop. So pumped up that he drove the 350-yard 8th green, he conceded the 9th to Homans when his ball landed in the sand once again and he missed a twelve-foot putt. It was only the third hole Homans had won all day, and the last.

Both men landed in the same bunker at the 10th—Jones needed two shots to get out—and took double bogeys. Jones was now four over par for the last four holes. For those who loved golf, and who loved Bobby Jones, the struggle to the finish line was becoming painful to watch.

Merion's 11th tee is at a far corner of the course and separated by a fence from a road where cars can be heard whizzing by. Members playing the hole today can stop to purchase drinks from women at a concession stand behind the tee. To the left, a modest plaque, fixed to a large stone by six long screws, attests to what occurred there on Saturday, September 27, 1930.

The 11th fairway bears off to the left and, at about the distance of a healthy tee shot, declines to a lower plateau. The feature is typical of several holes on the course where the greens are visible from the tee, but the landing areas are out of sight. The hole itself is set against a winding brook and, as Jones and Homans approached the tee, a horde of spectators came running out of the surrounding woods, down a small hill, and through the water to reach the green, 378 yards away.

Homans drove off to the left, and Jones followed with a fine tee shot that landed near the front of the brook about 300 yards away. The fairway was engulfed by onlookers who brushed aside marshals—and in some cases knocked them over—leaving the Marines to all but push the golfers through the crowds.

Both men reached the green with their second shots—Jones's ball came to rest twenty-five feet from the cup, Homans's five feet closer—and for a moment they were swallowed up by the crowd. When they reached the green, Jones took his putter from Rexford, stepped up to his ball, and the crowd fell silent.

He had the distance right, but the line was off just a bit. The ball rolled to the side of the cup and stopped almost at the edge. Homans's only hope of extending the match was to sink his long putt for a birdie. Wasting little time, Homans hit his ball, and for a moment it appeared to have a chance. Then, halfway to the cup, it broke a bit to the right. While it was still rolling, Homans walked not after his ball but, smiling broadly, toward Jones.

Jones did not hit his putt. His final act in achieving the Grand Slam was to shake Eugene Homans's hand.

The crowd tore the green apart and was well on its way to doing the same to Jones before Whitey Lloyd and his Marines pushed their way through. Somehow they got him off the green, down through the woods, and toward a few narrow planks that spanned the brook and led to the 12th fairway. As the escort party neared the bridge, a number of spectators already standing on it, including several women, were shoved off into the water. A few marshals wearing their red berets and armbands fell, too. The golfers and their cordon of guards made it safely across, then broke into a dogtrot toward the fairway, where they were again engulfed by the crowd.

Finally, with the Marines holding hands and forming a circle around the golfers, a semblance of order was restored. Jones and his entourage walked the length of the course to the clubhouse, cheered to the echo at every step. It was, Richardson wrote in the *New York Times*, "as triumphant a journey as any man ever traveled in sport."

Recalling the moment years later, Jones would say he felt a wonderful release of tension when he saw Homans coming across the green toward him. But in the Merion locker room immediately afterward he was far less sanguine. The image that came most vividly to his mind was crying like a baby after winning the 1926 U.S. Open at Scioto.

"What fun do I get out of tournaments?" he said to Jimmy Johnston. "None. You are merely on exhibition. This is my last amateur tournament. After today I am through with competitive golf."

But by the time they called him out to receive his fourth national championship trophy of the year, the stress that had been building for so long was, for the moment at least, finally gone. He wanted to thank the gallery for being so kind to him, Jones said. And he probably owed his life to those Marines.

In London, Bernard Darwin was exultant—"Bobby has now made of it what Mr. Peggotty called a 'merry-go-rounder,' and there is probably not one single golfer in the world who is not glad thereof," he wrote—while back home in Atlanta, Mary got the news when a reporter for the *Journal* called.

"That's grand," she said. And though the rest of the city reacted with excitement, there was nothing approaching the hysteria after his victory at Interlachen. The city had had its big blowout, and there would be no repeat. Jones would arrive at the Brookwood Station at nine-thirty Monday morning, it was announced. Those who wished to could come pay their respects, after which he would go directly home.

"There is no suggestion of a parade," one civic official said. "Bobby knows that Atlanta loves him."

20

Quitting the Memorable Scene

Even as he was beginning to conquer competitive golf as no one before him ever had, Jones found himself wondering what it would be like to give it up.

"Sometimes I get to thinking, with a curious little sinking away deep down, how I will feel when my tournament days are over, and I read in the papers that the boys are gathering for the national open or the amateur," he wrote in his youthful memoir *Down the Fairway*. "Maybe at one of the courses I love so well, and where I fought in the old days. It's going to be queer."

But when the time finally came, there was no such nostalgia. The pressure to win, which had begun in 1925 by his reckoning, was getting worse and worse, the pleasure he took from the game growing smaller and smaller. He could see where this led, he thought, and he wanted nothing to do with it.

"You take Walter Hagen and some of the others of my era," Jones said years later, "I think they lost their real enthusiasm for tournaments long before they were physically on the downgrade. I know I did."

And so, in an announcement released by the U.S. Golf Association in November, less than two months after his victory at Merion, Jones retired.

He had not planned to say anything official, Jones said, but he had signed to make a series of instructional films for Warner Bros. in Hollywood, and his thinking had changed. He was not convinced that the contract was a violation of the rules of amateurism—he had been writing instructional *articles* for years now—but "I am so far convinced that it is contrary to the spirit of amateurism that I am prepared to accept and even endorse a ruling that it is an infringement." He would never play professionally, Jones said, but "since I am no longer a competitor, I feel free to act entirely outside the amateur rule, as my judgment and conscience may dictate."

The announcement was front-page news on both sides of the Atlantic, and Jones was widely applauded. He had made a wise move, said Jerry Travers, whose record of four U.S. Amateur championships Jones had broken, because he had won all there was to win. He had retired with dignity, said the *London Observer*, and an editorial in the *New York Times* used the same word. "With dignity he quits the memorable scene upon which he nothing common did or mean."

Nobody, of course, was happier with the decision than Mary and the rest of Jones's family. "I am glad his tournament golf is over," his mother said. "I am tired of seeing him go away from home in good health and come home worn and exhausted."

Most of Jones's colleagues understood his reasoning—"I think Bobby Jones was so fed up on galleries, excitement and notoriety which comes under the heading of publicity, that he was sick and tired of it all," said Ouimet—but others were not so sure the decision was permanent.

"I don't think Jones will play again for a year or so," said Hagen, "but when he comes back I believe he will attract the biggest gallery that ever followed a golf player in any country. And being thoroughly human, he will like it. There's a contagion about the spotlight that champions cannot successfully resist. Few of them try to."

The pros on the PGA tour, well aware of what the retirement of the most popular golfer in the world would do to tournament attendance and the attention paid to the game, adopted a resolution encouraging him to enter "the world he has not conquered"—their own championship.

But Hagen was wrong, and the PGA was disappointed. Except for acceding to Masters chairman Clifford Roberts's request that he play in that tournament for the publicity value, Jones's career as a tournament golfer was over. He would play golf and plenty of it during the next two decades, but the pressure and the tension would be gone. "If I want to take 11 on a hole," he said, "I can now."

Darwin summed up Jones's retirement announcement by recalling the words of George Washington to the Continental Congress in 1784—"Having finished the work assigned to me, I retire from the great theater of action"—as well as the response: "Sir, you retire with the blessings of your fellow citizens."

Perhaps Jones would return to Britain for a friendly round someday, Darwin wrote. "Meanwhile we must wait to see him on his famous film. If it does not improve our golf—a thing past hoping for in some cases—it will at least give us a sight of a cherished friend."

PART III

The Best That Life Can Offer . . . and the Worst

21

Hollywood, Augusta, and Beyond

In 1939, Robert T. Jones Jr., attorney at law, moved his family into Whitehall, a columned eighteen-room mansion at 3245 Tuxedo Road in the center of Atlanta's fashionable northwest side. Whitehall had no meaning to the home's new occupants, but Jones did not object to living in a dwelling that bore a name as well as a number.

"Dad bought the house from a Dr. Childs and the name was on the mailbox when we moved there," Mary Ellen, the youngest of the three Jones children, who was born four months after he won the final leg of the Grand Slam, told Atlanta sportswriter Furman Bisher. "Dad just never did bother to take it down."

The house was set back from the road and all but out of sight behind a white spiked fence. Mary decorated it with Waterford chandeliers, Aubusson rugs, and European antiques, while Jones outfitted a trophy room and built an indoor gym in the back. "It was a huge barnlike thing with badminton courts in it," says Robert Marsden, who went to school with the three Jones children. "Spalding was his company, and if the feathers on the shuttlecock got beat up a little bit, there were two fifty-five-gallon barrels and you'd reach in and there were probably a thousand of them."

Life at Whitehall was all that might have been expected of Atlanta's most famous citizen. The staff included a cook, chauffeur, butler, maid, gardener, and night watchman. Two nurses later joined them. Bob Jones III and his sister Clara rode in horse shows at summer camp. Mary Ellen took golf lessons from Stewart Maiden ("To his outspoken disgust, I was a very poor student") without exactly understanding why it mattered. To the nun who asked her class to explain what their fathers did for a living, she said, "I don't know, but he has an awful lot of blue ribbons, so he must have won something."

It was not Jones's legal acumen alone that provided this elegant standard of living. Rather, as he was the first to admit, it was golf. No longer bound by the constraints of amateurism, he could now cash in on the demand his fame had created over the years, a fame that had reached its crest with his victory at Merion.

Far from reacting tentatively to this huge change in his life—the world's most celebrated amateur selling his services on the open market—Jones embraced it. Just as giving up competition had relieved him of the pressure he had been laboring under, signing a movie contract with Warner Bros. was a liberating act as well. "I was surprised and delighted that I experienced a new sense of freedom," Jones wrote. "Suddenly I realized that there had been considerable strain attached to the job of maintaining a strict amateur position." From now on, he said, he could entertain business proposals that appealed to him without having to worry about whether they ran afoul of U.S. Golf Association regulations.

So while Jones may have become a full-time lawyer in the popular imagination, the time he spent practicing his profession in the years immediately after his retirement gave way to other pursuits. "I found that you can't work at the law and too many other things at the same time," he said. Especially when there were so *many* other things in his life all of a sudden and they were so interesting.

Jones had no sooner returned to Atlanta after winning the Grand Slam than Clifford Roberts, a New York financial adviser he had met some years earlier, suggested they look into building a golf course 150 miles down the road in Augusta, where he had often played before. But even as that project began to take shape, Jones was "already deeply involved in enough golfing projects to preclude, at least for many years, my taking any serious interest in other activities."

"I began to realize that golf was the only thing in the world I really knew very much about," he wrote. "And since all phases of the game had interested me, why should I make an effort to put it away from me? It was not necessary to play for money, or to teach, or to run a golf shop. I could serve the game in other ways and let it serve me."

And serve him it did, in one way or another, for the rest of his life.

Jones was still at Harvard when he sketched out his first club designs. He was supposed to be reading English history, he said, but like college students everywhere, he found his mind idly drifting toward the golf course. What a beautiful driver, he thought, as he examined the drawings that made good use of his mechanical engineering training, and he sent them off to a designer at the A. G. Spalding & Brothers sporting goods company. The firm made several prototypes, and the club turned out to be "a monstrously powerful implement" that added yards to his shots. Jones was hooked and began designing other clubs.

Now, years later, he was able to devote himself to mass production, and he worked with Spalding's designers to produce clubs that would bear his name. The first set went on sale in time for the 1932 Christmas trade and quickly became so popular that Spalding had trouble keeping them in stock. Jones denied later suggestions these were the first matched clubs produced in the United States, but his natural modesty did not prevent him from claiming they were the best. The irony was that the clubs had steel shafts, which had first been introduced some years earlier and were now taking over the game. Jones's own clubs always had been made of hickory.

Over the years, more than two million Bobby Jones clubs were sold, and they remained on the market until 1973. Coming as they did with a Spalding vice presidency, a membership on the company's board of directors, and a "substantial block of stock," the clubs played a large part in securing his financial future.

Designing a golf course that would quickly become one of the most famous in the world, and sets of golf clubs that were similarly all the rage, were not the only activities that kept Jones from his law office in the first months after he announced his retirement. In January 1931 he appeared on his first NBC radio broadcast, sponsored by the

Lambert Pharmaceutical Company, whose ads, which must have sounded jarring to some listeners, promised men would find "Lister-ine Shaving Cream as valuable to your shaving comfort as Bobby's advice is to your game."

The shows were uneven—how was he supposed to teach golf without pictures?—and Jones, who sounded nervous and out of his element, was not happy with the results. Neither, he suspected, was Lambert, though its executives never complained, and the series ran for twenty-six consecutive Wednesday nights.

Jones's movie shorts for Warner Bros., on the other hand, were a triumph.

"Did I enjoy it?" he recalled years later of his stay in Hollywood. "Hell, yes, I'll never forget it. . . . I never had a more delightful experience."

Jones's arrival on the West Coast in March 1931 was big news, par-ticularly in the movie community, which was as starstruck as many of its fans. At first, Warner Bros. used only its own actors in the films, but soon stars from other studios were clamoring to take part. Intrigued by Jones's celebrity and excited about the chance to take lessons from him, they demanded a chance to be in the series, and their employers, realizing the publicity they would receive from being associated with Jones, acquiesced. "Paramount allowed me to go over because of the esteem they had for Bobby Jones," Richard Arlen, the star of *Wings*, which won the first Academy Award for best picture, in 1927, told the writer Robert Cantwell. "It was a loan that wasn't often done in those days. It was probably the greatest two weeks I ever spent."

W. C. Fields, James Cagney, Edward G. Robinson, Walter Huston, Loretta Young, Douglas Fairbanks Jr., Joe E. Brown, and a host of other popular actors of the day appeared in the films. They com-prised the most famous cast ever to be assembled for a series of short subjects, and they worked for free. "The top actors and actresses donated their time," said George Marshall, who directed the series, which was largely shot at the Flintridge Country Club, north of Los Angeles. "It was a privilege to have Jones work on their game."

Marshall, who got his start directing Westerns in 1916 and who was used to turning out four or five full-length features a year, out-lined the series after coming to Atlanta to meet with his star. A four-handicap golfer himself, Marshall was playing with Jones at East

Lake when he saw a man following them. He had come down from the North for four straight winters to trail Jones around the golf course, he said. Just watching him play was enough to knock five strokes off his score.

Inspired, Marshall called Keeler, who had signed to do the narration, and said he had a plan. In each ten-minute short, Jones would come across a different actor struggling to play golf and would demonstrate the correct method. A story line would be developed that would have Jones using one club per episode. Jones suggested starting with the putter and working up through the short irons to the longer clubs. Each film would end with Keeler, in imitation of the then-popular serial *The Perils of Pauline*, saying, "Watch for the next episode of Bobby Jones's *How I Play Golf* coming soon to your theater."

The plots of the shorts were silly—Cagney and Robinson played Chicago-style gangsters, Brown a wisecracking comic, Young a lovelorn girl trying to distract her father and run off with her boyfriend—and there were times when Jones was all but lost among such professional scene stealers. But in the end his message came across. With films of his flawless swing matching the words, and with the looks and bearing of a leading man himself, Jones was a natural. His calm demeanor and deep southern accent—talkies were still relatively new, and his voice was much remarked on—combined to make him a presence on the screen despite, or perhaps because of, the fact that he was clearly no actor. "The first Bobby Jones reel is a darb!" said *Motion Picture Daily*, and other critics were equally charmed.

The films were an instant success, playing in six thousand theaters around the country before audiences of twenty million to thirty million. Warner Bros. quickly made plans for another series, to be shot a year later. In part, this popularity was due to moviegoers' fascination with seeing some of their favorite stars in a different light—relaxed and clearly enjoying themselves. It was almost as if, Cantwell suggests, they were showing home movies.

Jones brought his family with him to Los Angeles ("My nurse used to tell me of all the famous movie stars I had met," said Mary Ellen, who was three months old at the time, "but I remember none of that"), which made his first golfing venture away from the tournament trail even more pleasant. Not to mention the fact that the two series of shorts he made for Warner Bros. as the Depression was tightening its grip, earned him some $250,000.

And so Jones settled into a comfortable existence in the town of his birth among the people who knew him best. His family life was satisfying, and his business ventures away from the golf course prospered. He owned Coca-Cola bottling plants in Pittsfield, Massachusetts, and Rutland, Vermont, sat on a number of corporate boards, had some holdings with Roberts and a stake in his grandfather's textile mill in Canton as well as the earnings from his law firm.

Altogether, Dick Miller estimates in *Triumphant Journey*, Jones had a net worth of $2 million. This was not wealth of the sort possessed by some of his friends—both Roberts and Coca-Cola president Robert W. Woodruff could have bought and sold him many times over—but for a man who professed not to care about great riches ("What is the use of all that money? Just enough to be even and kind to everyone"), it was more than enough to provide every luxury the family of a southern gentleman required.

The one extended period he spent away from home was a year in Europe as an intelligence officer in World War II. In England, his unit was involved in the planning for D-Day, and though it landed on a Normandy beach the day after the main invasion, it still came under artillery fire. He was mustered out as a lieutenant colonel and, as Stephen Lowe notes in *Sir Walter and Mr. Jones*, seldom had much to say about his military career. "Can't talk about those things, you know," he once teased a reporter.

Even before he first walked through the fruit orchard that would become Augusta National, Jones had had glimpses of it. The Augusta Country Club, where he had played many rounds over the years, lies just beyond the fence at the far end of the course, which is now the famous landscape of "Amen Corner," where the hopes of so many would-be Masters winners have come to grief. But not until the spring of 1931, when he and Roberts drove in through the front of the property, did Jones realize he had found the "house in the high woods" Hilaire Belloc had spoken of.

"The long lane of magnolias through which we approached was beautiful," Jones wrote. "The old manor house with its cupola and walls of masonry two feet thick was charming. The rare trees and shrubs of the old nursery were enchanting. But when I walked out on the grass terrace under the big trees behind the house and looked down over the property, the experience was unforgettable. It seemed that this land had been lying here for years waiting for someone to lay a golf course upon it."

Roberts took an option on the land for $70,000—it was estimated he could have bought it for half that amount a few years later, as the Depression caused real-estate prices to continue to fall—and asked a number of wealthy businessmen, many of them friends of his and Jones, to subscribe $5,000 each. Several checks were written on the spot, and the full amount was quickly subscribed.

To design the course, Jones never considered anyone other than Alister Mackenzie. From his first look at Cypress Point in 1929, and from the conversations he had had with Mackenzie about the theory of golf course design, he knew he had found his man.

Born in Yorkshire, England, Mackenzie studied medicine at Cambridge, but while serving as a surgeon during the Boer War, he became interested in the Boer soldiers' talent for remaining hidden in open country. Soon he was an adviser to the British government on camouflage, and during World War I he wrote the army's training manual on the subject.

After the war, Mackenzie gave up medicine to join a firm of golf course architects and, several years later, left for the United States. Without exactly hiding his birthplace, Mackenzie was perfectly happy to be taken for a Scotsman—his father was Scottish and his mother English—and he often wore kilts—even, notes Charles Price, at formal dinners instead of a tuxedo.

Mackenzie's theory of course design emphasized two principles above all: the setting should determine the layout, and the course should be playable by everyone. Not for him the glut of bunkers and the punishing high rough of other famous courses. The only purpose of rough, Mackenzie said, was to lose balls and frustrate golfers. Jones, who wanted a course that could be enjoyed by golfers of every ability, could not have agreed more. Though Augusta National has undergone a number of changes over the years, it is still distinctive for its wide fairways and lack of rough and bunkers that offer strategic escape routes to players of lesser skill.

The one difficulty Mackenzie did build into his courses was on the greens. He liked them large and rolling, and designed them to accommodate elaborate drainage systems. Asked how he built in such tricky undulations, he once said he told the contractor to "employ the biggest fool in the village and tell him to make all the greens flat."

Mackenzie went to work quickly on the huge new layout—at 365 acres Augusta National covered more than twice the ground of courses elsewhere—and Jones, who often accompanied him to measure the distance shots would have to travel from various positions on the course, gave him his head. With out-of-work farmers in the area willing to work from dawn to dusk for as little as 25 cents an hour, the course was ready for play in a year.

The formal opening of Augusta National took place in January 1933, when eighty members and a few friends arrived on a private train from New York chartered by Roberts. For $100, each man received round-trip transportation—the Pennsylvania Railroad supplied Pullman cars, diners, and club cars—and three days at Augusta's Bon Air Vanderbilt Hotel, with meals and transportation to and from the club. Even the fact that it was cold and wet during their stay did not keep the members from enjoying their new playground, perhaps because kegs of corn liquor were stored in tents at the 1st and 10th holes.

Mackenzie was missing from this celebration and, though he came to Augusta after major construction work was finished, he never saw his handwork with the grass in place and ready for play. He died in 1934, a few months before the first Masters was played.

As soon as the course was completed, Roberts went to work on the U.S. Golf Association to try to schedule an upcoming U.S. Open for a date in April, when Augusta was in bloom. When the organization pointed out that the Open was always held in June, Roberts had another idea: Augusta National would host a tournament of its own.

Grantland Rice offered the shrewd suggestion that the tournament be held late in March, when many of the nation's top sportswriters were heading north from baseball's spring training camps. The Augusta National Invitation Tournament was a hit from the start and quickly became a signature event on the golf calendar. Other tournaments may have had many of the best golfers in the country, after all, but only one had Bobby Jones.

Jones thought calling the tournament the Masters was presumptuous, but had no choice once the press picked it up from Roberts. Nor could he resist Roberts's request that he play in the tournament for the publicity value, particularly since the playing partners he regularly thrashed in friendly matches at East Lake and charity exhibitions could attest that there was nothing wrong with his game. A few weeks before the first Masters was played in 1934, for instance, he shot 65 at Augusta National. He was only thirty-two years old. Why shouldn't he think of winning?

Jones practiced hard for the tournament, but he never had a chance. His putting was an embarrassment, and he was startled to see that his usual prematch jitters, which he had always welcomed as an indication he was concentrating, never went away. Playing with friends, he was as good as ever—at least he liked to think so—but now that he had given up the pressure of tournament golf, there was no going back. He had taken so much punishment in his effort to win tournaments over the years, he said, that he simply could not will himself to go through it again. It was one last indication of how much competitive golf had taken out of him, and how wise he had been to give it up.

Jones finished the first Masters with a score of 294, ten shots behind Horton Smith, who won while playing with a Bobby Jones model driver. Jones never did that well in the tournament again.

It was force of habit that prompted Jones to bring his golf clubs when he and Mary, along with Grantland Rice and Robert Woodruff and their wives, sailed to England en route to the 1936 Olympics in Berlin. Certainly, he was not expecting to play on the trip, nor was he pleased with the way he had been hitting the ball lately. But when Woodruff said he and his wife and a few other friends were going to spend several days at Gleneagles before heading to the Continent, Jones decided to go along. He shot two rounds of 71 on the historic course and suddenly was feeling better about his game.

Sitting at dinner during their final evening and discussing arrangements to return to Southampton and the boat for Germany, Jones felt a pang of longing. He was so close to St. Andrews. If he looked out across St. Andrews Bay, he could almost see the Old Course. How could he not play it one more time? The party made plans to drive in for lunch, after which Jones would play a round and they would all take the night train to London. A chauffeur was sent ahead to write down his name along with Woodruff's for an afternoon tee time.

Norman Boase, the captain of the Royal and Ancient, hosted the travelers for lunch and arranged for Willie Auchterlonie, the club professional who had won the British Open in 1893, and Gleneagles pro Gordon Lockhart to join the group. But when Jones arrived at the golf course, he wondered if there had been some mistake. There must be a tournament going on, he thought as he saw the huge crowd that had gathered at the first tee.

But the mistake was his. The crowd was there to see him.

Someone had seen the name R. T. Jones Jr. on the sign-up sheet, the word had quickly spread through the small college town, and thousands of people had stopped what they were doing and hurried to the golf course. "I looked out to the shopkeepers on South and Market Street," says Gordon Christie, who worked in his family's bicycle shop. "One shopkeeper went to another and said, 'Bobby Jones is coming.'" Soon, stores were shuttered all over town, with only hastily written signs explaining the proprietors' absence: "Bobby's back."

Woodruff took one look and immediately dropped out of the match. A mediocre golfer, he had no intention of putting his game on display before such a huge gathering. The crowd grew so animated when it caught sight of Jones that it appeared he might be kept from the golf course as well. He was besieged by spectators and signed autographs before Boase and a few others came to the rescue and took him inside the clubhouse for a few moments to allow the excitement to subside a bit.

Back out on the tee, Jones and his partners had to wait twenty minutes as attempts were made to clear enough of the crowd off the fairway to allow the golfers to hit their tee shots. The delay gave a number of cameramen, who had rushed to the course, time to fire off shot after shot.

Finally the round began, and with it a scene never before seen on a golf course: three men out for a casual Monday afternoon game of golf followed around by an almost deliriously excited gallery in numbers worthy of a national championship. Rice estimated the crowd at six thousand at its peak, while the *St. Andrews Citizen* put the number at four thousand. It was an astonishing turnout for a match that had not been publicized and had been posted only a few hours earlier. "If only we had known a day in advance," one spectator told Rice, "we'd have had twenty-five thousand people here. They would have walked from a hundred miles away."

As he followed the crowd, which included everyone from elderly men to couples with small children in tow and babies in their arms, Rice found himself looking at people's eyes. The emotion he saw brought a lump to his throat. For a supposedly unemotional people, he thought, the Scots were certainly letting themselves go. "He should be king of Scotland," a spectator told him. "This is where he belongs."

The gallery grew larger as word of the match continued to spread, and with no marshals to exercise even minimal control, it ran all over the golf course without regard for its own safety. At least two people were hit by flying golf balls. Nobody was complaining, however, because the round had barely begun when it became clear that Jones was playing some of the best golf of his life.

He sank a twelve-foot putt at the 2nd hole for a birdie and pitched within three yards at the 6th for another. At the par-3 8th, he hit a beautiful 4-iron that faded around a small mound obscuring the flag and came to rest eight feet from the hole. The resulting birdie, which was followed by a par, gave him a nine-hole score of 32, which matched his start in the finest round he had ever shot at St. Andrews—his 68 in the 1927 British Open. It was almost as if, a few Scotsmen might have been thinking, the Old Course was glad to see him back, too.

It could not last, of course. Jones's troubles on the back nine began with his old friend, the 11th hole, where he had torn up his scorecard fifteen years before. His second shot was too strong, bounced off the green, and landed in a bunker on the far side. It was the first of five fives coming in, and he finished with a score of 72.

Still, Jones had acquitted himself well and thrilled the crowd. And when he sank a long putt for a birdie at the 18th, hundreds of spectators, in one last demonstration of unlikely British emotion, raced across the green to join him. Jones made it to the clubhouse, where he signed everything thrust into his hands—books, papers, postcards, even cigarette wrappers—for half an hour before he finally was led away.

"I would not have missed this experience for anything," he told the reporters who had planned to be anywhere but at the golf course that day. "I said before that it was worthwhile crossing the Atlantic for the pleasure of playing the Old Course and I am still of that opinion."

Though Jones would always remember his final round at St. Andrews as one of the great days of his life, for almost a quarter of a century he kept one story of what had happened there to himself. It was one of those things a man does not talk about, he said. But finally, in his last book, *Golf Is My Game*, he relented. He was sensing his mortality now—"this may be my last utterance on the subject of golf," is the way he put it—so perhaps he could be forgiven for relating one more reason why he had come away smiling.

He had just made his last great shot on the Old Course, Jones said, the 4-iron off the 8th tee he had placed so exquisitely within eight feet of the hole. He had stepped back to place his club in his bag when he heard his caddy, a young man whose name he had long since forgotten, say under his breath, "My, but you're a wonder, sir."

22

"White as the Ku Klux Klan"

Shortly before dawn on December 24, 1955, a maintenance crew arrived at the Bobby Jones Golf Course in northwest Atlanta and removed racial epithets that had been smeared in yellow paint on its benches and pavilion.

When newspaper reporters, photographers, and television crews arrived several hours later, there was no sign of the vandalism—and no story for them to cover. A clever ruse by Mayor William Hartsfield made sure that the first black golfers ever to play on one of the city's municipal golf courses would tee up several miles away rather than, as had been expected, at the one named after Atlanta's favorite son.

Jones was pleased when, on December 30, 1933, Atlanta named its new municipal course after him. He was so delighted, in fact, that when a thousand people wearing heavy coats and mufflers to ward off the winter cold showed up at the inauguration ceremonies, he played a full 18 holes in a biting wind. Making some excellent shots and sinking every putt in sight, he shot a 67.

The Bobby Jones Golf Course was built in Peachtree Battle Memorial Park, the site of the climactic Civil War Battle of Peachtree Creek, and ranked with any municipal layout in the South, said Everett Millican, chairman of the Atlanta Parks Commission. He had his eye on some federal funds to help with the construction of a club-house, Millican added, referring to a program in the new Roosevelt administration's Works Progress Association in which some six hundred golf courses were built around the country to provide employment and recreation during the Depression. "I spent a very enjoyable afternoon," Jones said, "and the course is a tribute to the efforts of those responsible for its creation . . . I am sure that it will prove popular with golfers."

There was no question of any black Atlantans playing the Jones municipal course at that time, of course. Just as they were not welcome at any of the city's sixty-two tennis courts, twelve baseball diamonds, seven football fields, and one indoor basketball court, they were not allowed on any of its seven golf courses. Unless, as Pete McDaniel noted in *Uneven Lies: The Heroic Story of African-Americans in Golf*, they were carrying another man's bag.

The one course that did welcome Atlanta's black golfers was the Lincoln Country Club, which was founded in 1927 and quickly became a popular place to see and be seen in the African American community. The price was right—a membership cost only $12—the food was good, and the camaraderie at the bar was lively. The presence of slot machines and the fact that, in contrast to many white country clubs, women were admitted as members added to Lincoln's popularity. Social memberships for those who did not care for golf sold for $6. "If you weren't seen at Lincoln on the weekends, you weren't part of the in-crowd," Charles T. Bell, whose family owned a real-estate firm on Auburn Avenue, told McDaniel.

The only real drawback to Lincoln was the quality of the golf. A nine-hole course with no hole longer than three hundred yards and a cement block clubhouse, it was poorly maintained and frustrating to players with any real ability who wanted to challenge and improve their games. "The greens looked like someone had taken a lawn mower, cut an area, and put some sand on it," Bell said. "Most of us were former caddies, so we knew how a golf course should look."

Over the years, some of the club's more serious golfers made several attempts to improve the course, but they all failed. After a particularly bitter argument over the installation of an irrigation system in 1951, one of the dissidents, Hamilton Holmes, a physician who played on an all-black golf circuit and won a National Negro Seniors title, was asked to resign his position as a director of the club. With his sons Oliver and Alfred, Holmes joined a score of other dissatisfied golfers at meetings in Bell's office to vent their frustrations and decide what to do next.

At one of these gatherings, Alfred Holmes said the words that put in motion a fight that would reach all the way to the U.S. Supreme Court: "To hell with trying to get them to fix up Lincoln. Let's go and play Bobby Jones."

Unlike his brother, Oliver Wendell Holmes, who was a minister known for his conservative ways, Alfred Holmes—everyone called him Tup—liked to speak his mind straight out. He had played for the golf team at Tuskegee Institute, then gone to work for Lockheed Aircraft in Marietta, Georgia, where he became a union shop steward. While others in the room were shocked by his suggestion, Bell agreed immediately, and the two men devised a plan.

One member of the group, Kusuth B. Hill, would go on ahead to integrate Bobby Jones Golf Course by stealth, and they would follow. With his light skin and blond hair, Hill had often been taken for white, and it was no different this time. A short time after Hill teed off, Bell and Holmes followed him to the course and were turned away. "The head pro told us straight out we couldn't play, that they didn't allow no niggers at Bobby Jones," Bell said. "We said, 'Is that right? Well, there's one on your course right now.'" Hill was quickly rounded up, and the party was ejected.

Two years later, after innumerable strategy sessions in which Tup Holmes took the lead, the golfers filed a lawsuit aimed at forcing the city to desegregate its parks and golf courses. Technically, they won when a federal judge ruled that Atlanta must allow them to play at any municipal course available to whites. But the city's response— that they would be allowed on the courses only when whites were not playing and certainly not on weekends—made the victory a hollow one. They decided to appeal to a higher court.

John H. Calhoun, a businessman who was president of the Atlanta chapter of the National Association for the Advancement of Colored

People, threw the weight of his organization behind the suit despite some dissent within the black community. Why spend the NAACP's time and money on this case, some wondered, when so few blacks played golf? Why not accept the court decision as a victory and move on to more important battles? But the case went forward under the direction of an NAACP lawyer brought in for the occasion, Thurgood Marshall.

An appeals court in New Orleans upheld the original ruling, but on November 7, 1955, a unanimous U.S. Supreme Court reversed it. Citing *Brown v. Board of Education*, which had been handed down the year before, as precedent, the Court outlawed segregation in Atlanta's parks, playgrounds, beaches, and golf courses.

"I appreciate the decision beyond all expression," said Hamilton Holmes. "We know that it is right that we should be allowed to play on the city courses as taxpaying citizens. We understand how to play the game of golf and the courtesies of the game. You can be sure we will do what is right."

The response of their opponents was less gracious.

As racial slurs appeared on the benches and pavilions at Bobby Jones Golf Course, the Holmeses households began receiving threats. "As soon as you hit the house, the phone calls started," Isabella Holmes, Tup's wife, recalled in an interview with the Atlanta History Center in 1998. "The children were afraid. I was afraid. It was a frightening time."

Many state and city politicians were equally intransigent.

"Comingling of the races in Georgia state parks and recreation areas will not be tolerated," said Governor Marvin Griffin. "I can make the clear declaration that the state will get out of the park business before allowing a breakdown in segregation in the intimacy of the playground." If it were up to him, Griffin said, he would plow up the city's golf courses and plant alfalfa.

"It is obvious that the NAACP is able to obtain from that Court any decision respecting segregation that is designed to further its program to force intermarriage," the state attorney general, Eugene Cook, said.

"It will probably mean the end of most public golf courses, playgrounds, and things of that type," said U.S. senator Herman Talmadge, who, as governor of Georgia at the time of the *Brown* decision, had predicted that "blood will run in Atlanta's streets" and who was a leading national spokesman for segregation, which he said was the work of God. "If He had wanted one race and one color, He would have created them," Talmadge told a national television audience on *Meet the Press* after the historic ruling outlawing separate but equal schools. "When He segregated them, it was good enough for me."

The city should consider leasing or selling its recreational facilities to private individuals, Talmadge said, a statement that led to mockery in some quarters. The South might be willing to sacrifice public education to preserve its prejudices, scoffed the *Nation*, but it is hard to believe it would ever give up golf.

The one elected official who had no immediate public reaction to the decision was William Hartsfield. A shrewd politician, the mayor knew he had to pick his steps carefully between a white population in danger of being aroused by the inflammatory statements of its leaders and a black citizenry that suddenly found the law on its side. Most important, Hartsfield knew, was for the city to remain calm.

Moving quickly, he met with more than a hundred employees of the city's golf courses. If segregation meant closing the courses down altogether, he said, their jobs would disappear. Considering the small number of black golfers who would show up, was defying the law really worth it? And besides, the mayor noted, there was no question of integrating the *showers* at the three public courses that had such facilities. The employees agreed to go along.

Hartsfield was just as direct with Bell and Tup and Oliver Holmes, whose father had decided he had created enough history and would not join the first group of black golfers to play on a public course in Atlanta. If they played Bobby Jones, Hartsfield told them, there were bound to be problems. More than just the press and television cameras would be there; angry whites bent on making trouble were sure to join them.

"They told me they had promised the television people they would appear," Hartsfield later remembered. "I said, 'Those TV boys aren't interested in watching you hit the ball. They want to get pictures of you getting beat up.'"

Again, the mayor's arguments prevailed and Bell, the Holmes brothers, and a few of their friends went to the North Fulton course several miles away. As they drove up, Bell saw a white man unpacking his golf bag look up in astonishment. "He made a beeline to the clubhouse," Bell said, "to let them know the niggers were coming."

But there were no disturbances and, in fact, the new golfers were welcomed warmly. "Fellows, we're glad to have you here," one white golfer told them, and as they passed a foursome on the course, a man called out, "I want to see a birdie next time."

Realizing that they had been duped, reporters and cameramen raced to the course and caught up with the black golfers on the 4th hole. "Nobody shot under par after that," Bell noted with a laugh years later, although Tup Holmes shot a one-over-par 36 on the front nine and finished with a more than creditable 79.

Driving home after their historic round, Bell and the Holmes brothers passed Bobby Jones Golf Course, where three black golfers were playing. Nobody knew who they were, but they seemed to be enjoying themselves. Other golfers who followed them in the ensuing days encountered some harassment, but such reports disappeared almost entirely within a month. The issue began to fade from public scrutiny.

One significant factor in the acceptance of Hartsfield's plan was the backing of many of Atlanta's civic leaders, chief among them Robert W. Woodruff. Though his natural allies were some of the same politicians urging defiance of the Court's order, the president of Coca-Cola understood the damage that could be done to the city by a potentially violent dispute, and he let it be known that he supported Hartsfield. Another sign of the support of the city's power structure came in an editorial in the *Atlanta Journal* that said that while the Court's decision was in "fundamental error," it was the law of the land and should be obeyed.

But one voice that was not heard in the matter, either while it was being resolved or at any time in the future, was that of the man for whom the golf course at the center of the struggle was named.

There is no dispute over the regard in which Jones was held by the black people he came in personal contact with during his lifetime.

Without exception, they viewed him with respect and admiration. From Camilla, the black maid of his childhood days whose home he remembered visiting with such delight, to Woodrow Bryant, a caddy at East Lake who later became its clubmaker and enjoyed Jones's special trust, his behavior was as courteous and polite as it was with anyone else he encountered. The black men who caddied for Jones, who waited on him, who chauffeured him, and who, in his final years, attended to his personal needs, all remembered him as kind, generous, and intolerant of any cruelty toward them.

Seth Ray, a New York investment banker whose grandfather, T. J. Ray, was a fixture at East Lake for many years, tells several typical stories.

"Mr. Jones took him under his wing," Ray says of his grandfather, who began working in the East Lake clubhouse as a teenager and later became Jones's caddy and a chauffeur for his family. "He told me once he was in the clubhouse shining shoes when a man spat on him and called him a name. Mr. Jones heard it and became extremely angry. He really dressed the man down and said you will not speak to my caddy in that manner."

T. J. Ray also told of an incident during Jones's triumphant stopover in New York after sailing home from Britain in 1930. Jones had sent word asking that Ray be included in the contingent that came up from Atlanta on the Bobby Jones Special and, after the ticker-tape parade up Broadway, Ray appeared on a platform with the rest of the Jones party.

"During the celebration, Mr. Jones was introducing people," Seth Ray says. "He said, 'One of my young caddies is here,' and pointed to my grandfather and there was booing in the audience. He said, 'Don't you boo T. J. He's part of my family.'" Not a word of this appeared in the press at the time, but T. J. Ray, who continued to work for Jones for many years, told his grandson to make sure the story was never forgotten.

When it came to race relations in the larger context of public policy, however, Jones's views were far more ambiguous. It was not that he was indifferent to politics. To the contrary, there is ample evidence of his interest in the issues of the day and of his willingness to make his voice heard. This was particularly true during the last decades of his life, the politically turbulent 1950s and 1960s.

In large part, Jones's activism was due to his friendship with Dwight D. Eisenhower, whom he had met in 1947 and who became a frequent visitor to Augusta National during his presidency. Jones joined Eisenhower's 1952 campaign, introduced him at a rally in a large Atlanta auditorium, and the two men conducted an extensive correspondence that lasted until Eisenhower's death in 1969. But beyond his affection for Eisenhower and his stated desire to build a viable Republican Party in the South, Jones had very definite political views, which he was not at all reticent about expressing.

During a debate over what Eisenhower called a "crippling cut" in the budget for one of his defense proposals, Jones sent a telegram to his congressman, James C. Davis, saying it was "unthinkable that our mutual security program should be handicapped in any way. There could be no more effective answer before the world to the insults of the Communist dictator [Nikita Khrushchev] than for the Congress to vote enthusiastically the full appropriation for this program."

When Davis opposed John F. Kennedy's proposal to form the Peace Corps as "just another catchy slogan" the following year, Jones wrote approvingly, "It seems since we are all fighting a rearguard action anyway, we should be grateful even for small success in delaying the march of the New Frontier."

The King-Anderson Bill, Jones wrote to Representative Charles Weltner of a 1964 precursor to Medicare, was a "further unwarranted extension of the dominance of the federal government in our society. It is my opinion that private insurance companies can handle this situation much better without increasing Social Security taxes, which are already burdensome on employers and employees alike."

As for pending tax legislation that would affect him personally, Jones wrote Talmadge in 1969 that it "would result in beneficiaries of irrevocable trusts which I created in 1938 owing an estimated $100,000 of income tax in the future, none of which would be owed under existing law." Talmadge responded that he fully concurred.

And while Jones's correspondence with Ralph McGill, the Pulitzer Prize–winning editor and publisher of the *Atlanta Constitution*, consisted largely of good-natured jibes back and forth between friends with opposing political views, there were times when it grew more serious. He was wrong to support Kennedy in his dispute with U.S. Steel president Roger Blough, Jones lectured McGill, who, as a young sportswriter, had often written about Jones and remained one of his most devoted admirers.

Yet for all of Jones's interest in politics, he never addressed himself to the central domestic issue of the times. Nowhere in his copious correspondence, or in the memory of those who knew him, does the subject of race or the struggle for equal rights arise.

"My office adjoined his for ten years," says Jones's law partner Arthur Howell, "and I can't remember any discussion of race with Bob. If somebody asked me where he was on all this, I'd tell you I don't know. I don't think he ever discussed it with anybody."

"None of my research shows that he ever said, or did, anything," says Catherine Lewis, the curator of a permanent exhibit devoted to Jones at the Atlanta History Center, whose book *Considerable Passions: Golf, the Masters, and the Legacy of Bobby Jones* discusses the controversy over integrating the Bobby Jones Golf Course. "With all the folks that write about Jones, and all the resources we share, you'd think there would be something, and there's not. That's sort of stunning."

And just as no journalist bothered to ask Jones what he thought of the attempt to integrate the course that bore his name, neither was he questioned about his views on race at any other time. "I could have asked," says Frank Hannigan, who was a U.S. Golf Association official for twenty-eight years before becoming an adviser and commentator on ABC's golf telecasts. "I knew a lot of Augusta National members and they'd invite me into the clubhouse and we'd sit around and talk. I knew Jones's son and daughter-in-law very well. I could have asked them, but I never did. I regret it."

"There was a kind of deference to public figures that we don't hold today," says Lewis, explaining why Jones was never asked for his opinion about racial matters, particularly as they related to golf. It was a deference Jones enjoyed for the rest of his life.

The only recorded instance of Jones speaking about race, and the equal-rights demonstrations sweeping the South, came in a tale told by Eisenhower in 1956. As he tried to balance calls for him to back a modest civil rights bill against those warning him to go slow, says Eisenhower's biographer Stephen E. Ambrose, quoting notes taken at a meeting of Republican congressional leaders, he repeated "a little story he had heard from Bobby Jones down at Augusta; one of the field hands was supposed to have said, 'If someone doesn't shut up around here, particularly those Negroes from the North, they're going to get a lot of us niggers killed.'"

But despite Jones's silence, there are clues as to his views on race and civil rights. What they indicate is that, like many white southerners of the time, he chose not to become involved. There is no record of Jones supporting segregation in any aspect of southern life—or on southern golf courses—just as there is no indication that he opposed it publicly. What is on the record is his private support of two of the most intransigent segregationists of the time.

Letters from Jones to Georgia senators Richard Russell and Herman Talmadge can be taken as expressions of personal friendship—and in Talmadge's case of the fact that he relied heavily on Arthur Howell for advice on tax legislation. ("Herman would call me at eight in the morning and ask what I thought," Howell says. "I'd tell him and he'd say, 'Great. Look, Arthur, would you mind sending me that immediately by Western Union? And put it in third-grade English.'") But the fact that both men were defiantly opposed to court-ordered integration, and that they were Democrats, did not disqualify them from admiration in Jones's eyes.

"You can be very sure of the enthusiastic support of Mary and me in any race you may have for the United States Senate," Jones assured Russell in 1965 after the senator wrote in some agitation about "completely false rumors" that he was thinking of stepping down. "You will hear from me again as soon as I learn you have opposition."

"I haven't got much money these days, and I am hoping you won't need much in the coming election," Jones wrote to Talmadge in 1968, "but I do want to send you the enclosed as a token of my support and friendship. We very much need you in the United States Senate."

Similarly, Jones's private opposition to Lester Maddox in his successful run for governor in 1966 was based not on Maddox having chased black demonstrators out of his restaurant with an ax handle. Rather, it was a reflection of the Atlanta power structure's opinion that Maddox was a buffoon who was bad for business.

"I don't think that anybody thought Lester had any capacity to be governor," says Howell, who, after working with five Georgia governors on state funding programs, refused to allow the law firm to have anything to do with Maddox and supported his opponent, Bo

Callaway. "Bob knew exactly why I quit working for Lester. You just don't work for anybody who doesn't know anything about government. We were all Bo Callaway supporters."

Twice in the last decade of his life, Jones did involve himself privately in the subject of black golfers playing alongside white ones. Once, it was in response to criticism of qualification standards for the Masters, which Lee Elder did not integrate until after Jones's death. The other occasion hit even closer to home—at his beloved East Lake.

If Jones had an out when it came to the controversy over the Masters, it was Clifford Roberts. Though Jones's name and reputation had been the key to establishing the tournament by drawing golf's greatest players, it was Roberts's organizational ability, his friendship with wealthy and powerful businessmen, and his instincts for public relations that built it into a force of nature. The Masters had become not only the most prestigious tournament in the world, but also the inspiration for rapturous odes to the beauty of Augusta National that became a rite of spring on America's sports pages and television sets every April.

The combination of Jones's natural reticence and declining health pushed him more and more into the background as the years went by. Except for annual pilgrimages to his cottage on the course by old friends, golf officials, and the sportswriters he had known the longest, and his appearance at the awards ceremony when the tournament ended, he was seldom seen or heard from.

Roberts, on the other hand, was everywhere. Waspish, imperious, and with little regard for anyone unlike himself—"He regarded shortened Italian names as evidence of sinister behavior," Frank Hannigan says—he ran the Masters as his own private kingdom. "He was a complete authoritarian and that's the way he ran Augusta National," says Frank Chirkinian, who directed the Masters telecasts for CBS for thirty-eight years. "He proved conclusively that democracy was an ineffectual form of governing because it led to corruption and confusion. Under autocratic rule, nobody is confused. It works."

As the unchallenged leader of Augusta National, Roberts bore the brunt of the debate over whether the Masters should admit black players—and he loved every minute of it. Whether or not it is true, as charged by Charlie Sifford, the top black professional golfer in the country in the 1950s and 1960s, that Roberts once said, "As long as I live, there will be nothing at the Masters beside black caddies and white players," his conduct spoke volumes.

Charlie Harrison, a solid amateur golfer from Atlanta who played in two Masters, remembers an information packet each player received when he registered in 1973. "The first thing in it was a telegram Masters officials had received from various members of Congress stating that all professional sports had been integrated and it was time for the Masters to integrate," Harrison says. "They said Lee Elder is a great player and the Masters should do the right thing and invite him." Also included was Roberts's response, in which he obviously took great pride. "He said something like, 'Gentlemen, you do me great honor taking your valuable time away from running the country to try to help me run my golf tournament.'"

Jones was incapable of this sort of sarcasm, or of taking a strong hand against Roberts even if he had chosen to do so. He was joking when, in an application to the U.S. Golf Association in 1965 for a ceremonial restoration of his amateur standing, he listed his occupation as "assistant" and his employer as "Clifford Roberts," but it did define their relationship in terms of the Masters.

Jones was not immune to the controversy over who could play in the Masters, though, and in 1969 he was provoked into revealing his views at length in several letters to one of America's most popular sports columnists, Jim Murray of the *Los Angeles Times*. Murray was known above all for three qualities—his wild and sometimes scathing sense of humor, his love of golf and the men who played it, and his fierce sense of social justice. Charlie Sifford gave him the opportunity to indulge all three.

Writing before the Los Angeles Open in January 1969, Murray referred to the fact that the bylaws of the PGA contained a Caucasians-only clause until 1961, making it "the recreational arm of the Ku Klux Klan." Then he quoted Sifford about what happened when he complained about not being invited to the Masters. "I get this letter from Bobby Jones telling me to stop threatening him," Sifford said. "I don't threaten any man. I *get* threatened."

Murray's column quickly made its way to Jones, who responded more in sorrow than in anger, and pledged Murray to secrecy. "In almost fifty years of close association with the press," Jones wrote, "I have never known a newspaperman to violate a confidence. It is in reliance upon your respect for this tradition that I am sending you this letter with enclosures."

He had not threatened Sifford, Jones wrote. In fact, he had never met him and had only written to him once—the previous year, in response to Sifford's criticism of the Masters' qualification standards. He was enclosing that letter, Jones said, and would leave it to Murray to judge whether it contained any threats.

It did not. The letter was, however, patronizing from start to finish. Jones's letter to Murray was addressed to "Dear Mr. Murray," which was his custom when writing to people he did not know well. The one to Sifford began "Dear Charlie."

"I am somewhat doubtful that you were quoted accurately in the rest of your remarks," Jones wrote. "Since I do not believe that you uttered any belligerent threats, I want to ask you if it will not be better in future if you point out that you have seen no mention of color or race in the Masters tournament qualifications . . . and that you have every reason to believe that you will be invited whenever you fulfill one of these qualifications. . . . Personally, I can see no advantage either to you or the club to encourage newspaper reports of this nature."

Murray was not persuaded. Less than a week later, after Sifford won the Los Angeles Open, Murray wrote another column that contained more of his biting wit: "The proposition before the house now, is how does Charlie go about crashing the last barricade to membership in golf's front-of-the-bus—play in the Masters." Murray also wrote to Jones saying that surely there must be some way to invite Sifford to the Masters as a way of making up for all the years he and other black golfers had been barred from full professional participation in the sport.

Again, Jones responded with a courteous two-page letter—his increasingly desperate physical condition was evident in the painstaking, childlike scrawl of his signature—in which he said "Honorable disagreement is by no means a bar to friendship."

He then reviewed for Murray the Masters' requirements in detail. (The field was then heavily weighted toward amateurs, former

Masters competitors, and the top money winners on the PGA tour. "Charlie could get in if he were the Chinese or Turko-Roman champion, or runner-up in the Formosa Open, or the All-Madrid City Championship," Murray wrote.) He was following the progress of Sifford toward qualification, Jones said, and he hoped he would qualify "so that we may have the question disposed of on the basis of performance." But the tournament could not "invite a man simply because he is black."

While not mentioning Jones, Murray hooted at this reasoning three months later, as the attention of the golf world was centered on Augusta National: "The circumstances are well known, but I will recount them briefly here, to the accompaniment of the 'Battle Hymn of the Republic' and a recitation of the Gettysburg Address." Past Masters champions, he noted, were allowed to choose a player to be added to the field, and only one of them, Art Wall Jr., had voted for Sifford. The headline over the column was "White as the Ku Klux Klan."

But if Jones never faltered in his belief that no player should be invited to the Masters "simply because he is black," he also subscribed to its corollary: no one should be kept *off* a golf course when he was entitled to be there because of his color. Once again, however, his views were expressed only in private, and the result was a blot on the record of the golf course he knew best.

In May 1965, Charlie Harrison returned a call from Jim Brett, the starter at East Lake, where 36-hole qualifying for the upcoming U.S. Open would take place the following day. Harrison had won several city championships and a Southern Amateur title but had never played in an Open and was excited about the chance to qualify on his home course.

"He's not here," said Woodrow Bryant, who picked up the phone, when Harrison asked for Brett, "but I know what he wants to tell you. He wants to tell you who you're playing with tomorrow."

"I already know that," Harrison said. "Somebody named George Johnson. Do you know him?"

"Yeah, I know him," Bryant said, "He's colored, plays out at Lincoln."

"Can he play?" Harrison asked.

"He's a good player," Bryant replied.

Whether purposely or not, Bryant did not share this knowledge with Brett, and when Johnson arrived at East Lake the following morning and said "I'm here for the U.S. Open qualifying," the starter reacted in the only way that could possibly have occurred to him.

"The caddy shack is right over there," Brett said, pointing off in the distance.

"I've got a player's certificate," Johnson said, and he handed it over.

Those witnessing the scene said Brett was speechless and quite literally spinning in his tracks as he tried to come to terms with what he was confronting—the first black player on record ever to play at East Lake.

"Fine," he finally said. Johnson headed for the first tee.

Though nervous at the start, Johnson quickly settled down and played excellent golf until, on the final few holes, his game fell apart and his score approached 80. Harrison, in the meantime, shot a 69, his best round ever in Open qualifying. Excited and pleased with himself, he headed toward the clubhouse for lunch when something occurred to him. Where would Johnson eat? In the caddy shack? Surely not in the public restaurant on the course? Wait a minute, Harrison thought. They were trying to qualify for the U.S. Open together, weren't they?

"George, there's a players' luncheon in the clubhouse," Harrison said. "Do you have time to get a bite to eat?"

"Great," Johnson replied. The two men went inside and made themselves at home.

Except for an elderly woman who complimented Harrison on the fine round he had played under *those* circumstances, the rest of the day proceeded without incident. Harrison qualified for the Open, Johnson did not and went home.

Soon, Harrison began hearing whispers. "Some of the members, some friends of yours even, think you ought to get kicked out of the club," Tommy Barnes, a longtime East Lake member, told him. Larry Martin, the president of the Atlanta Athletic Club, which ran East Lake, did not make the threat explicit, but he asked Harrison to write a letter explaining why he had brought a black man into the East Lake clubhouse.

And then Harrison began hearing something he feared far more than losing his East Lake membership. If the U.S. Golf Association required the Atlanta Athletic Club to allow black players on its grounds, it would refuse to host qualifying events, which, for either the Open or the U.S. Amateur, it did every year.

"That affected me selfishly because it certainly was an advantage if I could qualify on my own home course," Harrison said four decades later of his decision to approach East Lake's most renowned member for help. "It wasn't all that noble."

Harrison had known Jones casually since he was a boy hanging around East Lake in the 1940s. "I remember my daddy telling me any time you see Mr. Jones over there practicing, you go and watch," he says. "Once my cousin, Tom Cousins, and I were over at the swimming pool and I said, 'You know, the greatest golfer that ever lived is play- ing today. We ought to go watch him play a hole.'" The boys jumped in a 1932 Pontiac that belonged to Harrison's grandfather, sped around behind the 13th green, and hopped over a fence just in time to see Jones hit an 8-iron from the fairway. The ball hooked around an oak tree guarding the left side of the green and landed a foot and a half from the hole.

"I said, 'See, he does it every time,'" Harrison says. "We didn't even watch him putt out. We just went on back to the girls at the swimming pool."

Years later, after winning his Atlanta city championships, Harrison joined the firm that handled some of Jones's insurance, and when Harrison's boss, Bill Leidl, asked if he would like to visit Jones at his office, he jumped at the chance. "We got the insurance business out of the way and for some reason, he started telling us how he prepared for a golf tournament and I'm just all ears," Harrison says. "He said he always took two weeks off prior to a tournament and didn't come to the office at all. He would just go play golf every day or, if it rained, he would read a book.

"I nudged my boss in the elbow and said, 'Bill, that sounds like a good idea,' and Jones leaned across the desk and said, 'Aw, goddamn, Harrison, I'm not talking about the city championship!'"

But now Harrison was approaching Jones on a more serious mat- ter and was not sure what to expect. The important thing to empha- size, he thought as he told Jones of the letter he had been asked to write, was not the fate of his membership but the possibility of East Lake withdrawing from U.S.G.A. events. He was delighted when Jones agreed that would be a mistake. "The real key, I think," Harrison says, "is that it was 1965 and the civil rights movement was really going and Martin Luther King was doing his marching and there was a lot of criticism of the Masters for not allowing a black to play."

"Charlie," Jones said, "I am on record, in writing, in the office of Augusta National, that anyone who qualifies for Augusta will play regardless of race, color, or creed. You've just got to meet the qualifying standard."

"Would it be all right if I used your name?" Harrison asked. "I think it would carry a lot more weight if I suggested in the letter that you agreed with me."

"I certainly do agree," Jones said, and he gave his assent.

Harrison's letter to Martin was brief. During the time George Johnson spent in the clubhouse, he "had behaved himself in a gentlemanly manner and gave no cause for criticism." While the directors might face problems from his presence, he hoped the club would not "alter its support of U.S.G.A.-sponsored tournaments." And then, in one sentence near the end, Harrison fired his biggest gun: "I feel that Bob Jones will concur in my desire that the Club continue its major contribution to the game of golf."

Harrison cannot explain why he did not make his point with greater force. Why he did not say, "I have spoken with Bob Jones and he has told me to say he agrees with me." Or, "I have spoken with Bob Jones, who said he agrees with me, and would be happy to discuss this with you personally."

"I don't know, that's just the way I wrote it," Harrison says. "I had no reason not to say Bob Jones will write you a letter or anything else. I wanted to give them the opportunity to talk to him if they wanted to. But if they did, it didn't do any good."

The East Lake board of directors was unmoved. Making no mention of Harrison's invocation of Jones's support, Martin's response was wordy, but the message it contained was clear enough: the club would entertain no more unauthorized guests in its clubhouse.

"It is the desire of the Board of Directors to direct the operation of the Atlanta Athletic Club in a manner which would be in accordance with our concept of a private club as we know it," Martin wrote. "We

believe that this concept of a private club is basic with the vast majority of our members. Any decisions we make will be based on this
belief and will govern the way in which we try to run all of our facilities, including the matter of tournaments." From now on, Martin
wrote, the board would be required to give specific approval before
hosting outside tournaments. Which was to say no more U.S.G.A.
events at East Lake.

There is no record of Jones going beyond Harrison's carefully
phrased statement or taking the matter up with the club's directors
personally. Like Harrison, he simply acquiesced. The two men never
spoke of the subject again, or of anything else to do with black and
white golfers playing together. "I wasn't on any crusade where I
would call Bob Jones back and say, 'This isn't happening,'" says Harrison. "I made my pitch and accepted the fact we weren't going to
have any more tournaments."

Within the next three years the Atlanta Athletic Club sold the two
East Lake courses—one had been added to the original layout in
1930—and relocated to a new golf course in Duluth, a suburb north-
east of Atlanta closer to the homes of the many members who had
long since left the city behind. In 1970, a public housing project was
built on the site of the second course, and it quickly became the center of one of the most crime-ridden, drug-infested neighborhoods in
the city. The original golf course fell into disrepair.

During the next several decades, Harrison began to come to terms
with what the reaction to his casual invitation to George Johnson had
represented. By then, Harrison had, much to his surprise, become the
director of a black-owned bank and, even more astonishingly, had
moved into a house overlooking the East Lake's 3rd green in 1994.
"My wife always wanted to live in an old home and this one was built
in 1856 and had a great Civil War history," Harrison says. "The first
two years we slept on the second floor because so many guns were
being shot off outside at night."

Today, the neighborhood is safer and the course is once again as
beautiful and inviting as it was when Alexa Stirling, Perry Adair, and
Little Bob Jones were learning how to play golf by imitating Stewart
Maiden's swing. Tom Cousins, Harrison's cousin with whom he had

witnessed Jones's fine shot at the 13th hole five decades earlier, and who had become a prominent Atlanta real-estate developer, bought the property in 1993 and began to reclaim the surrounding area.

With a $15 million federal grant, Cousins tore down the crime-infested public housing project, replaced it with a five-hundred-unit complex, and set about restoring both the East Lake course and the clubhouse in Jones's memory. Cousins persuaded eighty companies to buy corporate memberships to help with this revitalization and also arranged for East Lake to be opened for clinics at which minority youngsters were taught the basics of golf.

At one of these clinics, a television reporter asked Harrison if he had ever envisioned himself introducing black children to golf at East Lake. His answer spoke for an entire generation of Atlantans, a generation that included Bobby Jones.

"I never gave it a thought," Harrison said. "I was only worried about making pars and birdies and not three-putting the next green. I grew up with a white line on the bus and with separate water fountains and with the fact black people couldn't stay at the same hotel and had to walk around to the back steps of the Fox Theater. It never dawned on me. I was at the beginning of a learning process of the injustice of what was going on then. And I'm still learning."

It is important, Catherine Lewis says, to guard against what historians call "presentism"—observing events of the past in the light of current practices and beliefs. By this standard, it is unfair to judge what Jones did, and what he did not do, to promote equality in the sport that, had he spoken out, would have had to listen.

Still, it is interesting to contemplate what might have happened had Jones challenged the directors of East Lake publicly, had he told them to their faces that the course should continue as a venue for all legitimate contestants in U.S. Open and Amateur qualifying.

Or had he asked past Masters champions to exercise their right to add a player to the tournament by selecting Charlie Sifford.

Or when the Supreme Court handed down its decision barring segregation at the Bobby Jones Golf Course, had he announced that he would meet Charles Bell, and Hamilton, Tup and Oliver Holmes, at the first tee, where they would have their picture taken together.

.   .   .

In 1983, Atlanta mayor Andrew Young participated in ceremonies changing the name of the city's Adams Park Golf Course to the Alfred (Tup) Holmes Memorial Golf Course. Charles Bell took part in the event, but Holmes, and his father and brother, were present only in the memories of the few remaining veterans of the battle they had led.

The three men had all died within two years of each other in the 1960s and were buried in a cemetery adjacent to the Lincoln Country Club, which, after losing most of its members to municipal courses like the one named after Bobby Jones, had closed some years before.

23

"I've Been Having Some Numbness in My Limbs"

On August 15, 1948, a round of golf was arranged at East Lake as a farewell to Henry Lindner, the club's assistant pro, who was off to a new job in Charlotte, North Carolina. Along with two of his friends, Charlie Yates and Tommy Barnes, Jones joined the group as it teed off on the back nine.

As the match progressed, Lindner noticed something peculiar. Though he was a scratch golfer himself, he was certainly no Bobby Jones, who, even in his mid-forties, was still a formidable striker of the ball. But Jones was using a longer club from similar positions on the fairway, and Lindner could not restrain his curiosity.

"Mr. Jones," he said as they stood on the first fairway waiting for the group ahead of them to leave the green, "I notice you've been playing a 4-iron where I've been playing a 5."

"I've been having some numbness in my limbs," Jones replied, with no further elaboration.

Later in the round, as he was crossing the bridge to the 6th green, which the East Lake members called the island hole, Jones turned to Charlie Yates and said he would not be playing any more golf for a while; he had decided to have an operation. Two under par after 16 holes, Jones hooked his tee shot into the woods, played out for a double bogey, then parred the 18th to finish with a 72. It was the last round of golf he ever played.

"I had no idea until I saw a headline in the paper a day later," Barnes told Furman Bisher. "'Jones Enters Emory Hospital for Tests.' Funny thing, he was two under par coming into the 8th hole [Jones's 17th] and he finished even par as a cripple."

Jones had often felt the pain in his neck and his shoulder. A crick, or a creak, or a click, he called it. Sometimes the pain was so great he could not raise his backswing to its normal height, or bend over to putt properly. Once it had caused him to consider withdrawing from a tournament—the 1926 British Amateur at Muirfield—but he played through the pain and lost to Andrew Jamieson, the "small nobody" who all but apologized for beating him.

"I felt, and I am sure heard, the muscle up the left side of my neck give a loud, rasping creak like a rusty hinge," Jones wrote of the sensation when he woke up the morning of the match. The pain was never that severe again, but the clicking and the stiffness recurred often during his career.

Doctors were consulted, one after another. Whirlpool treatments were prescribed, and osteopathy. Jones even had a few teeth pulled in deference to the odd theory they might somehow be poisoning his system. It was amazing, Clifford Roberts thought when Jones told him years later how often his neck and shoulder had hurt, that X-rays had never been taken. Nobody had considered the problem might be in his spine.

Nor did Jones ever consider his condition might have been exacerbated by a close call during a practice round at East Lake in 1929 when, after lightning struck so close to his group at the 12th hole he could feel a tingling in his spikes, he and his partners ran for the clubhouse. As they arrived at the entrance to the locker room, another bolt hit a large double chimney just above their heads. A falling brick collapsed the umbrella Jones was carrying and caromed onto his shoulder, where it left a six-inch-long scratch and ripped his shirt open to the waist.

It had been a brush with death, Jones said years later in the casual manner of a man telling a good war story. He even got the year wrong, writing in *Golf Is My Game* that the accident had happened prior to the 1930 U.S. Amateur, although Paul Gallico had written about it in a magazine article the year before. Jones's near miss by the car jumping the curb near his office ("Look out, mister!") occurred a few weeks later, Jones said, perhaps unconsciously joining the two incidents together because it made a better story that way: "The Two Strokes of Fate That Saved Bobby Jones's Grand Slam— and His Life."

This much about 1930 was true, however. The year of Jones's greatest triumph also was the year when the intimations of the condition that would one day reduce him to a helpless, painful immobility were most in evidence.

In March, before the Southern Open in Augusta, Jones lifted his head off the pillow one morning and felt "a click on the lower part of the left side of the back of my neck." He did not hear the sound, he told Keeler, but he could feel it for the next few days. Playing his practice round, Jones checked his backswing several times, had trouble making his normal pivot, and could not bend over to putt properly. He played poorly and, Keeler reported, was prepared to try massage and infrared heat treatments if his condition did not improve. His participation in the tournament was in doubt.

A few days later, Jones won the event by 13 shots, by far the easiest victory of his historic year. "I honestly think he was hitting the ball better than I ever saw him before," Keeler wrote. "His old-fashioned crick in the neck apparently has yielded to modern treatment."

Jones also felt the pain during the Grand Slam itself. During his stopover in Washington, D.C., en route to Merion, he played an exhibition and developed a crick in his shoulder that he attributed to wet weather. His first order of business in Philadelphia, he told reporters upon his arrival, was to find an osteopath. Again, he played without further pain, and won the easiest of his Grand Slam victories.

There was another curious incident in 1930, at Hoylake as Jones was winning the British Open. He was then at the peak of his physical powers, so Henry Longhurst had no reason to take much notice of what a doctor friend told him. It was only many years later, when Jones, then confined to a wheelchair, sent Longhurst a copy of *Golf Is My Game* that the veteran British journalist recalled the moment in one of his columns for the *Sunday Times*.

"I know," Jones wrote on the book's first page, "that my physical affliction was not derived in any sense from playing the game."

"And yet I wonder." Longhurst mused. "Though not tall, Jones was sturdily built. In his superbly graceful swing, he reached positions which many of us could not attain with the aid of pulleys—his left arm as straight as a ramrod high above his head on the backswing, and his right arm high and straight on the follow-through."

And then Longhurst recounted what the doctor had said as they stood together watching Jones play at Hoylake: "Well, I am sorry, but I do not see how the human spine can stand that sort of thing forever."

"Jones should know best," Longhurst wrote, "but I have often wondered whether the doctor was right."

Longhurst's column made its way to Jones, who sent a polite letter of disagreement. "Regarding the observation of your doctor friend at Hoylake," he wrote, "I think I should tell you that according to the observation most acceptable to me, golf had nothing to do with my present disability. It is not, as has so often been written, the result of arthritis or injured spinal structure. The diagnosis calls it syringomyelia. It is said to be a slow growth of fibrous tissues in the spinal cord itself."

That Jones never deviated from this view—"my trouble did not result from pressure on the cord, but was attributable to a spinal cord disease known as syringomyelia," he wrote a friend in 1958—indicates that he did not truly understand the nature of his condition. There is compelling evidence that the damage to his spinal cord, which made his final years so difficult, was caused by problems with the spine itself and was made worse by the pressure he put on it playing golf. This evidence also indicates that he may not have been afflicted with the disease long associated with his name—syringomyelia.

The spinal cord is made up of hundreds of thousands of microscopically thin nerves, which, bundled together, achieve the consistency of toothpaste. Syringomyelia is a rare disease in which a cyst forms within the cord, elongates over time, and destroys the center of the cord. This results in progressive weakness in the back, shoulders, arms, and legs; an inability to feel extremes of hot and cold, especially in the hands; severe headaches; and extreme, chronic pain.

Although a great deal of information about Jones's illness, his two operations, and the steady decline of his physical condition has been made public, the answer to the question of whether he actually had syringomyelia may lie in files at Emory University Hospital in Atlanta, files Jones's heirs have declined to release.

In recent years, several nerve specialists have asked to see the records, including T. Glenn Pait, a neurosurgeon and the founding director of the Jackson T. Stephens Spine and Neurosciences Institute at the University of Arkansas. With Stephens, who was one of Roberts's successors as chairman of the Masters, Pait has written *Golf Forever: The Spine and More, a Health Guide to Playing the Game*, which deals extensively with sports injuries and their prevention. A further request by this author also was denied by a representative of the Jones family.

"We've been approached about this matter many times," says Bob Jones IV, a psychologist who is alone among the seven Jones grandchildren in favor of releasing the material relating to the original diagnosis. "I thought perhaps if it was written about in a peer-reviewed medical journal it could be helpful to people, but the rest of the family saw it differently. The general feeling has been that my grandfather was very private about it, therefore we will be very private about it. He didn't want to be remembered for a disease, and we've always tried to respect that."

What the doctors would most like to see are two myelograms, X-rays after injections of an oil-based dye into the space around the spinal cord, that were taken in 1948 and 1950. While a myelogram would not allow them to see the interior of the cord—that was not possible until magnetic resonance imaging revolutionized diagnostic techniques in the 1980s—it does let them assess its exterior condition. "Syringomyelia forms a balloon inside the cord," says Pait. "The dye comes up and you can see the ballooning. The myelogram is going to show whether the spinal cord is being squeezed from the outside or expanded from the inside."

Pait believes that Jones's myelograms would show the former— the spine impinging on the cord—which would indicate nothing wrong with the cord itself at that time. "See these little bumps here?" Pait asks, pointing to a reproduction of a myelogram in a textbook. "Something is blocking the dye. Those are bone spurs. I think that's what Bob Jones had—a spine problem. Whatever spinal cord problem he had came from that."

What the 1948 myelogram disclosed can be inferred from the action taken shortly after it was read. Jones was operated on for the removal of a bone growth from the back of his neck. "The myelogram didn't show syringomyelia or they wouldn't have done the operation they did," Pait says. "There was no widening of the spinal cord. It was being squeezed. The operation was to relieve disc pressure. Syringomyelia has nothing to do with a disc."

At first, Jones seemed to understand this. In 1949, when he was still hopeful the operation would lead to improvement, he told the writer Robert Ruark that his spine had become twisted out of shape and the pressure on a nerve was affecting his legs. He also told Ruark that he learned of his condition while drinking. "I would take a couple of snorts and sit down to the table," Jones said. "Then I would find I couldn't get up. My head would be clear and I'd be cold sober, but I couldn't work my legs."

But the surgery was not a success, and another operation, in 1950 at the Lahey Clinic in Boston, also failed. It was not until 1956, eight years after the first operation on Jones's neck, that he was told he had syringomyelia—that the problem was not with his spine, but the spinal cord. The doctor making the diagnosis was H. Houston Merritt, a professor of neurology who was the dean of the faculty of medicine at Columbia University in New York, the author of a widely used textbook, and a revered figure in the relatively new field of neurosurgery.

"He was a powerhouse," says Pait, who is a former chairman of the history section of the American Association of Neurological Surgeons. "He was an incredible neurologist who had a very special interest in the diseases of the spinal cord."

Merritt's status in the field made his word gospel. In diagnosing a disease of the spinal cord, he was assigning a name to the condition that had put Jones in a wheelchair. By then, the matter was academic. The operations had failed, and the fact that Jones had lost all feeling in his hands during the past few years indicated his spinal cord was now injured beyond repair. But for the historical record, Linton Hopkins, a neurologist at Emory who has studied the case and whose interest in Jones led him to write a memoir of East Lake titled *Where Bobby Learned to Play*, thinks Merritt may have gotten the diagnosis wrong. Pait is sure of it.

"The diagnosis of syringomyelia as we know it today was just not possible with the imaging they had in the '40s," Hopkins says. "It's a problem of nomenclature. The word 'syringomyelia' means different things today than it did then. We'd have to have Houston Merritt sitting here in front of us to ask him what he meant by that word. My own speculation is that Merritt used that term to include a spinal cord dysfunction due to external compression. I wouldn't call it that. I would call it central cord syndrome from external compression."

Pait takes this argument one step further, noting that toward the end of his report summarizing his examination of Jones, Merritt mentions "osteophytic encroachment of the intervertebral foramen" and then states "The history and findings were felt to be consistent with the diagnosis of syringomyelia."

"No, they weren't," Pait says as he reads those words nearly fifty years later. "Osteophytic means bone spurs—that's what the X-rays he looked at showed—but because Merritt found some upper and lower neuron lesions, which indicate irritation of the spinal cord, he concluded that it was syringomyelia. But the lesions were due to changes in the spinal cord caused by pressure from the spine. Syringomyelia is intrinsic to the cord. I'm convinced he was wrong."

Over the years, there has been some speculation that the two operations on Jones's spine might have harmed it further, but Pait doubts it. The surgeons—Edgar Fincher in Atlanta and Gilbert Horrax in Boston—were giants in the field, and they did what they could for a patient searching desperately for whatever help they could give with the equipment and techniques then available.

"It wasn't anybody's fault," Pait says. "It was the only treatment option in the 1940s and '50s. They didn't have the techniques. He had these problems at a time when the whole concept of surgical disc disease was in its infancy. We were just beginning to understand it better. Bob Jones fell into that learning curve. And who knows? Had he not undergone surgery, he might have gone downhill much quicker. It's much more difficult to back off and do nothing than to do something."

But while all this makes for interesting speculation, the key point remains. The original damage Jones suffered was to his spine, and the fact that it went ignored and untreated despite so many warning signs over such a long period of time is, along with the pain and immobility of his final years, the great tragedy of his life. It is also—and this is why doctors would like to know more of the details—at the heart of what Jones's condition has to teach golfers, and the public at large, today.

Jones suffered from cervical spondylosis. Another name for it is golfer's spine. A common degenerative condition of the spine, it is caused by changes in the discs between vertebrae, which then begin to impinge on the spinal cord. Most often this is due to age, but repetitive twisting of the spine also can aggravate the condition.

"Every golfer will have a neck and back problem at some time," Pait says. "Look at how many golfers today miss tournaments because of neck and back pain. They are evaluated and treated, they see trainers and physical therapists and when they're better they return to playing golf. You can't do what Bob Jones did. You can't go right back on the golf course without doing something about it. That's what he has to teach us. To listen to your body."

At the time Jones was playing, however, exercise was not in vogue ("The best exercise for golf is golfing"), either for prevention or rehabilitation. Pait all but winces as he reads Jones's description of his condition before his 1926 match with Jamieson.

"He says the muscles in his neck felt like a rusty hinge," Pait says. "But that would be bone, not muscle. He's having joint problems in his neck—along with numbness and tingling—which means there are some arthritic changes going on. But what does he do about it? What does he do for the next twenty years? He continues to abuse his neck. Was there any rehabilitation? Was there any reconditioning? He went to osteopaths, who in those days did manipulation. Could that have aggravated the situation if he had a big osteophyte in there? I don't know."

Pait speculates that Jones's problems may have been intensified by the flying bricks that struck him during the lightning storm at East Lake in 1929. "It probably aggravated some preexisting condition that was caused by playing golf over and over again," he says. "All those cricks in his neck he kept talking about—it just kept on progressing."

As for Jones's letter to Longhurst saying his doctor friend at the 1930 British Open was wrong about the pressure he was placing on his spine, Pait disagrees. "He was on to something," he says. "When you're looking at somebody hitting the ball as powerfully as Jones, who looks as if he needs pulleys to get himself into position, it can be very tough on your spine. He had this incredible swing but he didn't ever do anything to *prepare* that swing. If he was a young golfer today, his condition would have been diagnosed and he would be in a training program to strengthen the musculature of his neck. But unlike golfers of today, he went out cold and just hit. He played golf with an unprepared spine."

After making his diagnosis of syringomyelia, Merritt wrote to Dr. Frank M. Atkins, Jones's physician in Atlanta, and closed on a note of despair: "I regret we have nothing very constructive to offer to help this fine gentleman."

"Merritt was a very straightforward guy so imagine what he must have told Jones," Pait says. "That must have been one long trip home. He probably went into a depression."

Though Merritt did recommend "therapy in the cervical and lumbar thoracic regions," it is unclear whether Jones underwent sustained treatment or rehabilitation. In any case, his condition steadily deteriorated for the next fifteen years, until his death. This is, Pait believes with the benefit of hindsight, a great pity.

Some sort of neck-strengthening exercises might have been possible, and perhaps a cervical collar to reduce pain by supporting his neck. "It wouldn't have changed the outcome," he says, "but it might have provided some degree of comfort." And surely, Jones should have been told to stop smoking and drinking—he admitted to thirty cigarettes and "two to six drinks a day"—and to eliminate the four cups of coffee a day he drank.

"We'd certainly make him change his habits today," Pait says. "Smoking and drinking cause a vascular compromise. He needed all the blood he could get to his spinal cord. His breathing, his oxygenation, his endurance were greatly compromised. But remember, at that time smoking was considered a good thing. Doctors did television commercials saying how relaxing it was. I would not be surprised if his physician recommended it."

.   .   .

The great irony of Jones's decline is that for all the time and energy he spent worrying about the mental stress of golf ("I encountered golfing emotions which could not be endured with the club still in my hands"), he ignored the physical pain that would, in the end, be far more damaging. The mental pressure disappeared as soon as he retired from tournament golf—it did not bother him a bit when he could not recapture his old competitive form in his annual appearances in the Masters—but his physical condition grew more and more desperate. And, as Jones's letter to Longhurst shows, he was incapable of contemplating the possibility that the game he loved, the game he had excelled at like no one else, could have exacted such cruel revenge.

In the end, it is not possible to make a definitive judgment about what might have been. It is only possible to wonder.

Suppose Jones had never taken up golf, Pait is asked. Might his spine not have degenerated the way it did?

"Maybe not," he replies.

Might the disease to his spinal cord—whether it was syringomyelia or something else—not have developed?

"I don't think so. He may have had a continually aging spine, but there wouldn't have been the rigors he put himself under playing with an unprepared spine."

Might he not have ended up a helpless invalid in a wheelchair?

Pait pauses, looks again at the reproduction of a myelogram in the textbook, and finally answers.

"I don't know," he says. "Maybe not."

24

"Will Ye No' Come Back Again?"

Day by day, month by month, year by year, Jones's condition deteriorated. Yet with a great exertion of will and effort, he continued to put in full days at his law office and to make public and social appearances.

"He went from cane to crutches to wheelchair," says Arthur Howell, who occupied the adjoining office at Jones and Howell. "But he always had that terrific mental capacity." And indeed, Jones actively participated in the life of the firm—much of the work had to do with his Coca-Cola interests—and in the affairs of the numerous companies he served as a director.

Occasionally his disabilities were almost forgotten, as when Howell welcomed him back from a business trip by entering his office and asking, "Hey, Bob, how are you?"

"Oh, God, don't ask me that," Jones replied. Howell silently chastised himself for having been so thoughtless.

For the most part, though, Jones's condition simply could not be ignored, by himself or those around him. "He would get up here on a quarterly basis," says his cousin Louis, of the Jones family firm's board of directors meetings in Canton. "He'd get out of the car and they'd load him into his wheelchair. It was very difficult for him. He had to have somebody assist him in practically all the normal things you need to do in life."

What an effort it was for Jones to keep to his schedule, Ed Miles, his old high-school friend who wrote for the *Atlanta Journal*, thought after paying him a visit: "The lengthy torture of the dressing routine, arduous task of eating, laborious transfers from bed to wheelchair to office chair, completed only when, with bent hands between his knees, he shifted one badly swollen ankle and foot and then the other to the footrest with which his office chair was fitted. And how can one describe the feelings when finally he settled back, turned on his twisted almost apologetic grin and said, 'Well, you old so-and-so, what's on your mind?'"

This graciousness, this ability to put his visitors at ease, was much remarked on by those who saw him, including Alistair Cooke, the renowned British journalist with whom Jones had corresponded but did not meet until a few years before he died.

"My first impression was the shock of seeing the extent of his disability," Cooke wrote, "the fine strong hands, twisted like the branches of a cypress, gamely clutching a tumbler or one of his perpetual cigarettes in a holder. His face was more ravaged than I had expected, from the long-endured pain I imagine, but the embarrassment a stranger might feel about this was tempered by the quizzical eyes and the warmth his presence gave off."

But while Cooke was startled, at least he had known something of what to expect from all that had been written about Jones's condition over the years, and from what could be seen during his annual televised appearances at the Masters awards ceremony. There had been far less warning some years earlier when, after a long absence, Alexa Stirling returned to East Lake.

She was Alexa Stirling Fraser now, the wife of Wilbert Fraser, a Canadian ophthalmologist she had met at the 1923 Canadian Open and had married two years later in a gala celebration at East Lake that also served as a farewell to a beloved daughter.

The Frasers lived in Ottawa, and Alexa competed in Canadian and U.S. championships for a number of years before retiring to devote herself to her husband and children. The only reminder of her past glories—three U.S. and five Canadian Women's Amateur championships—were her thirteen consecutive Ladies' Club championships at the Royal Ottawa Hunt Club.

Alexa could hardly refuse her invitation to the fiftieth Anniversary of the U.S. Women's Amateur at East Lake in 1950, nor did she wish to. She had just been elected to the Ladies' Professional Golfers' Association Hall of Fame—Keeler had been her sponsor—and Jones, who had been named the tournament's honorary general chairman, had written, asking her to come. Word of her return after a quarter of a century created a stir in Atlanta, and when her train arrived at Peachtree Station, she was greeted by a crowd of reporters.

Alexa knew a little of Jones's condition but nothing of its severity, and was startled when she was told Jones was waiting for her at the top of the stairs. "He really couldn't walk downstairs!" she wrote years later in an article for *Reader's Digest*. "Until this moment, I hadn't quite believed it."

Halfway up the stairs, she finally caught a glimpse of him and "felt as if a steel band had suddenly clamped itself around my chest. On the retina of my memory was impressed the picture of a handsome young man in knickers, swinging a golf club with tremendous power and grace. In tragic contrast there stood before me a man slumped on two canes, a brace on his right leg, his face gray."

Slowly, they made their way to Jones's car, Alexa growing more and more upset as she noticed Jones was not walking but dragging his feet along the floor, his face set in a grimace against the pain. They chatted of old times as Jones drove—the act was difficult for him, but he had insisted on giving his chauffeur the day off—as if nothing were out of the ordinary. "Bob was not self-conscious about his problem," she wrote. "He simply ignored it."

During the next few days, however, Jones spoke of his illness in a way he had not with his Atlanta friends or associates. Perhaps it was because he and Alexa had known each other since they were children, and she would not be staying long; her presence would not serve as a reproach to having spoken frankly about himself for once in his life. Or perhaps he just needed to talk to *somebody* other than Mary and his doctors. The moment came as they were having lunch on the East Lake terrace when Jones suddenly broke into a sweat and reached into his pocket for two small pills.

"The doctor said I should take them when the pain gets too bad," he said.

He had raised the subject, Alexa thought, and she mustered up the courage to ask how he remained so cheerful in the face of his disability. At first, Jones made a joke of it.

"One morning a few weeks ago, I woke up without remembering my condition," he said, "and I stepped out of bed to walk to the bathroom. I fell flat on my face, of course. I lay on that floor and beat it with my fists and cursed at the top of my voice. For ten minutes, nobody dared come near me. I would have bitten them."

Alexa smiled and said that the fact he could laugh at himself certainly showed he had adjusted to his condition. His response told her that for once she had misread her old friend.

"Adjustment?" he said. "If adjustment means acceptance, I'd say no. I still can't accept this thing. I fight it every day. When it first happened to me I was pretty bitter, and there were times when I didn't want to go on living. But I did go on living, so I had to face the problem of *how* I was to live. I decided that I'd just do the very best I could."

But if Alexa was among the first friends Jones told of his despair, she would not be the last. During the next two decades, he would again succumb to a bitterness that is at odds with the portrait so often painted of a man who played it "as it lies" and told a journalist "we will not speak of it again. Ever."

A number of Jones's letters in his final years, and those of his secretary Jean Marshall, expressed a deep anguish. But it was one he wrote in 1968 to Houston Merritt, who had told him twelve years earlier that his condition was not immediately life-threatening, in which all his agony, and his wish for a merciful death, came flooding out. "I hope you will appreciate that I am saying this with all the good humor of which I am capable," he told Merritt, "but I am getting pretty fed up with this 'relatively good prognosis.' My life, day and night, is about as nearly miserable as one could imagine."

What he wanted Merritt to tell him, Jones wrote, was "based on averages, and perhaps somewhat on conjecture, how much longer am I likely to endure this condition? As a corollary of this, again based on averages, what is the most likely way in which my exit may be achieved?" Merritt flew to Atlanta to visit with Jones and his doctors but could give no satisfactory answers.

·   ·   ·

Before she returned home, Alexa drove with Jones to a clinic where he was receiving physiotherapy and watched as he climbed out of the car; pulled himself up on his crutches; and, dragging one leg after the other, slowly made his way to the door. When, after what seemed like an eternity, he finally made it, he turned and flashed a triumphant smile—one she remembered from their days as children at East Lake when he had just made a good shot and was feeling proud of himself.

"Well," Jones called from the doorway, "I didn't bogey *that* hole."

The winner of the 1950 U.S. Women's Amateur at East Lake was an attractive young woman named Beverly Hanson. After the tournament, she visited an Atlanta hospital where she was photographed kissing a patient full on the mouth. "She sure tasted good," said O. B. Keeler. He died of liver cancer the following month at age sixty-eight.

He would do the very best he could, Jones had told Alexa, and he did.

He took up bridge with a vengeance. He fished for bass with his friend Charles Elliott, a writer for *Outdoor Life*, in a specially constructed boat with a swivel seat that allowed him easy access to his tackle box and his lunch. He became more and more involved in politics, wrote *Golf Is My Game*, and collected his old Bell Syndicate instructional columns into *Bobby Jones on Golf*. Both books were highly praised and sold well. He attended concerts, hosted the Masters, served on various civic committees, and attended banquets—often as the guest of honor. And he never lost his sense of humor.

"Thank you, gentlemen," Jones said when, as the last man to enter a banquet hall, he received a standing ovation. "I can only assume that little show was because I am the only man here who was smart enough to bring my drink in with me." Laughter filled the room.

Linton Hopkins, the Emory University neurologist, marvels at Jones's refusal to disengage from the world around him. "There are so many people afflicted by spinal cord dysfunction who can take hope from this man," Hopkins says. "He is a model of how people in wheelchairs can use their intelligence and sense of humor, along with rehabilitation, pain control, and the support of their families and friends, to lead a full life. That's the message of Bobby Jones. He lived a full life, even while he was so weak. To me, that's extremely powerful."

And, indeed, Jones was surrounded by his family and friends, who made regular visits to Whitehall. Stories are told of regular Sunday afternoon bridge-and-martini parties that sometimes ended with him and Mary passed out on the couch. "We would wake them up at seven o'clock Sunday night," Clara remembered, "and say, 'What about dinner?'"

Bob Jones IV retains an indelible image of being brought into a television room off the bedroom, where Mary had him sit in her chair next to his grandfather. He would place a cigarette in a holder, insert it into Jones's mouth, and hold up a flame so it could be lit. Then, because Jones could no longer move his hands to his mouth, he would occasionally remove the cigarette.

"Every once in a while I'd forget and leave it clenched in his teeth," says Jones, who was twelve years old at the time. "But he was always very patient with me."

In 1958, Jones undertook the most arduous journey of his invalid years, and the most emotional one of his life: a return to St. Andrews.

Even before he was named captain of the U.S. team that would compete in the inaugural World Amateur championship in October 1958, he was determined to attend. It would be, he knew, his last chance to visit the course that had meant so much to him.

Jones was confined to a wheelchair much of the time by then—it was extremely difficult for him to walk with crutches, and he seldom attempted it—and the preparations for the trip prompted a blizzard of transatlantic correspondence. There was the flight to Prestwick for himself, Mary, Bob III, and Mary Ellen to be arranged. (Clara stayed home with her two young children.) There was a car to take the party across Scotland, and hotel reservations. And there was something never before seen at St. Andrews: a motorized golf cart.

He would need it to get around the course, Jones wrote to the Royal and Ancient. Could the edict that forbade such machines on the Old Course, where they were viewed as abominations, be suspended? Quickly, word came back that St. Andrews would be happy to do whatever it could for the comfort of Bobby Jones. The news made headlines in Scotland.

What about electricity for the cart? Jones asked. He had heard that British current would not work on his American model. Would he have to ship over weighty automobile batteries, along with the acid to power them? That would not be a problem, Jones was told. The proper batteries were available in Scotland. (The batteries were not strong enough, though, and volunteers had to be enlisted to push his cart off the course.)

Very well, Jones replied, although he was beginning to have his doubts about the entire trip. Maybe he was silly to try it, he wrote Joe Dey at the U.S. Golf Association. But then he added, "Nevertheless, I do want to have another look into Hell Bunker."

The flight itself also was far from routine, as the plane lost an engine en route and was turned back to Newfoundland. But at last the party made it and drove across Scotland to St. Andrews, where they arrived at night. In spite of the delay, the late hour, and a persistent drizzle, Jones found a small group of townsmen waiting to greet him at Rusack's Hotel.

"It is good to see you back," one of them said.

"It's good to be back," Jones said. "It has been a long time."

Though he could hardly contain his delight at being back in St. Andrews, Jones did have one major disappointment: none of his former British competitors had been able to come, though many sent messages of congratulations. Sid Roper telegraphed from Nottingham. Henry Cotton said he had made previous plans and could not break them. Roger Wethered said it was hard for him to get around much anymore. Cyril Tolley sent his "sincerest regards and deep affection, sorry you are not playing."

The most effusive regrets came from Bernard Darwin, who, at age eighty-two, was three years from the end of his life. "Long journeys and championship gatherings make me rather too tired nowadays and I have to stay at home." Darwin wrote. "I know you will get an exuberant welcome and I only hope you won't be killed with kindness or oratory. The Scots, with all due respect to them, are much too fond of speeches."

Jones responded to each man but did not bother to hide his regret at the absence of his old friends. "I must confess a very keen disappointment that I did not have the pleasure of seeing either you or Roger," he wrote Tolley. "I had so very much hoped that you would both be on hand."

Shortly before Jones left for Scotland, he received a telegram from the St. Andrews town clerk, C. H. Mackenzie:

DESIRE CONFER FREEDOM OF CITY ON OCCASION YOUR VISIT NEXT MONTH. CABLE ACCEPTANCE.

The Town Council apologized for the abruptness of the invitation, Mackenzie wrote a few days later, but the idea had occurred to its members only recently. The details of the ceremony had yet to be worked out, he said. Jones would receive more information later.

Jones had assumed that the Freedom of the City award must be something on the order of receiving a key to the city, which in New York and Atlanta had been little more than an excuse to get the recipient's picture, not to mention the mayor's, in the newspapers. But when he met with the town clerk, he learned it was an honor that was given infrequently, and had gone to an American only once before: in 1759, to Benjamin Franklin.

The event would take place at Younger Hall, where the graduation exercises from St. Andrews College were held as well as most of the town's large civic events. Robert Leonard, the St. Andrews provost who was to present the award, would be wearing his crimson robe with wide ermine collar and his chain of office. They would need a copy of his speech, Jones was told, and his heart sank. A prepared speech? He had always spoken off the cuff. "At this point," he wrote, "the matter was assuming alarming proportions."

On October 9 Jones was brought into the seventeen-hundred-seat auditorium—the tickets had been snapped up quickly, and hundreds of people waited outside—with Mary, Bob III, and Mary Ellen through the back entrance, and they made their way to the stage. A prayer was read, and the citation on the award by the town clerk, who was wearing the white wig of his office. Then Leonard welcomed him back to St. Andrews and cited some of his greatest moments on the Old Course.

Though the privileges of the Freedom of the City award were homely, Leonard said—honorees were allowed "to catch rabbits, take divots and dry one's washing upon the first and last fairways of the Old Course"—the intentions of those who offered them were not. He was to feel as at home in St. Andrews as he was in Atlanta.

"Now, Bob," Leonard said after handing him the proclamation in a small silver casket adorned with the seal of the city, "the ordeal is yours."

Jones was determined to walk the few feet from his seat on the stage to the lectern, and Mary Ellen was in almost physical pain as she watched him struggle to his feet with the aid of his two walking sticks. He's not going to make it, she thought. But he did.

Jones had not been sure what to say. Several times during the past few days, he had renewed his apology to the town clerk for being unable to supply a written copy of a speech. He felt "a gnawing fear that I might get up before the audience and draw a complete blank." But now that he stood before the crowd, he knew what he wanted to say. His notes remained in his pocket.

At first, Jones spoke humorously in reviewing his career at St. Andrews. It was kind of Leonard, he said, not to have mentioned his adventures at the 11th hole in 1921. His only excuse for that travesty was that he had reached the ripe old age of nineteen and did not know much about golf. He had done rather better than that afterward, he noted, but the memories of St. Andrews that meant the most to him had little to do with championships. "After all," he said to much laughter, "you know if you enter a tournament and don't cheat and happen to make the lowest score, they have to give you the cup."

Jones spoke of winning the British Amateur in 1930 and of how moved he had been by the crowds that turned out to see his impromptu round in 1936. "That was a great day for me," he said. He pointed to the silver casket and said, "And now I have this."

Then Jones spoke the words that eliminated all laughter from the hall: "I could take out of my life everything except my experiences at St. Andrews and I would still have had a rich and full life. When I say now to you, 'Greetings, my friends of St. Andrews,' I know I am not presuming because of what has passed between us. Now I officially have the right to feel at home in St. Andrews as much as I, in fact, always have done."

The applause was deafening, and when Jones was assisted into his golf cart and driven with Leonard down the center aisle through the hall and out of the building, people wept and reached out to touch him as well as his wife, son, and daughter. "I felt like the queen of England," Mary Ellen said. Strains of "Will Ye No' Come Back Again?" filled the room as the golf cart left the building and then a tearful hush.

"It was a deeply moving moment with a deadly finality to it," wrote Pat Ward-Thomas. "Everyone knew that St. Andrews would never see him, or anyone like him, again. Herbert Warren Wind and I left the Hall together and some minutes passed before either of us could trust his voice."

Wind also described the ceremony in an article for *Sports Illustrated* that so moved Jones he wrote the magazine's publisher a note of appreciation. But Wind's greatest tribute to his friend came upon his death. "As a young man," he wrote, "he was able to stand up to just about the best that life can offer, which is not easy, and later he stood up with equal grace to just about the worst."

One of the last photographs of Jones playing golf was taken in late 1947 or early 1948. The setting was not East Lake or Augusta National, but a course that was being built in north Atlanta, one that Jones, Robert Woodruff, and Dick Garlington, another close friend, had been thinking about for some time. Robert Trent Jones, the golf course architect who was chosen to design the course, recalled years later that it was at a meeting where Jones explained their plans to a dozen or so friends and influential Atlantans where he learned the meaning of clout.

"Fellows, it's taking me five or six hours to play a round at East Lake," Jones said, speaking of the course's growing popularity. "If I have to do that I'm going to give up golf." He and Garlington had picked out the property, Jones said, and Trent Jones had made the preliminary drawings. Now only one thing remained to be done: raise the money to purchase the land. "I would like your support," he said. "I'll need a check from [each of] you by next Monday morning."

"He got the money," Trent Jones told Randy Guyton of *Links Magazine*, and not long afterward scores of wealthy Atlantans found themselves members of their city's most exclusive and beautiful golf club. "Many people became members because Bobby Jones pointed the finger at them," said Jack Glenn, the president of Peachtree from 1973 to 1975. "Some didn't play golf and some didn't even know which end of the stick to hold."

With its magnolias, pines, azaleas, and dogwoods—and its plantation-home clubhouse that, because General Sherman had spent a night in 1864, had been spared a fiery end—Peachtree soon became a favored retreat for many of Atlanta's most prominent citizens. Some even were heard to whisper the ultimate heresy—that they preferred it to Augusta National.

Jones was never physically able to play the course, but no one disputed to whom it belonged. With no Clifford Roberts to reign over him, he controlled the life of Peachtree, from its membership rolls to its menus. The food did not have to be fancy, he said at one meeting, but it would be nice if it had a hamburger it could be proud of.

There were no bureaucratic formalities, says Robert Marsden, who joined the club at age twenty-six thanks to a financial dispensation he owed to his friendship with the Jones children, and the fact that he had played golf at Georgia Tech. Jones simply said what he thought ought to be done, and it was. "At one of the meetings he said, 'We don't need cocktail parties, we don't need wedding receptions, we don't need a lot of entertaining,'" Marsden says. "'All we want is a place for people to change their shoes and get a couple of stiff drinks.' But it was never, 'Let's have a vote,' or 'I'm going to impose this.' He just said what he wanted done and Mr. Woodruff and the rest did it."

One of Jones's first decisions was to hire Stewart Maiden as Peachtree's professional. Maiden had long since left East Lake to capitalize on his fame as Bobby Jones's teacher by opening the Stewart Maiden Golf School near Grand Central Station in New York. Maiden did well for a while, charging $20 an hour for lessons and designing his own line of "Grand Slam" clubs for Hillerich & Bradsby. But as Maiden's marriage failed and his drinking increased, Jones, who had kept in touch over the years, grew increasingly concerned.

"He saw it as a place for Stewart Maiden to live out his years," Marsden says of Peachtree. "I went out there, and there was Maiden giving lessons at the first tee. 'Hit the damn ball. Hit the damn ball.' That's all he ever said. He died not long afterward."

Maiden's death, at age sixty-two, came not long after he suffered a stroke. He died in a hospital room on the same floor where Jones was recovering from the first operation on his spine. Out of concern for his own precarious health, Jones was not told until three days later.

One May evening in the mid-1950s, Marsden arrived at Peachtree for its annual meeting, which was held in the men's grill on the second floor, when Jones intercepted him. "Bobby, I've got to the point where I can't get up the stairs," he said. "Let's go out on the porch and have somebody serve us out there."

The two men ate steaks and chatted as the meeting progressed without them, and Marsden realized he was witnessing Jones's swan song at Peachtree. Though he was transported to the club for a few special events afterward, he was no longer a part of its daily life. From then on, his most regular visits to a golf course were his trips to Augusta National in April, when the sport made its annual pilgrimage to what had become its most celebrated tournament. For those who saw Jones only infrequently—and even for those who met with him more often—the experience could be jarring.

When Ward-Thomas arrived in Augusta in 1961, he was startled at what had transpired in the three years since Jones's trip to St. Andrews. "By then the change in Jones was heartrending to see," he wrote. "He could no longer walk; his hands were too frail to lift a glass and a supply of cigarettes had to be arrayed in holders within easy reach. It seemed as if his body had become too fragile to support the splendid head, which never lost its noble outlines, but the mind remained wonderfully sharp, the humour lively and the manner unfailingly gentle."

"It was terrible," says Frank Chirkinian, who visited Jones each year before directing the Masters telecasts for CBS, of his rapid deterioration. "He could not do anything. At the end, he was down under a hundred pounds—it was just a pitiful sight—and I would think of all those old black-and-white pictures of Bob Jones. God, what a handsome man!"

Occasionally Jones would be wheeled out onto the golf course to watch a little of the tournament. Old friends might come by to exchange a few words—"You'd say, 'Mr. Jones, it's a beautiful day, a great tournament,'" says Marsden, "and he'd say, 'Thank you very much'"—but members of the gallery, who in better days might have said hello or asked for an autograph, maintained a respectful distance. "Mostly, they left him alone," Marsden says. "Every year he was worse. You would look at him and it would break you up. You would think, 'How much more can he take?'"

By 1968, Charles Price noted, Jones's eyes were bloodshot, his arms atrophied to the size of a schoolgirl's, his ankles so swollen they spilled over the edges of his shoes. "To sign his name, he used a ball-point pen inserted in a rubber ball and a spring device that helped to support his hand and wrist." Seeing that it was difficult for Jones to light his cigarettes, Price would pull out one of his own, which gave him an excuse to light them both. Not long before Jones died, Price received Jones's lighter in the mail, along with a note: "You weren't fooling me a bit."

The 1968 Masters was Jones's last—he sent word the following year that he was "just not up to" making the trip—and it led to the last great legendary tale of his life. Perhaps fittingly, the story of his removal from the televised Masters award ceremony—during which he would preside over the presentation of the green jacket to the winner and briefly interview him—has been told several ways. But finally, thirty-five years later, Chirkinian provided an authoritative account.

When Jones arrived at the tournament, Roberts was appalled at his frail appearance. "I will never let that happen to me," he told J. Richard Ryan, the attorney who handled the Masters' television contracts. (He didn't; Roberts committed suicide in 1977.) Roberts was so upset that he decided Jones should not appear on the telecast; but he was unable, or unwilling, to confront his old friend. So he blamed it on CBS. The ploy might have worked with no one the wiser but for the suspicions of the one person from whom Jones could not hide his disappointment.

"How could you?" Mary told Chirkinian when he, along with Bill MacPhail, CBS's director of sports, arrived at Jones's cottage for his annual pre-tournament visit.

Chirkinian could not believe his ears. Mary had always been the embodiment of southern courtesy, and they had always gotten along beautifully. Yet here she was so angry, she was speaking to him through clenched teeth. What the hell have I done? he wondered.

"How could I what?" Chirkinian asked, and he turned to MacPhail as if to say, "Did you do something you didn't tell me about?" MacPhail shrugged, then turned on his heels and left.

"How could you do that to Bob?" Mary said.

"Do what to Bob?"

"Remove him from the presentation ceremony?"

"I did not. I fully expect him to be there."

Mary paused for a moment and then said, "I knew it. That son of a bitch Roberts. I knew he was behind this."

Roberts had told Jones CBS was afraid he might die on the air, she said. Chirkinian explained again he knew nothing about it and then went into Jones's bedroom. There, to his relief, they spoke pleasantly for two hours of every golfing matter under the sun *except* the telecast. "It was just small talk while the dignitaries of the world of golf were outside waiting to come in and say hello," Chirkinian says. "He just kept them waiting while we talked. I don't think in my entire life I've met a more gentle man than Bob Jones."

There was no question of Chirkinian confronting Roberts on his subterfuge—"When you work on a year-to-year contract, you tread lightly; we weren't going to stir anything up," he says—although he is certain Mary told Jones the truth.

"Of course she did," he says. "I would bet my life on that."

Despite Jones's knowledge of Roberts's betrayal, friends say there were no signs of bitterness between them, and they continued to correspond and work together on Masters arrangements. These were among the last characteristically gracious acts of Jones's life, because even before 1968 his relationship with Roberts had begun to decline. Members of Jones's family will not discuss the details of the falling out, but there was no such reticence at the time from his son, who was on the Augusta National board of directors.

"Young Bob had a real animus toward Cliff," Chirkinian says of Bob Jones III. "I got all kinds of reports from within the body of the club that he was very upset with him and that he made his feelings quite apparent."

Though it was later reported that Roberts was not invited to Jones's funeral because of this animosity, Bob Jones IV says that was not the case. "That had nothing to do with it," he says. "It was my grandfather's explicit wish that he did not want anybody not from the immediate family. He wanted to be remembered in life, not at a funeral. Cliff could have gotten his nose out of joint—it wouldn't have been the first time—but my father never said a thing about it. It was not an issue that anyone ever mentioned in the family."

Though Jones continued to go to his law office until about a year before he died—an ordeal that required more and more assistance and was painful for others to observe—the last three years of his life saw him gradually disengage from the public and turn inward. He and Mary left Whitehall in 1969 and moved into an apartment on Peachtree Road, where they received a few friends and their children and grandchildren. His correspondence during this period—and that of his secretary Jean Marshall—sums up both the generosity he had shown to friends and strangers alike throughout his life and the increasing desperation he was feeling as he neared the end.

"My hands are badly crippled," he wrote John H. Smith, an official at a Rhode Island golf club who had asked him to inscribe a booklet to the club in 1970. "I am not willing to undertake to write all of the notation you suggest, but I am willing to sign 'Bob Jones' on your booklet as best I can. My secretary can fill in the legend you suggest in a reasonable facsimile of my handwriting, if this will be satisfactory."

"I have been about as low as a snake can ever get," he wrote Herbert Warren Wind in 1971. "Should I make any noticeable recovery one of these days, I will try to write you." A few months later, Jones did write again, apologizing for not having done so sooner. "I wish sincerely, Herb, that I could write you a friendly, newsy letter," he said. "But such is beyond me. I am sure you will understand."

"I am sorry I shall not be able to sign this letter, Peter, because the crippling in my hands has grown worse and I am no longer able to write," he wrote to Peter Ryde at the *Times* of London. "I think, however, you will recognize the old habits of expression that I have had for so long."

As the final year of Jones's life wore on, Marshall, who had been his personal secretary since 1956, was forced to take over the correspondence, a chore that left her more and more distressed.

"I wish Mr. Jones were able to write to you and to send his Christmas greetings personally . . ."

"I know you will be disappointed to have a letter from me. If only Mr. Jones were able to write, I know he would want to . . ."

"Mr. Jones has enjoyed your last two letters and has asked me to tell you that he would like to write to you if he ever feels well enough . . ."

"I am sorry to tell you that Mr. Jones is very seriously ill now and is unable to sign autographs . . ."

"I am enclosing for your fund-raising auction a book, *Bobby Jones on Golf*. He is too ill at this time to autograph it, but perhaps its value will be enhanced if I tell you that it is now out of print . . ."

Before the 1971 Masters, Marshall wrote to Price, who had pleaded with Jones to try to come to the tournament, if only for a day: "Heaven knows I wish he could be there. Even when he is able to see me for a few minutes and go over matters, he is too weak to dictate or have an audience with anyone—hardly able to have a thought beyond his immediate needs."

The end came on December 18, when Jones's heart simply gave out. He had converted to Mary's faith, Catholicism, several days earlier, an act that Marshall said gave him a great deal of comfort. He was buried in Atlanta's Oakland cemetery beneath a white marble tombstone that reads simply: ROBERT TYRE JONES, JR. BORN 1902, DIED 1971.

Not long before Jones died, Mary Ellen said, he told a friend, "If I had known it would be this easy, I wouldn't have been so worried about it."

Sources and Acknowledgments

This book is the product of scores of interviews and a great deal of prowling through libraries, museums, newspaper and magazine archives, and dusty cupboards in golf course clubhouses in the United States and Britain.

Virtually everyone I spoke with in person and on the phone—and corresponded with via e-mail—contributed to my understanding of Bobby Jones and the era in which he lived and played golf, but three men should be mentioned up front. This is because in addition to the information they provided, they were so helpful in suggesting others I should speak with and documents I should read that might otherwise have escaped my attention.

The first is Bob Jones IV, who, in several meetings and many conversations, was unfailingly generous with his time and insights. Jones suggested several avenues of inquiry that were extremely important in telling the story of his grandfather's life and career, and I am grateful for his friendship and his help.

The second is Sidney L. Matthew, who, by acclamation, is considered the Bobby Jones of Bobby Jones historians. A lawyer in Tallahassee, Florida, Matthew has filled his home with Jones memorabilia, including an impressive collection of his golf clubs, and his office with books, magazine articles, newspaper clippings, and photographs. A good deal of this output was written by Matthew himself, and he also has overseen handsome reprints of *Bobby Jones on Golf* and O. B.

Keeler's two biographies of Jones, and produced a documentary film narrated by Sean Connery. This makes the help he offers to other writers who wander into his territory all the more generous.

Two of Matthew's books, *The Life and Times of Bobby Jones* and *Champions of East Lake*, are unsurpassed as comprehensive, profusely illustrated collections of Jones lore. My portraits of O. B. Keeler, Robert P. Jones, Alexa Stirling, Stewart Maiden, and others owe a great debt to these works, and I owe my thanks to Matthew—and to his two alarmingly competent assistants, Gwynne Chason and Cindy Thompson—for his encouragement and his help.

The third is James Collier, the "unofficial" archivist of St. George's Hill Golf Club in Surrey, who, after passing along information about Cowan Shankland, a club member who was one of Jones's victims in the 1930 British Amateur, supplied me with material about a number of his other opponents published in Britain I might not otherwise have seen.

Collier's happiest discovery came one day in an e-mail: "Eric Fiddian is still alive at 93!, with a marvelous memory of his golfing exploits." Not long afterward, my wife and I spent a long and happy afternoon with Eric and Pearl Fiddian at their home at Hanley Swan, Worcestershire, listening to Jones's last surviving opponent in a championship tournament speak movingly of their match in the 1930 British Amateur—and of golf and golfers three quarters of a century ago.

I had similar good fortune when I ran into Tom Seaver at a traveling exhibit of the Baseball Hall of Fame at Chicago's Field Museum and asked if his father had ever discussed his memories of Jones. "My father," Seaver said of the man who had come so close to being Jones's last Grand Slam opponent, "is ninety-two years old and living in California and he would *love* to talk to you about Bobby Jones." And he handed over his phone number.

"One thing you will learn about me," Charles Seaver said during one of our lengthy conversations, "is that I have a very good memory." He was right about that, and this volume is richer for it. Seaver died at the age of ninety-three, in October 2004.

·   ·   ·

One of the great pleasures of working on this book was discovering the true meaning of southern hospitality. Without exception, all of those I spoke with who had known, worked with, or played golf with Jones were forthcoming with their reminiscences and patient with my questions. Even when the subject matter strayed into areas not likely to burnish the Jones legend, they were honest and reflective, and I thank them for that.

Charlie Harrison, Arthur Howell, Robert Marsden, Tommy Barnes, Charlie and Dorothy Yates, Louis Jones, John Imlay, and John Ridley all had stories for me, many of which appear in these pages. Others with valuable reminiscences included Seth Ray, who told me of his grandfather, T. J. Ray, who caddied for Jones; Frank Chirkinian, who elaborated on the interview he gave to *Golf Digest* in 2003 concerning Jones's falling out with Clifford Roberts; and Frank Hannigan, who has long been one of golf's keenest observers.

Drs. T. Glenn Pait and Linton Hopkins were critically important to my understanding of Jones's debilitating illness. I am especially grateful to Dr. Pait for his time and hospitality during my visits to Little Rock and for arranging for me to spend a pleasant hour with former Masters chairman Jackson T. Stephens.

I was also fortunate to be able to speak with the surviving relatives of a number of Jones's opponents. These included PGA tour professional Tommy Armour III, who told me of his grandfather; Tom Watrous, who had much to say about his father; Doris Watt, George Watt's granddaughter, and a whole host of people who helped me learn the story of the enigmatic Sid Roper: Stephen Roper, Stan Roper, Geoffrey and Andrew Parr, Harry Johnson, Nigel Balchin, and Eamonn Gavigan of the *Nottingham Evening Post*.

It was also a pleasure to be able to speak with Hall of Fame golfer Patty Berg and Bill Kidd, the longtime head professional at Interlachen. And a special thank you to former president George H. W. Bush for speaking with me about the incidents concerning Jones and his father, Prescott Bush, and grandfather George Walker.

Others who helped were St. Andrews historian Gordon Christie, whose memories of Jones and St. Andrews are invaluable; Leo Trachtenberg, whose mention of "Bobby Jones Night" at Texas Guinan's 300 Club in an article in *City Journal* led me to the lively coverage of that event in the New York press (and to Louise Berliner's book *Texas Guinan, Queen of the Nightclubs*); William Heyck, professor of history at Northwestern University, whose insights into life in Britain in the years surrounding World War I were enlightening; Jeb Stuart of the Princeton athletic department, for digging out information on Eugene Homans; and Glenn Greenspan, the director of communications at Augusta National, for answering a number of questions.

I am particularly grateful to Linda McCoy Murray, who has kept the name of her late husband alive through the Jim Murray Memorial Foundation, for providing me with Jones's letters to Murray; and to Catherine Lewis for taking time from her work at the Atlanta History Center, and her lovingly curated permanent exhibit devoted to Jones, to offer a great deal of help.

Any writer undertaking a project of this scope is almost certain to impose on his writer friends at some point, and I am no exception. Bill Brashler (and his wife, Cindy), Bryan Di Salvatore, John Schulian, John Fried, and the late and sorely missed Steve Neal were all kind enough to hear me out and offer guidance as I was getting started. Furman Bisher, Jon Roe, John Hopkins, Scott Simon, Jack Berry, Jack Saylor, Art McCafferty, Joel Boyd, Lynn Sweet, Reid Hanley, Brian Hewitt, Jeff Rude, and Steve Hummer were among those who offered help along the way, and I am in their debt.

My visits to the four Grand Slam courses were immeasurably enhanced by the men who showed me around, pointed out where some of the key events of the tournaments occurred, described how the courses had changed since 1930—and how they had not—and answered many questions. Jock Olson, the head pro at Interlachen, Merion historian John Capers, Hoylake secretary Christopher Moore, and St. Andrews links superintendent Gordon Moir and caddie manager Rick Mackenzie all have my thanks for the time they spent with me, the publications they made sure I read, and the insights they provided.

No one can write a book like this without developing a profound respect for the librarian's art. I did much of my research at the Harold

Washington Library Center in Chicago, where Mary Dempsey's staff was always helpful, spent a great deal of time in the library of Emory University in Atlanta, and later branched out to libraries and archives from Minneapolis to London, Nottingham, Liverpool, and St. Andrews.

Those who were particularly helpful were David Smith at the New York Public Library; Debby Miller and Alison Purgiel at the Minnesota Historical Society; Kathy Shoemaker, Naomi Nelson, Randy Gue, and Teresa Burk at Emory's Robert W. Woodruff Library; Michelle Carver at the Center for Research Libraries in Chicago; Morna Gerrard at the Georgia State University Library; Henrietta Paynegoodridge at the Auburn Avenue Research Library on African-American Culture and History in Atlanta; Herbert L. Pankratz of the Eisenhower Library in Abilene, Kansas; Cilla Jackson at the St. Andrews University Library; Judy Kingscott at the Local Studies Library in Nottingham; and Bill Loughman, who made his large private newspaper collection available to me.

As to the library at the U.S. Golf Association's headquarters in Far Hills, New Jersey, it is, in a word, irreplaceable. Its stacks represent a golf researcher's paradise that is filled to overflowing with books, bound copies of magazines extending back a hundred years and more, newspaper clippings, and U.S.G.A. programs and records. It is also the repository of many of Jones's letters, which are quoted so often in this book, and of an invaluable collection of oral-history interviews with famous golfers, and some not so famous, from an earlier time.

I spent two happy weeks in the Golf House library, where Doug Stark, Patty Moran, and Rand Jerris offered me a quiet corner, answered dozens of questions, gave me access to their copying machine, and made me feel at home. In the months that followed, Moran found the answers to many more of my questions and provided me with additional material. I am grateful to her, to Nancy Stulack, and to everyone at Golf House.

I also was made welcome at the British Golf Museum in St. Andrews by its assistant curator, Emma Jane McAdam, who provided me with a great deal of information by going back and forth to the library of the Royal and Ancient clubhouse across the way. Along with other writers, I look forward to the day when the R&A follows the U.S.G.A.'s example and allows researchers to enter its library, browse the shelves, and pursue their work on their own.

Along with Keeler's books, two full-scale biographies of Jones were helpful to me. *Triumphant Journey: The Saga of Bobby Jones and the Grand Slam of Golf* was written in 1980 by Dick Miller, who was kind enough to answer some questions. Stephen Lowe's *Sir Walter and Mr. Jones: Walter Hagen, Bobby Jones, and the Rise of American Golf* is a meticulously detailed dual biography that records the lives of these two very different men. I am grateful to Professor Lowe for meeting with me, letting me rummage through his files, and providing later assistance. *A Golf Story: Bobby Jones, Augusta National, and the Masters Tournament* by Charles Price also was useful, as was Martin Davis's *The Greatest of Them All: The Legend of Bobby Jones*, an elegant compilation of photos and essays.

Jones's own books, *Down the Fairway*, *Golf Is My Game*, and *Bobby Jones on Golf*, are, beyond their sheer readability, essential to reconstructing his career. Because Jones recorded his thoughts and actions so thoroughly, it is possible, by adding his accounts and those in Keeler's books to contemporary newspaper and magazine coverage—and to interviews given and articles written by some of his opponents—to understand his thinking and chart his shot-making in every important tournament he played.

The newspaper coverage itself was a revelation. Interest in golf had risen to such an extent by the 1920s that some publications ran shot-by-shot summaries of matches alongside lengthy stories. And though the *New York Times* and the *Times* of London provided thorough accounts throughout Jones's career, I often found the papers in the cities where the tournaments were played, particularly during the Grand Slam, to be more interesting.

There were five daily papers in Minneapolis and St. Paul in 1930, for instance, and their coverage of the U.S. Open that year was a delight to read. Similarly, the sixteen reporters assigned to the 1930 U.S. Amateur by the *Philadelphia Evening Bulletin* seemed to be having an awfully good time recording Jones's triumph in the final leg of the Grand Slam. Keeler's daily coverage in the *Atlanta Journal* and Ed Danforth's in the *Constitution* also were detailed and informative.

And during the tournaments in Britain, papers in Liverpool, St. Andrews, and Manchester provided a wealth of information and commentary.

The magazine coverage devoted to Jones at the time—most notably in the *American Golfer* and several British journals—also was useful, and all golf researchers owe a debt to the fact that magazines such as *Golf*, *Golf Digest*, and the now discontinued U.S.G.A. publication *Golf Journal* printed the reminiscences of so many of Jones's opponents in the decades following his retirement.

We also are fortunate that so many golfers of that era wrote books and magazine articles of their own. *The Walter Hagen Story*, recently reprinted in paperback, is an entertaining if not entirely reliable autobiography. Francis Ouimet, Chick Evans, Gene Sarazen, Byron Nelson, Cyril Tolley, Roger and Joyce Wethered, and others also wrote autobiographical books. Bernard Darwin's writings about golf are available in a number of books, including a multivolume series of reprints in Robert S. Macdonald's "Classics of Golf" series.

A number of books have been written about the origins of the Masters—Furman Bisher's *The Masters* is among the most informative—and it is interesting to note their different portrayals of Clifford Roberts. Steve Eubanks's *Augusta: Home of the Masters*, for instance, is a dark depiction of Roberts's methods and motives, while David Owen's *The Making of the Masters: Clifford Roberts, Augusta National, and Golf's Most Prestigious Tournament* offers a more benign interpretation.

Atlanta is fortunate to be so well served by historians. Franklin Garrett's massive multivolume history *Atlanta and Environs: A Chronicle of Its People and Events* is a painstaking re-creation of the city's past that contains copious newspaper citations. Gary Pomerantz's *Where Peachtree Meets Sweet Auburn* is a prodigiously reported and beautifully written account of its racial divide. *Living Atlanta: An Oral History of the City, 1914–1918*, edited by Clifford Kuhn, Harlen E. Joye, and E. Bernard West, gives voice to people with much to say about race relations in the city. I am grateful to Pomerantz and Professor Kuhn for answering some of my questions.

Others who have my thanks include Marty Elgison of the Atlanta law firm Alston and Bird, Gary Holaway at the Western Golf Association, Claudia and Jack Feagin for putting me up during my visits to

Atlanta, Northwestern University Professor Robert Coen for his assistance, Jim Kaplan, Grant DePorter, Jay Porter, Rick Bayliss, Eddie Papczun, Rowdy Harrington, Mary Stacy, and Lani Kline. Thanks also to *Chicago Sun-Times* publisher John Cruickshank, editor in chief Michael Cooke, and sports editor Stu Courtney for allowing me a leave of absence to pursue my research.

More thanks than I can express in just a few words go to my wife, Joan, for all her support and her help, which in this case included deconstructing the *British Road Atlas* as we made our way from London to Nottingham, Worcestershire, Liverpool, and St. Andrews. She was the first to read the manuscript, and as has been the case in the past, her critical eye was indispensable. Dave Kindred and Carol Slezak were also kind enough to read the manuscript and offer important suggestions. Thank you also to my agent, Mike Hamilburg, and his assistant Joan Socola, who were part of this project from its inception.

And finally thank you to Stephen Power, senior editor at John Wiley & Sons, who, as we were discussing some ideas one day, set this book in motion when he said, "What about Bobby Jones?"

Bibliography

Allen, Frederick. *Atlanta Rising: The Invention of an International City, 1946–1996.* Athens, Ga.: Longstreet Press, 1996.

Ambrose, Stephen E. *Eisenhower: Soldier and President.* New York: Simon & Schuster, 1990.

Barkow, Al. *Gettin' to the Dance Floor: An Oral History of Golf.* New York: Atheneum, 1986.

———. *The Golden Era of Golf.* New York: St. Martin's Press, 2000.

Behrend, J., P. N. Lewis, and K. Mackie. *Champions and Guardians: The Royal & Ancient Golf Club, 1884–1939.* Droitwich, Worcester, Eng.: Grant Books, 2001.

Berliner, Louise. *Texas Guinan, Queen of the Nightclubs.* Austin: University of Texas Press, 1993.

Bisher, Furman. *The Masters.* Birmingham, Ala.: Oxford House, 1976.

Burnett, Bobby. *The St. Andrews Opens.* Edinburgh: John Donald, 1990.

Campbell, Shepherd, and Peter Landau. *Presidential Lies: The Illustrated History of White House Golf.* New York: Macmillan, 1996.

Chapman, Kenneth G. *The Rules of the Game: A History of the Rules of Golf.* Chicago: Triumph Books, 1997.

Concannon, Dale. *Bullets, Bombs, & Birdies: Golf in the Time of War.* Ann Arbor, Mich.: Clock Tower Press, 2003.

Cooke, Alistair. *Alistair Cooke's America.* New York: Alfred A. Knopf, 1974.

Cotton, Henry. *A History of Golf Illustrated.* Philadelphia: J. B. Lippincott, 1971.

Cousins, Geoffrey, and Tom Scott. *A Century of Opens.* London: Frederick Muller, 1971.

Darwin, Bernard. *Golf.* London: Flagstick Books, 1999.

———. *Golf between Two Wars.* London: Chatto & Windus, 1944.

————. *Green Memories*. London: Hodder & Stoughton, 1998.

————. *A History of Golf in Britain*. London: Cassel, 1952.

————. *Tee Shots and Others. 1911.* Facsimile of first edition. Far Hills, N.J.: U. S. Golf Association, 1984.

Davis, Martin. *The Greatest of Them All: The Legend of Bobby Jones.* Greenwich, Conn.: American Golfer, 1996.

Di Salvatore, Bryan. *A Clever Base-Ballist: The Life and Times of John Montgomery Ward.* Baltimore: Johns Hopkins University Press, 1999.

Dumenil, Lynn. *Modern Temper: American Culture and Society in the 1920s.* New York: Hill & Wang, 1995.

Elliott, Charles. *East Lake Country Club History.* Atlanta: Cherokee, 1984.

Ellis, Jeffrey B. *The Clubmaker's Art: Antique Golf Clubs and Their History.* Oak Harbor, Wash.: Zephyr, 1997.

Eubanks, Steve. *Augusta: Home of the Masters.* New York: Broadway Books, 1998.

Evans, Chick. *Chick Evans' Golf Book.* Cincinnati: Old Golf Shop, 1978.

Finegan, James W. *A Centennial Tribute to Golf in Philadelphia.* State College, Pa.: Jostens, 1996.

Fountain, Charles. *Sportswriter: The Life and Times of Grantland Rice.* New York: Oxford University Press, 1993.

Garrett, Franklin M. *Atlanta and Environs: A Chronicle of Its People and Events.* New York: Lewis Historical, 1954.

Glover, John. *Golf: A Celebration of 100 Years of the Rules of Play.* London: Macmillan, 1997.

Graffis, Herb. *The PGA.* New York: Thomas Y. Crowell, 1975.

Graves, Robert, and Alan Hodge. *The Long Week-End: A Social History of Great Britain, 1918–1939.* New York: W. W. Norton, 1920.

Hagen, Walter, as told to Margaret Seaton Heck. *The Walter Hagen Story.* New York: Simon & Schuster, 1956.

Harper, William A. *How You Played the Game: The Life of Grantland Rice.* Columbia: University of Missouri Press, 1999.

Hilton, Harold M., and Garden G. Smith. *The Royal & Ancient Game of Golf.* London: London and Counties Press Association, 1912.

Hutchinson, Horace G. *Fifty Years of Golf.* Far Hills, N.J.: U.S. Golf Association, 1985.

Jones, Robert T. Jr. and O. B. Keeler. *Down the Fairway.* New York: Minton, Balch, 1927.

Jones, Robert Tyre. *Bobby Jones on Golf.* Garden City, N.Y.: Doubleday, 1966.

————. *Golf Is My Game.* Garden City, N.Y.: Doubleday, 1960.

Keeler, O. B. *The Bobby Jones Story.* Chicago: Triumph Books, 2003.

————. *The Boys' Life of Bobby Jones.* New York: Harper & Brothers, 1931.

————. *Confessions of an Average Golfer.* New York: Greenberg, 1925.

Kuhn, Clifford, Harlan E. Joye, and E. Bernard West. *Living Atlanta: An Oral History of the City, 1914–1918.* Athens: The University of Georgia Press, 1990.

Leuchtenburg, William E. *The Perils of Prosperity.* Chicago: University of Chicago Press, 1993.

Lewis, Catherine M. *Considerable Passions: Golf, the Masters, and the Legacy of Bobby Jones.* Chicago: Triumph Books, 2000.

Lowe, Stephen R. *Sir Walter and Mr. Jones: Walter Hagen, Bobby Jones, and the Rise of American Golf.* Chelsea, Mich.: Sleeping Bear Press, 2000.

MacDonald, Robert S., ed. *The Darwin Sketchbook.* Stamford, Conn.: Classics of Golf, 1991.

Mackie, Keith. *Open Championship Golf Courses of Britain.* Gretna, La.: Pelican, 1997.

Martin, H. B. *Fifty Years of American Golf.* New York: Argosy-Antiquarian, 1966.

Martin, Harold H. *William Barry Hartsfield: Mayor of Atlanta.* Athens: University of Georgia Press, 1978.

Mason, Herman Jr. *Black Atlanta in the Roaring Twenties.* Charleston, S.C.: Arcadia, 1995.

Matthew, Sidney L. *Champions of East Lake: Bobby Jones and Friends.* Tallahassee, Fla.: Impregnable Quadrilateral Press, 1999.

———. *Life and Times of Bobby Jones.* Tallahassee, Fla.: Impregnable Quadrilateral Press, 1995.

———. *Wry Stories on the Road Hole.* Chelsea, Mich.: Sleeping Bear Press, 2000.

McDaniel, Pete. *Uneven Lies: The Heroic Story of African-Americans in Golf.* Greenwich, Conn.: The American Golfer, 2000.

Miller, Dick. *Triumphant Journey: The Saga of Bobby Jones and the Grand Slam of Golf.* New York: Holt, Rinehart, & Winston, 1980.

Morton, W., and John M. Ohlman. *St. Andrews Golf.* Edinburgh: Market Street Press, 2000.

Murray, Francis. *The British Open: A Twentieth-Century History.* London: Pavilion Books, 2000.

Nelson, Byron. *How I Played the Game.* Dallas: Taylor, 1993.

Owen, David. *The Making of the Masters: Clifford Roberts, Augusta National, and Golf's Most Prestigious Tournament.* New York: Simon & Schuster, 1999.

Palmer, Arnold, and James Dodson. *A Golfer's Life.* New York: Ballantine Books, 1999.

Penna, Toney, with Oscar Fraley. *My Wonderful World of Golf.* New York: Centaur House, 1965.

Pomerantz, Gary M. *Where Peachtree Meets Sweet Auburn.* New York: Charles Scribner's Sons, 1996.

Price, Charles, ed. *The American Golfer.* New York: Random House, 1964.

————. *A Golf Story: Bobby Jones, Augusta National, and the Masters Tournament*. New York: Atheneum, 1986.

Salmond, J. B. *The Story of the R & A*. London: Macmillan, 1956.

Sampson, Curt. *The Masters: Golf, Money, and Power in Augusta, Georgia*. New York: Villard, 1998.

Sarazen, Gene, and Herbert Warren Wind. *Thirty Years of Championship Golf*. New York: Prentice-Hall, 1950.

Sifford, Charlie, and James Gullo. *Just Let Me Play: The Story of Charlie Sifford, the First Black PGA Golfer*. Latham, N.Y.: British American Publishing, 1992.

Stanley, Louis T. *A History of Golf*. London: Weidenfeld & Nicolson. 1991.

Stephens, Jackson T., and T. Glenn Pait, M.D. *Golf Forever*. Las Vegas, Nev.: Stephens Press, 2003.

Tolhurst, Desmond. *Golf at Merion*. Ardmore, Pa.: Merion Golf Club, 1989.

Travis, Jerome D., and James R. Crowell. *The Fifth Estate*. New York: Alfred A. Knopf, 1926.

Ward-Thomas, Pat. *The Royal and Ancient*. Edinburgh: Scottish Academic Press, 1980.

Wethered, H. N. *The Perfect Golfer*. London: Methuen, 1931.

Wethered, Roger, and Joyce Wethered. *Golf from Two Sides*. London: Longmans, Green, 1922.

Wind, Herbert Warren. *The Story of American Golf*. New York: Callaway Editions, 2000.

Index

NOTE: Page numbers in *italics* refer to illustrations.